Math in Focus

Singapore Math
by Marshall Cavendish

3B

Consultant and Author
Dr. Fong Ho Kheong

Authors
Chelvi Ramakrishnan and Michelle Choo

U.S. Consultants
Dr. Richard Bisk
Andy Clark
Patsy F. Kanter

Marshall Cavendish
Education

US Distributor

HOUGHTON MIFFLIN HARCOURT

COMMON CORE

© 2013 Marshall Cavendish International (Singapore) Private Limited

Published by Marshall Cavendish Education
An imprint of Marshall Cavendish International (Singapore) Private Limited
Times Centre, 1 New Industrial Road, Singapore 536196
Customer Service Hotline: (65) 6411 0820
E-mail: tmesales@sg.marshallcavendish.com
Website: www.marshallcavendish.com/education

Distributed by
Houghton Mifflin Harcourt
222 Berkeley Street
Boston, MA 02116
Tel: 617-351-5000
Website: www.hmheducation.com/mathinfocus

First published 2013

Math in Focus® Grade 3 Student Book B
ISBN 978-0-547-87574-3

Printed in United States of America

4	5	6	7	8		1401		18	17	16	15	14	13
4500403738								A	B	C	D	E	

Contents

10 Money

Look for **Practice and Problem Solving**

Student Book A and Student Book B	Workbook A and Workbook B
• **Let's Practice** in every lesson	• **Independent Practice** for every lesson
• Put on Your Thinking Cap! in every chapter	• Put on Your Thinking Cap! in every chapter

Look for **Assessment Opportunities**

Student Book A and Student Book B	Workbook A and Workbook B
• **Quick Check** at the beginning of every chapter to assess chapter readiness • **Guided Practice** after every example or two to assess readiness to continue lesson • **Chapter Review/Test** in every chapter to review or test chapter material	• **Cumulative Reviews** seven times during the year • **Mid-Year and End-of-Year Reviews** to assess test readiness

11 Metric Length, Mass, and Volume

12 Real-World Problems: Measurement

13 Bar Graphs and Line Plots

14 Fractions

15 Customary Length, Weight, and Capacity

16 Time and Temperature

17 Angles and Lines

18 Two-Dimensional Shapes

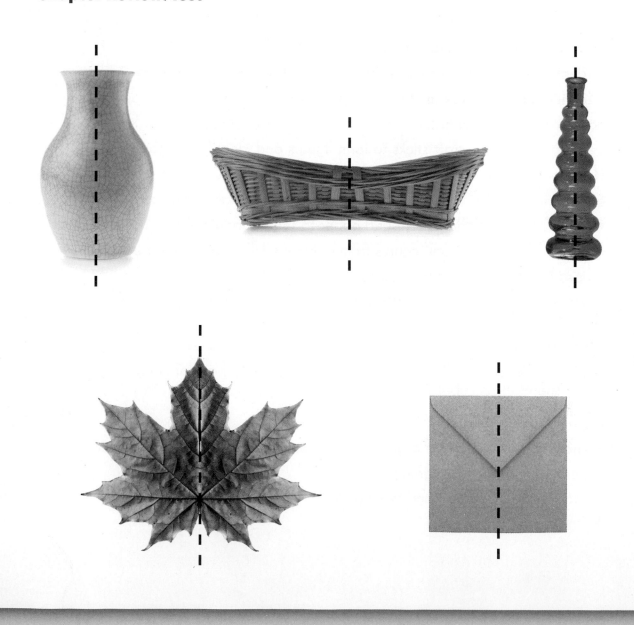

19 Area and Perimeter

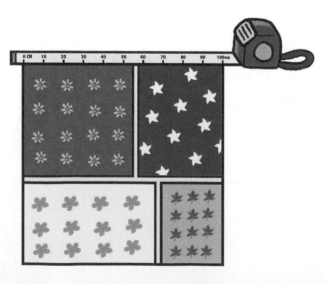

Welcome to

Math in Focus®

This exciting math program comes to you all the way from the country of Singapore. We are sure you will enjoy learning math with the interesting lessons you'll find in these books.

What makes *Math in Focus*® different?

▶ **Two books** You don't write in the ▢ in this textbook. This book has a matching **Workbook**. When you see the pencil icon  ON YOUR OWN, you will write in the **Workbook**.

▶ **Longer lessons** Some lessons may last more than a day, so you can really understand the math.

▶ **Math will make sense** Learn to use bar models to solve word problems with ease.

In this book, look for

Learn	Guided Practice	Let's Practice	ON YOUR OWN
This means you will learn something new.	Your teacher will help you try some sample problems.	You practice what you've learned to solve more problems. You can make sure you really understand.	Now you get to practice with lots of different problems in your own **Workbook**.

Also look forward to *Games, Hands-On Activities, Math Journals, Let's Explore,* and *Put on Your Thinking Cap!*
You will combine logical thinking with math skills and concepts to meet new problem-solving challenges. You will be talking math, thinking math, doing math, and even writing about doing math.

What's in the Workbook?

Math in Focus® will give you time to learn important new concepts and skills and check your understanding. Then you will use the practice pages in the **Workbook** to try:

▶ Solving different problems to practice the new math concept you are learning. In the textbook, keep an eye open for this symbol  ON YOUR OWN. That will tell you which pages to use for practice.

▶ *Put on Your Thinking Cap!*

   Challenging Practice problems invite you to think in new ways to solve harder problems.

   Problem Solving challenges you to use different strategies to solve problems.

▶ Math Journal activities ask you to think about thinking, and then write about that!

Students in Singapore have been using this kind of math program for many years. Now you can too — are you ready?

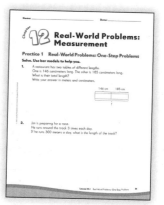

Chapter 10 Money

ABC Supermarket

BREAD

White	~~$3.00~~	$1.80
Whole wheat	~~$3.80~~	$3.20
Raisin	~~$4.20~~	$4.00

Wheat crackers	~~$1.50~~	$0.65
Graham crackers	~~$4.10~~	$3.75
Soda crackers	~~$6.00~~	$5.15

Sale

DETERGENT

Bathroom cleaner	~~$5.00~~	$4.80
Glass cleaner	~~$7.90~~	$6.50
Dishwashing liquid	~~$3.50~~	$3.30
Hand soap	~~$2.70~~	$2.50

Mom, look! The supermarket is having a sale.

My favorite wheat crackers are 85¢ less. May I buy 2 boxes?

If we buy now, we can save.

Sure.

Lessons

10.1 Addition
10.2 Subtraction
10.3 Real-World Problems: Money

BIG IDEA

▶ You can add and subtract money the same way you add and subtract whole numbers.

1

Recall Prior Knowledge

Counting to find the value

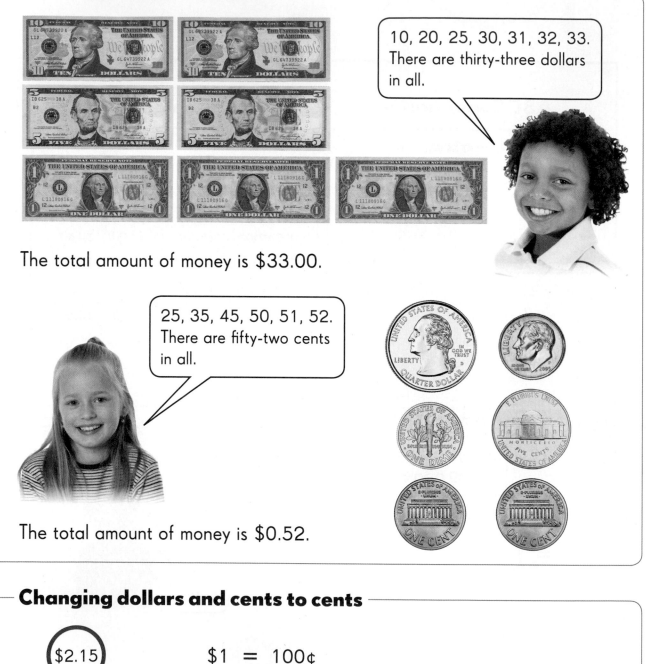

10, 20, 25, 30, 31, 32, 33. There are thirty-three dollars in all.

The total amount of money is $33.00.

25, 35, 45, 50, 51, 52. There are fifty-two cents in all.

The total amount of money is $0.52.

Changing dollars and cents to cents

$2.15

$2   15¢

$1 = 100¢
$2 = 200¢
$2.15 = 200¢ + 15¢
       = 215¢

Changing cents to dollars and cents

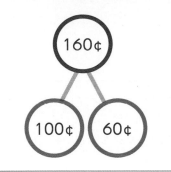

$100¢ = \$1$
$160¢ = \$1.60$

Adding and subtracting

```
   4 1 7          ¹1 8 5           8 9 5          ⁵1³
 + 3 0 2        + 7 6 2          - 5 3 4          ₆₄⁴4
 -------        -------          -------        - 3 7 8
   7 1 9          9 4 7            3 6 1          -------
                                                   2 6 6
```

✔ Quick Check

Change dollars and cents to cents.

1 $\$5.05 = $ ▢ ¢

2 $\$12.90 = $ ▢ ¢

Change cents to dollars and cents.

3 $180¢ = \$$ ▢

4 $3045¢ = \$$ ▢

Add.

5 $56 + 865 = $ ▢

6 $308 + 596 = $ ▢

Subtract.

7 $485 - 32 = $ ▢

8 $310 - 172 = $ ▢

10.1 Addition

Lesson Objectives

- Add money in different ways without regrouping.
- Add money in different ways with regrouping.

Learn Add the dollars using number bonds.

Dad buys a pack of cheese for $5.35.
He also buys a jar of peanut butter for $2.00.
How much does Dad spend in all?

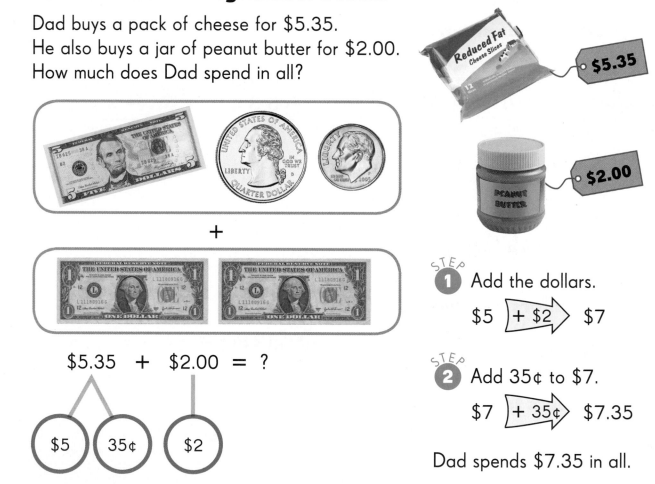

$5.35 + $2.00 = ?

STEP
1 Add the dollars.

$5 + $2 → $7

STEP
2 Add 35¢ to $7.

$7 + 35¢ → $7.35

Dad spends $7.35 in all.

Guided Practice

Add the dollars. Then add the cents to the dollars.

1 $2.15 + $7.00 = $ [ ]

2 $5.00 + $3.75 = $ [ ]

3 $6.45 + $4.00 = $ [ ]

4 $12.35 + $8.00 = $ [ ]

Add the cents using number bonds.

Mary buys a basket of apples for $3.20.
She also buys an orange for $0.55.
How much does Mary spend in all?

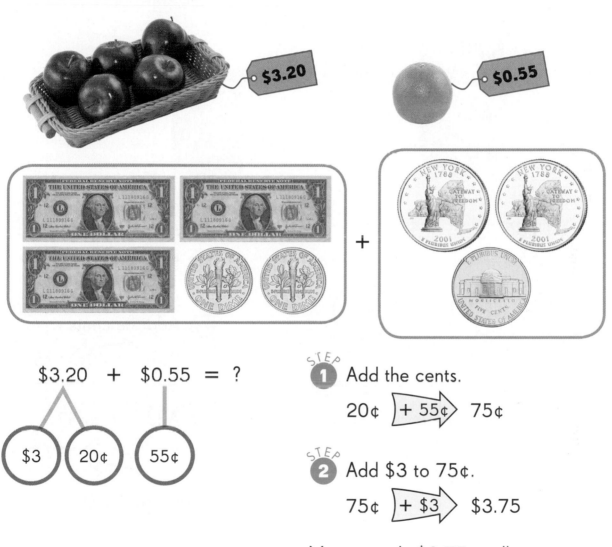

$3.20 + $0.55 = ?

$3   20¢   55¢

STEP 1 Add the cents.

20¢ + 55¢ ⟩ 75¢

STEP 2 Add $3 to 75¢.

75¢ + $3 ⟩ $3.75

Mary spends $3.75 in all.

Guided Practice

Add the cents. Then add the dollars to the cents.

5 $0.40 + $4.25 = $ _____

6 $5.40 + $0.55 = $ _____

7 $15.25 + $0.15 = $ _____

8 $3.25 + $0.65 = $ _____

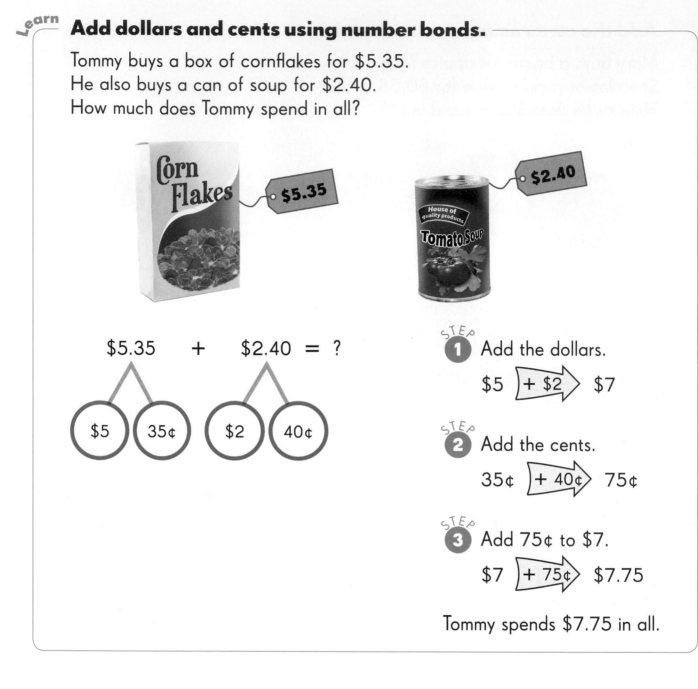

Learn **Add dollars and cents using number bonds.**

Tommy buys a box of cornflakes for $5.35.
He also buys a can of soup for $2.40.
How much does Tommy spend in all?

$5.35

$2.40

$5.35   + $2.40 = ?

$5   35¢ $2   40¢

STEP
1 Add the dollars.

$5 + $2 → $7

STEP
2 Add the cents.

35¢ + 40¢ → 75¢

STEP
3 Add 75¢ to $7.

$7 + 75¢ → $7.75

Tommy spends $7.75 in all.

Guided Practice

Add the dollars. Add the cents.
Then add the cents to the dollars.

9 $8.15 + $1.45 = $

10 $3.35 + $6.60 = $

11 $21.15 + $7.75 = $

12 $5.45 + $18.35 = $

Add the cents to make one dollar. Then add the dollars.

Mom buys a jug of laundry detergent for $9.15.
She also buys a bottle of fabric softener for $3.85.
How much does she spend in all?

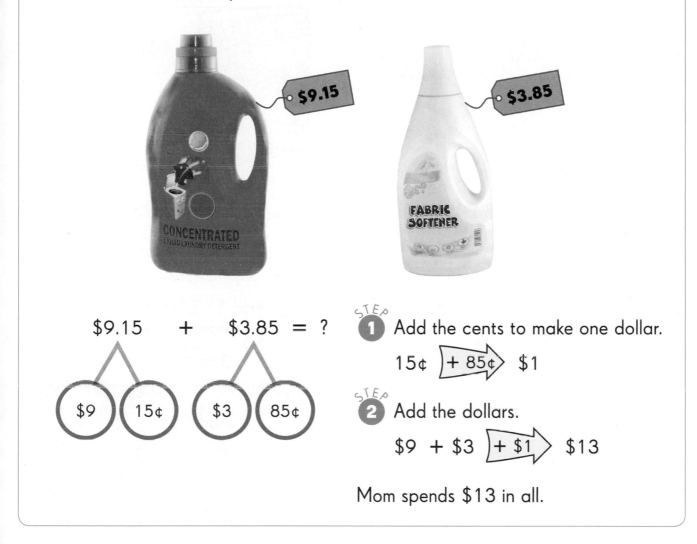

$9.15 + $3.85 = ?

$9   15¢ $3   85¢

STEP 1 Add the cents to make one dollar.

15¢ + 85¢ → $1

STEP 2 Add the dollars.

$9 + $3 + $1 → $13

Mom spends $13 in all.

Guided Practice

Add the cents to make one dollar. Then add the dollars.

13) $6.45 + $3.55 = $ ____

14) $7.35 + $8.65 = $ ____

15) $11.15 + $8.85 = $ ____

16) $14.25 + $15.75 = $ ____

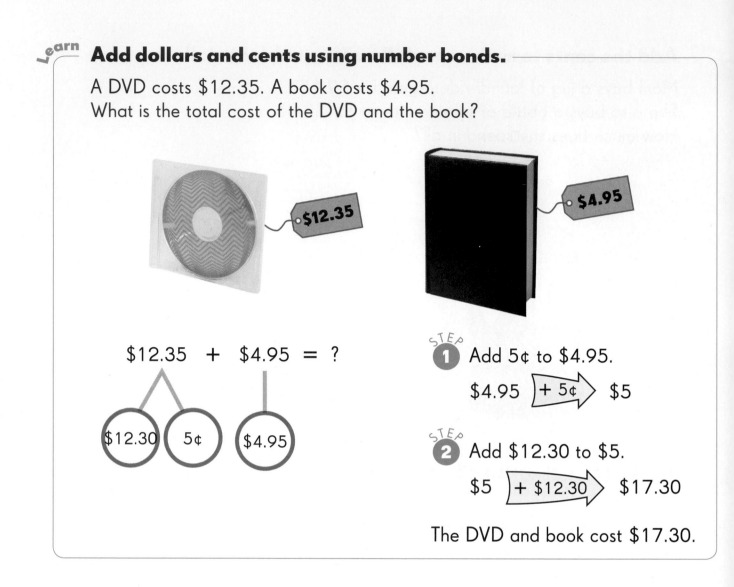

^{Learn} Add dollars and cents using number bonds.

A DVD costs $12.35. A book costs $4.95.
What is the total cost of the DVD and the book?

$12.35

$4.95

$12.35 + $4.95 = ?

$12.30   5¢ $4.95

STEP
1 Add 5¢ to $4.95.

$4.95 $+ 5¢$ $5

STEP
2 Add $12.30 to $5.

$5 $+ 12.30 $17.30

The DVD and book cost $17.30.

Guided Practice

Add. Use number bonds to help you.

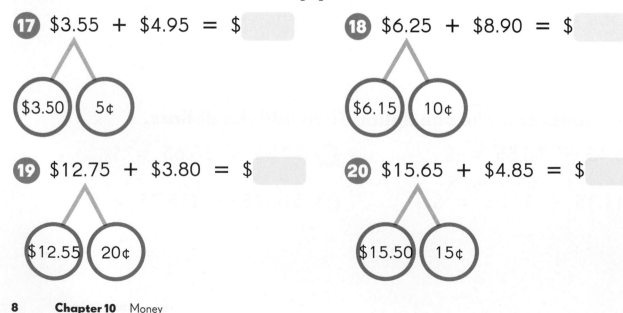

17 $3.55 + $4.95 = $ ____

$3.50   5¢

18 $6.25 + $8.90 = $ ____

$6.15   10¢

19 $12.75 + $3.80 = $ ____

$12.55   20¢

20 $15.65 + $4.85 = $ ____

$15.50   15¢

Add using the 'adding one dollar and subtracting the extra cents' strategy.

A tub of colored chalk costs $6.70.
A sketchpad costs $0.80.
What is the total cost of the chalk and the sketchpad?

$6.70 + $0.80 = ?

Adding 80¢ is the same as adding $1 and subtracting 20¢.

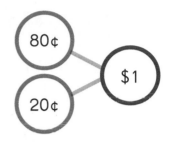

STEP
1 $6.70 $\boxed{+ \$1}$ $7.70

STEP
2 $7.70 $\boxed{- 20¢}$ $7.50

The chalk and the sketchpad cost $7.50.

Guided Practice

Find each missing amount.

21 $4.80 + $0.90 = ?

22 $23.65 + $0.95 = ?

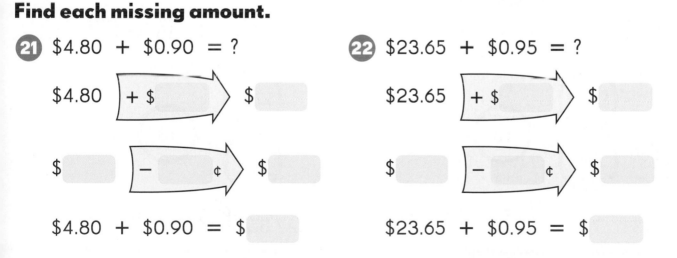

$4.80 + $0.90 = $ ⬚

$23.65 + $0.95 = $ ⬚

^earn **Add using the 'adding whole dollars and subtracting the extra cents' strategy.**

Mrs. Rodgers buys a dollhouse and a stuffed animal for her children. The dollhouse costs $15.80 and the stuffed animal costs $7.95. How much does she spend for the two toys?

$15.80 + $7.95 = ?

Adding $7.95 is the same as adding $8 and subtracting 5¢.

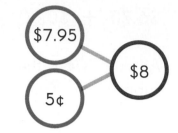

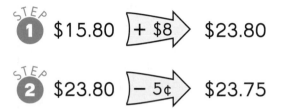

STEP **1** $15.80 + $8 ⟩ $23.80

STEP **2** $23.80 − 5¢ ⟩ $23.75

Mrs. Rodgers spends $23.75 for the two toys.

Guided Practice

Find each missing amount.

23 $16.70 + $5.85 = ?

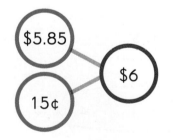

$16.70 + $5.85 = $ ▢

24 $27.85 + $7.65 = ?

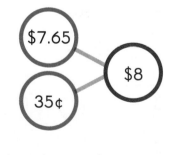

$27.85 + $7.65 = $ ▢

Change dollars and cents to cents. Then add.

$8.75 + $2.20 = ?

$$\begin{array}{r} \$8.75 \\ +\ \$2.20 \\ \hline \end{array}$$

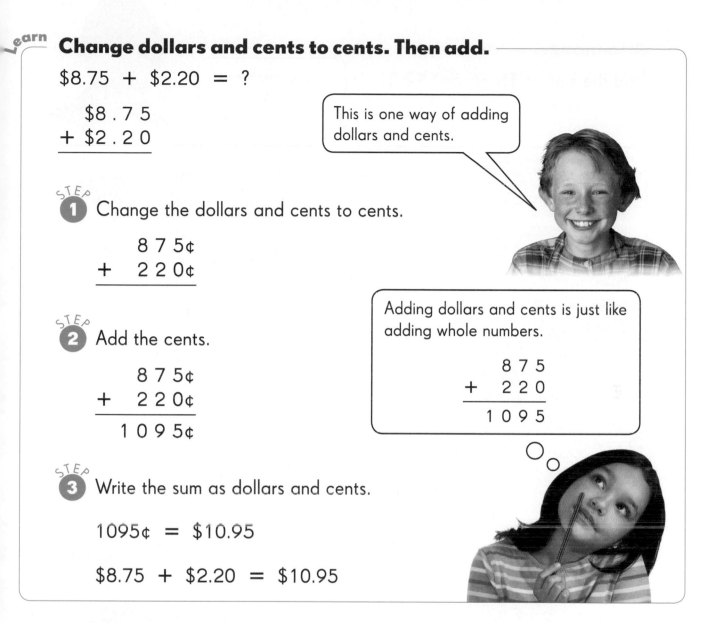

This is one way of adding dollars and cents.

STEP 1 Change the dollars and cents to cents.

$$\begin{array}{r} 875¢ \\ +\ \ 220¢ \\ \hline \end{array}$$

STEP 2 Add the cents.

$$\begin{array}{r} 875¢ \\ +\ \ 220¢ \\ \hline 1095¢ \end{array}$$

Adding dollars and cents is just like adding whole numbers.

$$\begin{array}{r} 875 \\ +\ \ 220 \\ \hline 1095 \end{array}$$

STEP 3 Write the sum as dollars and cents.

1095¢ = $10.95

$8.75 + $2.20 = $10.95

Guided Practice

Find each missing amount.

25 $9.30 + $15.45 = ?

$$\begin{array}{r} \$\ 9.30 \\ +\ \$15.45 \\ \hline \$24.75 \end{array}$$
→
$$\begin{array}{r} \boxed{}\ ¢ \\ +\ \boxed{}\ ¢ \\ \hline \boxed{}\ ¢ \end{array}$$

$\boxed{}$ ¢ = $ $\boxed{}$

$9.30 + $15.45 = $ $\boxed{}$

Learn

Add money.

Find the sum of $8.35 and $2.85.

Here is another way of adding dollars and cents.

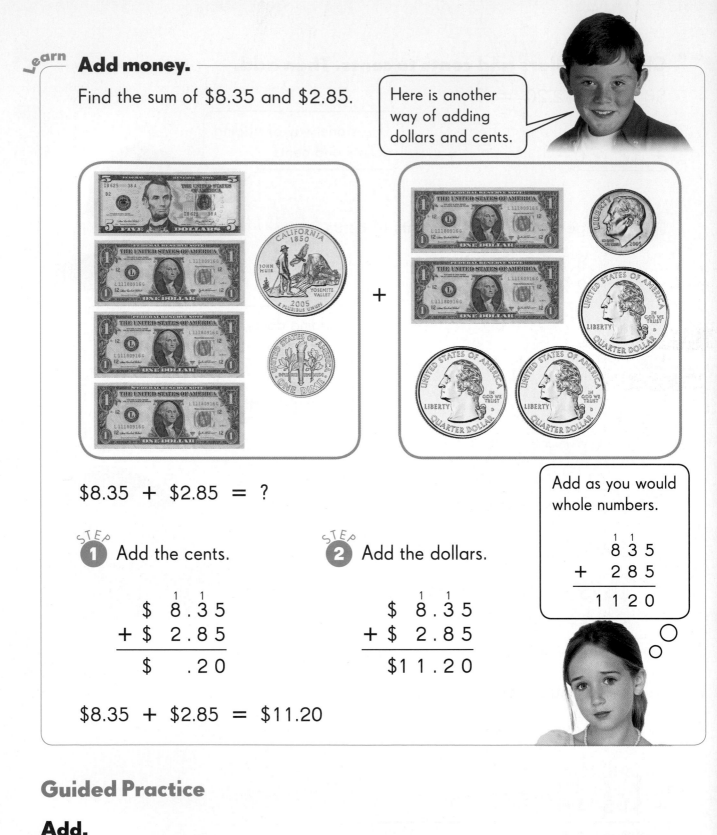

$8.35 + $2.85 = ?

Add as you would whole numbers.

$$\begin{array}{r} {}^{1}\ {}^{1}\\ 8\ 3\ 5 \\ +\ 2\ 8\ 5 \\ \hline 1\ 1\ 2\ 0 \end{array}$$

STEP 1 Add the cents.

$$\begin{array}{r} {}^{1}\ {}^{1}\\ \$\ \ 8.35 \\ +\ \$\ \ 2.85 \\ \hline \$\ \ \ \ .20 \end{array}$$

STEP 2 Add the dollars.

$$\begin{array}{r} {}^{1}\ {}^{1}\\ \$\ \ 8.35 \\ +\ \$\ \ 2.85 \\ \hline \$11.20 \end{array}$$

$8.35 + $2.85 = $11.20

Guided Practice

Add.

26
$$\begin{array}{r} \$\ \ 7.45 \\ +\ \$\ \ 9.75 \\ \hline \$\ \ \rule{2em}{0pt} \end{array}$$

27
$$\begin{array}{r} \$16.05 \\ +\ \$28.95 \\ \hline \$\ \ \rule{2em}{0pt} \end{array}$$

Hands-On Activity

WORK IN PAIRS

Materials:
• set of coins
• set of bills

Look at the advertisement.

Weekend Specials

Cat Food 60¢

Popcorn $4.50

Batteries $3.85

Raincoat $16.70

MP3 Player $85.40

Comb $1.10

Umbrella $9.30

STEP 1 Find each cost.

1 a can of cat food and a box of popcorn $ ____

2 an MP3 player and a pack of batteries $ ____

3 two combs $ ____

4 a raincoat and an umbrella $ ____

5 a raincoat and an MP3 player $ ____

6 two MP3 players $ ____

STEP 2 Your partner checks each amount using the set of money.

STEP 3 Take turns doing **STEP 1** and **STEP 2**.

Add.

1 $7.35 + $6.00 = $ ___

2 $5.45 + $0.35 = $ ___

3 $9.30 + $2.55 = $ ___

4 $25.35 + $24.65 = $ ___

Find each missing amount.

5 $7.50 + $4.90 = $ ___

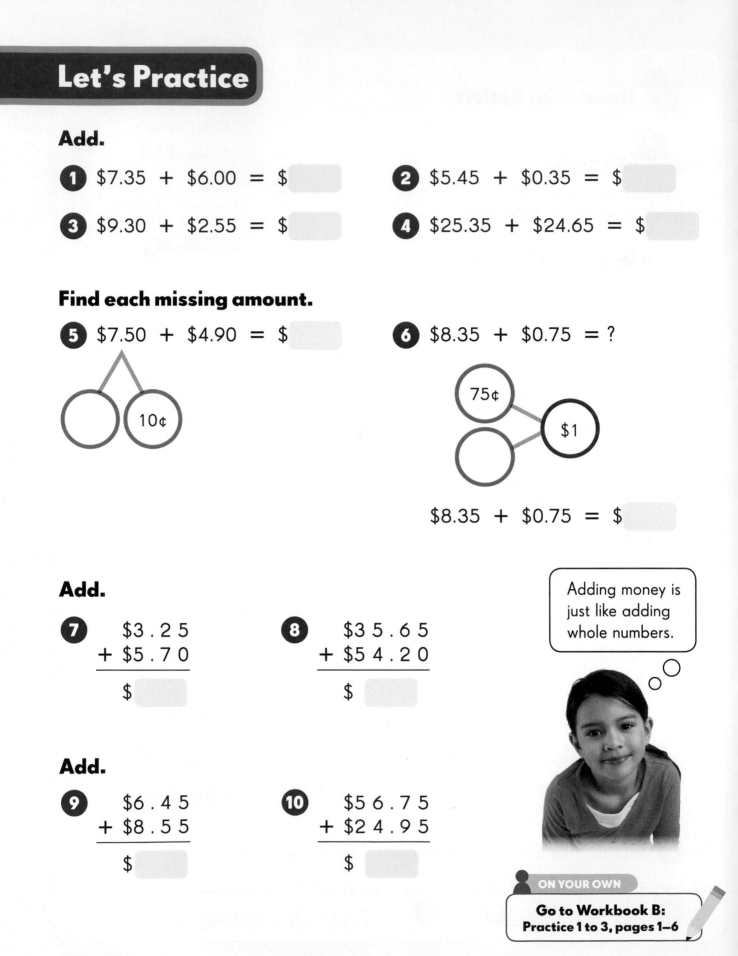

10¢

6 $8.35 + $0.75 = ?

75¢

$1

$8.35 + $0.75 = $ ___

Add.

7 $3.25
     + $5.70
     _____
     $ ___

8 $35.65
     + $54.20
     _____
     $ ___

Adding money is just like adding whole numbers.

Add.

9 $6.45
     + $8.55
     _____
     $ ___

10 $56.75
      + $24.95
      _____
      $ ___

ON YOUR OWN

Go to Workbook B:
Practice 1 to 3, pages 1–6

Lesson 10.2 Subtraction

Lesson Objectives

• Subtract money in different ways without regrouping.
• Subtract money in different ways with regrouping.

Learn **Subtract the dollars using number bonds.**

Tristan has $32.25.
He buys a pair of shoes for $21.00
How much money does Tristan have left?

$21.00

$$\$32.25 \ - \ \$21.00 \ = \ ?$$

$32   25¢ $21

STEP **1** Subtract the dollars.

$32 — $21 → $11

STEP **2** Add 25¢ to $11.

$11 + 25¢ → $11.25

Tristan has $11.25 left.

Guided Practice

Subtract the dollars. Then add the cents to the dollars.

1 $17.85 − $4.00 = $ ⬚   **2** $15.45 − $8.00 = $ ⬚

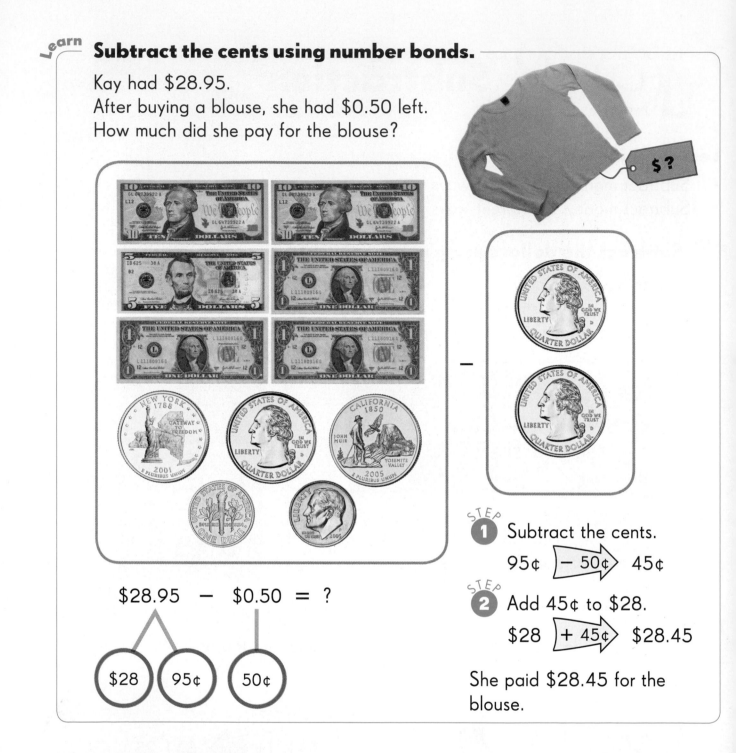

Subtract the cents using number bonds.

Kay had $28.95.
After buying a blouse, she had $0.50 left.
How much did she pay for the blouse?

$28.95 − $0.50 = ?

$28   95¢   50¢

STEP 1 Subtract the cents.
95¢ − 50¢ → 45¢

STEP 2 Add 45¢ to $28.
$28 + 45¢ → $28.45

She paid $28.45 for the blouse.

Guided Practice

Subtract the cents. Then add the dollars and cents.

3 $21.75 − $0.30 = $ [ ]

4 $18.80 − $0.50 = $ [ ]

5 $23.95 − $0.70 = $ [ ]

6 $32.50 − $0.40 = $ [ ]

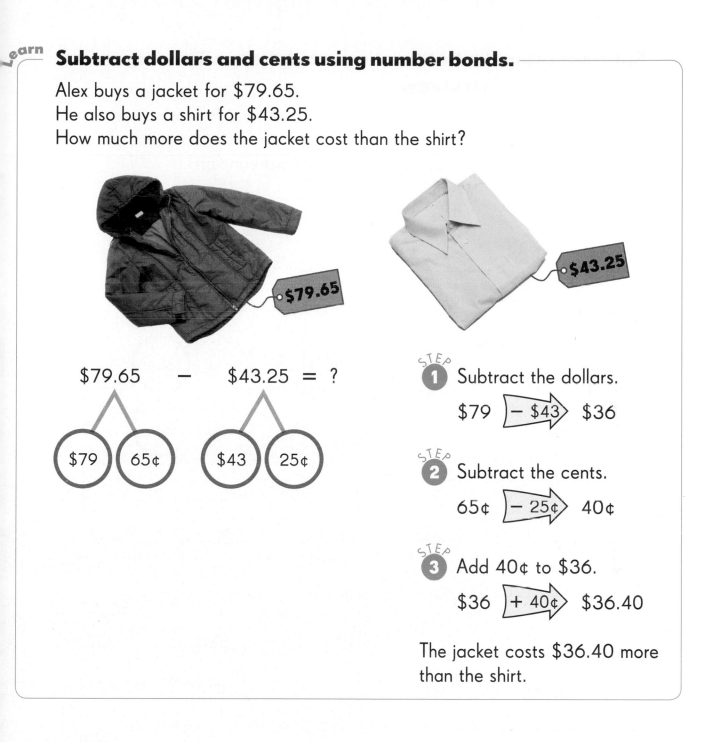

Subtract dollars and cents using number bonds.

Alex buys a jacket for $79.65.
He also buys a shirt for $43.25.
How much more does the jacket cost than the shirt?

$79.65

$43.25

$79.65 − $43.25 = ?

$79   65¢ $43   25¢

STEP **1** Subtract the dollars.

$79 − $43 → $36

STEP **2** Subtract the cents.

65¢ − 25¢ → 40¢

STEP **3** Add 40¢ to $36.

$36 + 40¢ → $36.40

The jacket costs $36.40 more than the shirt.

Guided Practice

**Subtract the dollars. Subtract the cents.
Then add the dollars to the cents.**

7 $65.75 − $12.45 = $ ____   **8** $78.65 − $23.05 = $ ____

9 $49.80 − $27.70 = $ ____   **10** $83.95 − $31.50 = $ ____

Learn **Subtract using the 'subtracting one dollar and adding the extra cents' strategy.**

A watermelon costs $4.70.
An apple costs $0.80.
How much less does the apple cost than the watermelon?

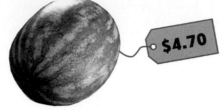

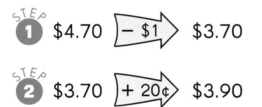

$4.70 − $0.80 = ?

Subtracting 80¢ is the same as subtracting $1 and adding 20¢.

```
   80¢
        $1
   20¢
```

STEP 1 $4.70 − $1 $3.70

STEP 2 $3.70 + 20¢ $3.90

The apple costs $3.90 less than the watermelon.

Guided Practice

Find each missing amount.

11 $5.60 − $0.90 = ?

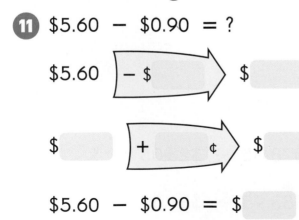

$5.60 − $ [ ] $ [ ]

$ [ ] + [ ] ¢ $ [ ]

$5.60 − $0.90 = $ [ ]

12 $12.55 − $0.95 = ?

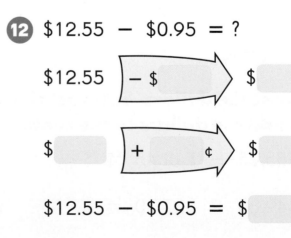

$12.55 − $ [ ] $ [ ]

$ [ ] + [ ] ¢ $ [ ]

$12.55 − $0.95 = $ [ ]

Subtract using the 'subtracting whole dollars and adding the extra cents' strategy.

Tim had $9.70.
He bought a cup for $4.90.
How much does Tim have left?

$9.70 − $4.90 = ?

Subtracting $4.90 is the same as subtracting $5 and adding 10¢.

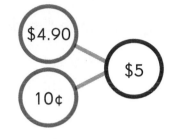

STEP 1 $9.70 − $5 ⟹ $4.70

STEP 2 $4.70 + 10¢ ⟹ $4.80

Tim has $4.80 left.

Guided Practice

Find each missing amount.

13 $8.40 − $5.80 = ?

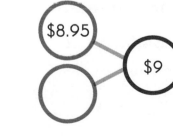

$8.40 − $5.80 = $ ⬚

14 $15.45 − $8.95 = ?

$15.45 − $8.95 = $ ⬚

Change dollars and cents to cents. Then subtract.

$9.65 − $4.30 = ?

$$
\begin{array}{r}
\$9\ .\ 6\ 5 \\
-\ \$4\ .\ 3\ 0 \\
\hline
\end{array}
$$

> This is one way of subtracting dollars and cents.

STEP 1 Change the dollars and cents to cents.

$$
\begin{array}{r}
9\ 6\ 5¢ \\
-\ 4\ 3\ 0¢ \\
\hline
\end{array}
$$

STEP 2 Subtract the cents.

$$
\begin{array}{r}
9\ 6\ 5¢ \\
-\ 4\ 3\ 0¢ \\
\hline
5\ 3\ 5¢
\end{array}
$$

> Subtracting dollars and cents is just like subtracting whole numbers.
>
> $$
> \begin{array}{r}
> 9\ 6\ 5 \\
> -\ 4\ 3\ 0 \\
> \hline
> 5\ 3\ 5
> \end{array}
> $$

STEP 3 Write the difference as dollars and cents.

535¢ = $5.35

$9.65 − $4.30 = $5.35

Guided Practice

Find each missing amount.

15 $11.85 − $4.55 = ?

$$
\begin{array}{r}
\$1\ 1\ .\ 8\ 5 \\
-\ \$\ \ 4\ .\ 5\ 5 \\
\hline
\$\ \ 7\ .\ 3\ 0
\end{array}
\longrightarrow
\begin{array}{r}
\boxed{}¢ \\
-\ \boxed{}¢ \\
\hline
\boxed{}¢
\end{array}
$$

$\boxed{}$ ¢ = $ $\boxed{}$

$11.85 − $4.55 = $ $\boxed{}$

Learn Subtract money.

Find the difference between \$27.30 and \$15.40.

Here is another way of subtracting dollars and cents.

−

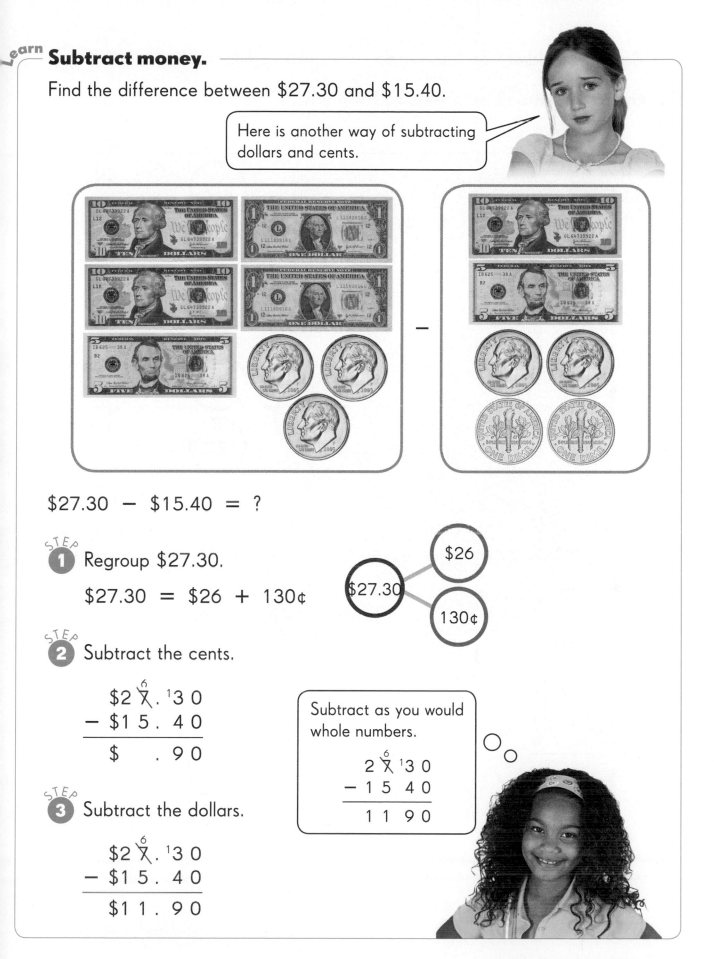

\$27.30 − \$15.40 = ?

STEP 1 Regroup \$27.30.

\$27.30 = \$26 + 130¢

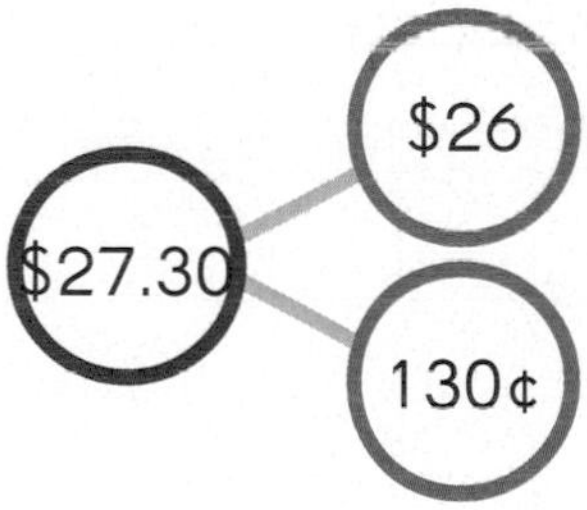

STEP 2 Subtract the cents.

$$\begin{array}{r} \$2\overset{6}{\not{7}}.\,{}^{1}3\,0 \\ -\ \$1\,5.\ 4\,0 \\ \hline \$\quad .\ 9\,0 \end{array}$$

STEP 3 Subtract the dollars.

$$\begin{array}{r} \$2\overset{6}{\not{7}}.\,{}^{1}3\,0 \\ -\ \$1\,5.\ 4\,0 \\ \hline \$1\,1.\ 9\,0 \end{array}$$

Subtract as you would whole numbers.

$$\begin{array}{r} 2\,\overset{6}{\not{7}}\ {}^{1}3\,0 \\ -\ 1\,5\ \ 4\,0 \\ \hline 1\,1\ \ 9\,0 \end{array}$$

Guided Practice

Subtract. Use number bonds to help you.

16 $ 1 8 . 3 0
     − $ 2 . 4 0

       $ ▢

Regroup.

17 $ 1 1 . 2 5
     − $ 3 . 1 5

       $ ▢

Regroup.

18 $ 2 5 . 0 0
     − $ 7 . 8 5

       $ ▢

Regroup.

19 $ 5 0 . 0 0
     − $ 2 4 . 7 0

       $ ▢

Regroup.

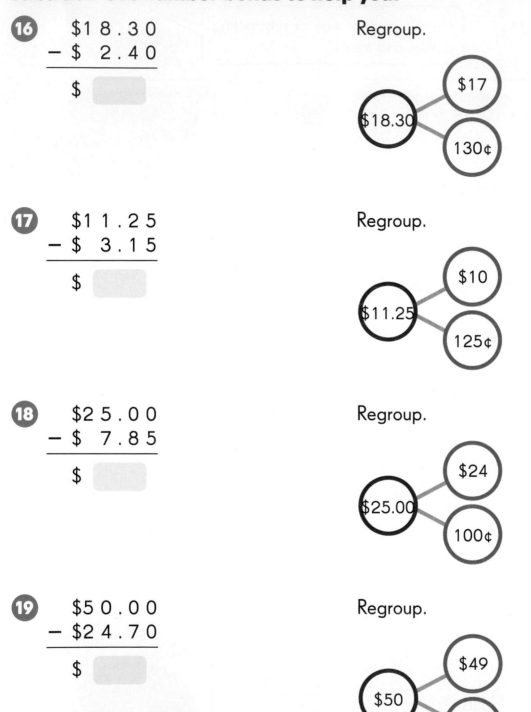

Let's Practice

Subtract mentally.

1 $9.45 − $5.00 = $ [ ]

2 $12.65 − $0.20 = $ [ ]

3 $23.85 − $0.40 = $ [ ]

4 $48.70 − $15.45 = $ [ ]

Find each missing amount.

5 $7.50 − $0.80 = ?

80¢
20¢
$1

$7.50 − $0.80 = $ [ ]

6 $15.35 − $6.75 = ?

$6.75
25¢
$7

$15.35 − $6.75 = $ [ ]

Subtract.

7
$1 2 . 6 5
− $1 1 . 3 0
‾‾‾‾‾‾‾‾‾
$ [ ]

8
$2 8 . 8 0
− $1 6 . 5 0
‾‾‾‾‾‾‾‾‾
$ [ ]

Subtracting money is just like subtracting whole numbers.

Subtract.

9
$8 . 2 5
− $3 . 6 0
‾‾‾‾‾‾‾‾‾
$ [ ]

10
$4 5 . 4 5
− $2 7 . 7 5
‾‾‾‾‾‾‾‾‾
$ [ ]

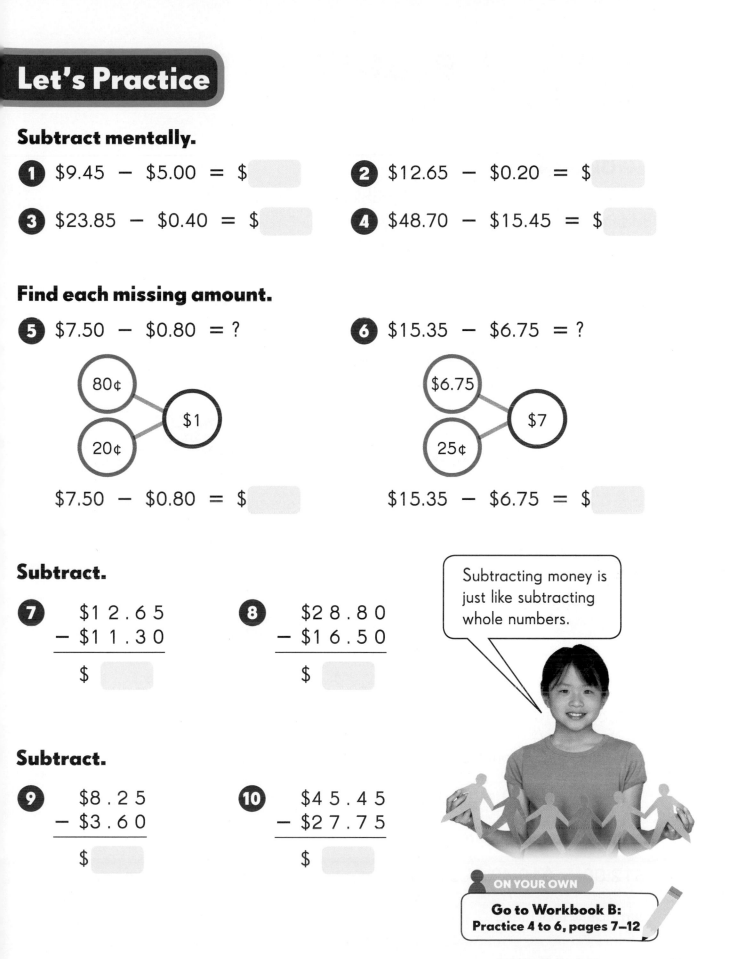

ON YOUR OWN

Go to Workbook B:
Practice 4 to 6, pages 7–12

10.3 Real-World Problems: Money

Lesson

Lesson Objectives

- Solve up to two-step real-world problems involving addition and subtraction of money.
- Write real-world problems for given situations.

Learn **Solve real-world problems using bar models.**

Nancy has $35.50.
She buys a necklace and has $29.30 left.
How much does Nancy spend on the necklace?

$35.50 − $29.30 = $6.20

Nancy spends $6.20 on the necklace.

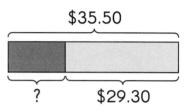

. . . .

Jim has $12 in his wallet. He buys a carton of fruit juice for $2.50 and a sandwich for $7.90. How much money does he have left?

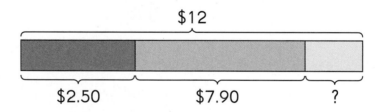

First, find the amount of money Jim spent.

$2.50 + $7.90 = $10.40

Then subtract this amount.

$12.00 − $10.40 = $1.60

Jim has $1.60 left.

Guided Practice

Solve.

1 Peter has $25.50. Sue has $18.75.
How much more money does Peter have than Sue?

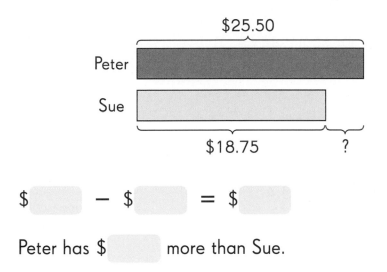

$25.50

Peter

Sue

$18.75   ?

$ [____] − $ [____] = $ [____]

Peter has $ [____] more than Sue.

2 A school sweatshirt costs $24.85.
A T-shirt is $3.40 less than the sweatshirt.
How much do the sweatshirt and the T-shirt cost in all?

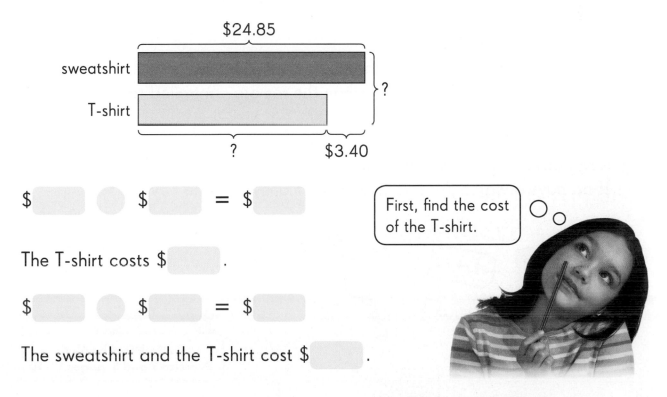

$24.85

sweatshirt

T-shirt   }?

? $3.40

$ [____] ⬤ $ [____] = $ [____]

> First, find the cost of the T-shirt.

The T-shirt costs $ [____] .

$ [____] ⬤ $ [____] = $ [____]

The sweatshirt and the T-shirt cost $ [____] .

Let's Practice

Solve. Use bar models to help you.

1 Katherine bought a towel for $7.90.
She has $18.75 left.
How much money did she have to start with?

2 A bag costs $12.35.
A T-shirt costs $2.65 more than the bag.
How much does the T-shirt cost?

3 Pele wants to buy a clock that costs $28.45.
He needs $2.20 more to buy it.
How much money does he have now?

4 Carrie buys a bunch of bananas for $3.80 and
some mangoes for $5.45. She has $16.50 left.

a How much do the bananas and mangoes cost?

b How much money did she have to start with?

5 A stuffed animal costs $28.45.
It is $15.20 more expensive than a remote controlled robot.
A comic book costs $7.90 less than the remote controlled robot.
How much does the comic book cost?

6 Kevin buys a CD-ROM and has $7.50 left.
If he buys a watch instead, how much money does he have left?

ON YOUR OWN

Go to Workbook B:
Practice 7 and 8, pages 13–18

PROBLEM SOLVING

Solve.

1 Grandma buys some tomatoes and carrots.
The total cost is $18.
The tomatoes cost $2 more than the carrots.
How much does she spend on the carrots?

tomatoes

carrots

$

$

2 Winona buys some pencils and erasers.
She spends $1.20 altogether.
The pencils cost $0.40 more than the erasers.
How much does she spend on the erasers?
Give your answers in cents.

Draw a bar model to help you.

ON YOUR OWN

**Go to Workbook B:
Put on Your Thinking Cap!
pages 21—22**

Chapter Wrap Up

Study Guide

You have learned...

Addition

1. $6.25 + $2 = ?
   First add the dollars: $6 + $2 = $8
   Then add the cents to the dollars:
   25¢ + $8 = $8.25

2. $5.60 + 25¢ = ?
   First add the cents: 60¢ + 25¢ = 85¢
   Then add the dollars to the cents:
   $5 + 85¢ = $5.85

3. $7.25 + $2.60 = ?
   First add the dollars: $7 + $2 = $9
   Then add the cents:
   25¢ + 60¢ = 85¢
   Then add the cents to the dollars:
   $9 + 85¢ = $9.85

4. $12.35 + $6.65 = ?
   First add the cents to make one dollar:
   35¢ + 65¢ = $1

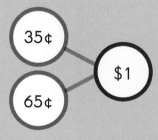

   Then add the dollars:
   $1 + $12 + $6 = $19

5. Use number bonds to add.
   $14.45 + $3.85 = ?

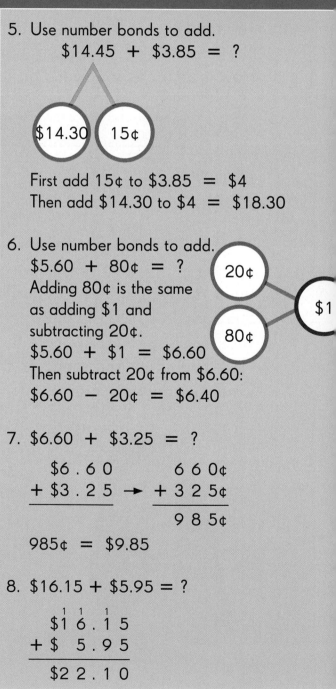

   First add 15¢ to $3.85 = $4
   Then add $14.30 to $4 = $18.30

6. Use number bonds to add.
   $5.60 + 80¢ = ?
   Adding 80¢ is the same
   as adding $1 and
   subtracting 20¢.
   $5.60 + $1 = $6.60
   Then subtract 20¢ from $6.60:
   $6.60 − 20¢ = $6.40

7. $6.60 + $3.25 = ?

   $6 . 6 0   6 6 0¢
   + $3 . 2 5 → + 3 2 5¢
   ─────────   ─────────
                  9 8 5¢

   985¢ = $9.85

8. $16.15 + $5.95 = ?

   ¹ ¹ ¹
   $1 6 . 1 5
   + $ 5 . 9 5
   ───────────
   $ 2 2 . 1 0

BIG IDEA

▶ You can add and subtract money the same way you add and subtract whole numbers.

Subtraction

1. $14.25 − $9 = ?
   Subtract the dollars: $14 − $9 = $5
   Add the dollars and cents:
   $5 + 25¢ = $5.25

2. $26.85 − $0.60 = ?
   Subtract the cents: 85¢ − 60¢ = 25¢
   Add the dollars and cents:
   $26 + 25¢ = $26.25

3. $99.45 − $56.25 = ?
   Subtract the dollars:
   $99 − $56 = $43
   Subtract the cents:
   45¢ − 25¢ = 20¢
   Add 20¢ to $43 = $43.20

4. Use number bonds to subtract.
   $14.70 − $0.90 = ?
   Subtracting 90¢ is the same as subtracting $1 and adding 10¢.
   First subtract $1 from $14.70 = $13.70
   Then add 10¢ to $13.70:
   10¢ + $13.70 = $13.80

   90¢ ── $1
   10¢ ──┘

5. Use number bonds to subtract.
   $11.70 − $8.90 = ?
   Subtracting $8.90 is the same as subtracting $9 and adding 10¢.
   First subtract $9 from $11.70:
   $11.70 − $9 = $2.70
   Then add 10¢ to $2.70:
   $2.70 + 10¢ = $2.80

   $8.90 ── $9
   10¢ ──┘

6. $8.95 − $6.30 = ?

   $$
   \begin{array}{r}
   \$8\,.\,9\,5 \\
   -\ \$6\,.\,3\,0 \\
   \end{array}
   \rightarrow
   \begin{array}{r}
   8\ 9\ 5¢ \\
   -\ 6\ 3\ 0¢ \\
   \hline
   2\ 6\ 5¢
   \end{array}
   $$

   265¢ = $2.65

7. $17.30 − $12.50 = ?
   Regroup $17.30.
   $17.30 = $16 + $1.30

   $$
   \begin{array}{r}
   \$1\ \overset{6}{\cancel{7}}\,.\,{}^{1}3\ 0 \\
   -\ \$1\ 2\,.\,5\ 0 \\
   \hline
   \$\ \ \ 4\,.\,8\ 0
   \end{array}
   $$

Chapter Review/Test

Concepts and Skills

Add mentally.

1 $3.45 + $8.00 = $ [ ]   **2** $6.25 + $0.35 = $ [ ]

3 $2.55 + $6.20 = $ [ ]   **4** $15.60 + $3.40 = $ [ ]

5 $8.35 + $1.95 = $ [ ]   **6** $12.70 + $0.90 = $ [ ]

7 $11.30 + $3.85 = $ [ ]

Subtract mentally.

8 $16.78 − $9.00 = $ [ ]   **9** $6.45 − $0.20 = $ [ ]

10 $8.65 − $7.25 = $ [ ]   **11** $5.40 − $0.90 = $ [ ]

12 $5.70 − $4.80 = $ [ ]

Add or subtract.

13
$$\begin{array}{r} \$70.48 \\ + \ \$ \ 9.65 \\ \hline \$ \ \ [\ ] \end{array}$$

14
$$\begin{array}{r} \$10.00 \\ - \ \$ \ 7.38 \\ \hline \$ \ \ [\ ] \end{array}$$

Problem Solving

Solve.

15 Randy wants to buy a calculator that costs $36.42.
He has only $27.09.
How much more money does he need?

16 Melvin gives $16.20 to his teacher for a book.
He pays $3.85 less for another book.
How much do the two books cost?

17 Sally and Joshua have the same amount of money.
Joshua pays $9.10 for a bag and has $16.25 left.
Sally buys a pen and has $19.60 left.
How much does the pen cost?

11 Metric Length, Mass, and Volume

Lessons

BIG IDEA

▶ Length, mass, and volume can be measured using metric units of measurement.

Recall Prior Knowledge

Using number bonds

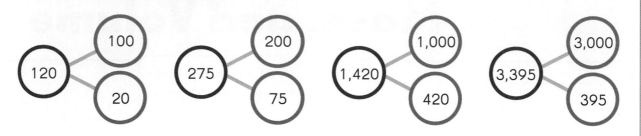

Measuring length in meters and centimeters

The meter is a unit of length.
It is a little longer than 3 feet.
It is used to measure length and height.

Stanley jumped 1 meter.

The cupboard is 2 meters tall.

The centimeter is also a unit of length.
It is used to measure shorter lengths.

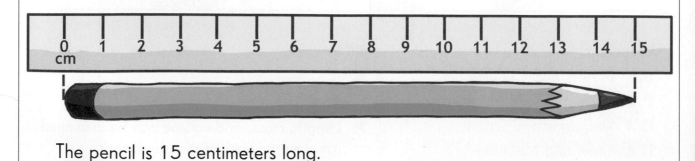

The pencil is 15 centimeters long.

Measuring mass in kilograms and grams

The kilogram is used to measure the mass of heavier objects.
The gram is used to measure the mass of lighter objects.

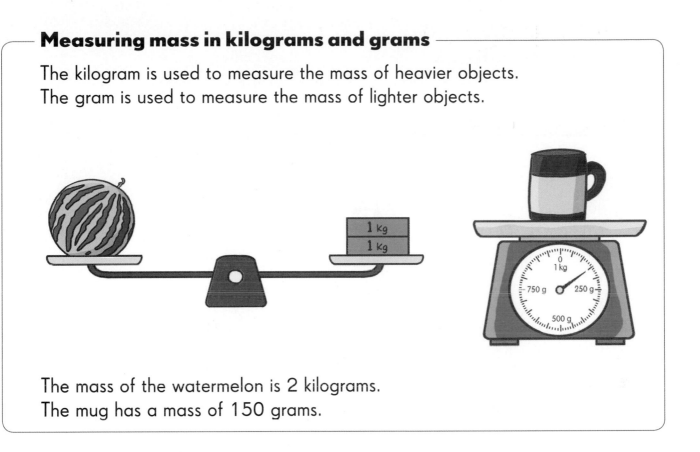

The mass of the watermelon is 2 kilograms.
The mug has a mass of 150 grams.

Measuring volume in liters

You can use liters to measure volume.

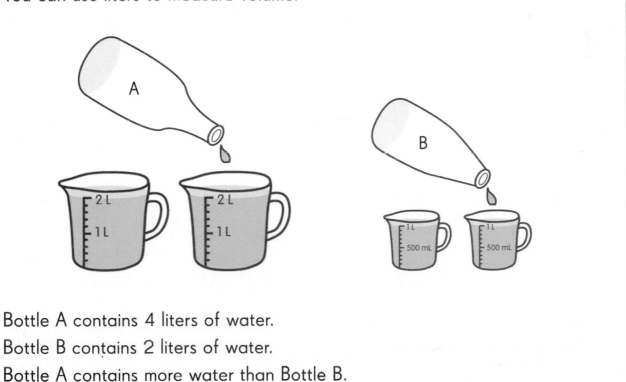

Bottle A contains 4 liters of water.
Bottle B contains 2 liters of water.
Bottle A contains more water than Bottle B.

1 The dog is ⬚1⬚ meter tall.

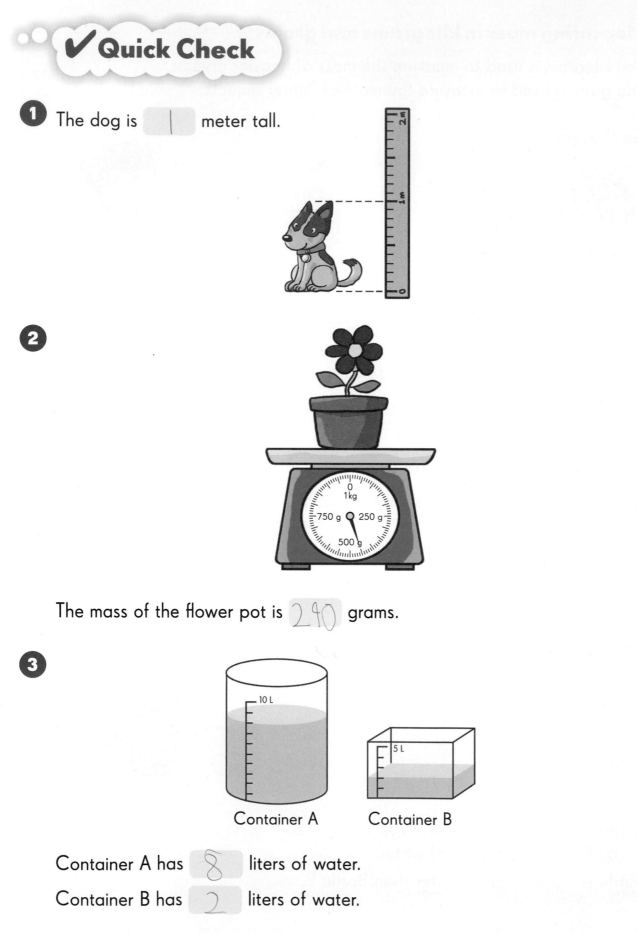

2

The mass of the flower pot is ⬚2.40⬚ grams.

3

Container A   Container B

Container A has ⬚8⬚ liters of water.

Container B has ⬚2⬚ liters of water.

Lesson 11.1 Meters and Centimeters

Lesson Objectives

- Use meters and centimeters as units of measurement of length.
- Estimate and measure length.
- Convert units of measurement.

Vocabulary
meter (m)
centimeter (cm)

Learn Use meters to measure length.

The length of the ribbon is 1 meter.

100 cm

70   80   90   100

The **meter (m)** and **centimeter (cm)** are units of length.

One meter is 100 times as long as 1 centimeter.
1 m = 100 cm

1 m

Learn Convert meters and centimeters to centimeters.

Kate's height is 1 meter 38 centimeters.
What is her height in centimeters?

$$1 \text{ m} = 100 \text{ cm}$$

1 m 38 cm

38 cm

1 m 38 cm = 100 cm + 38 cm
= 138 cm

Kate's height is 138 centimeters.

Guided Practice

Complete.

1 The length of a car is 4 meters 56 centimeters.
Find the length of the car in centimeters.

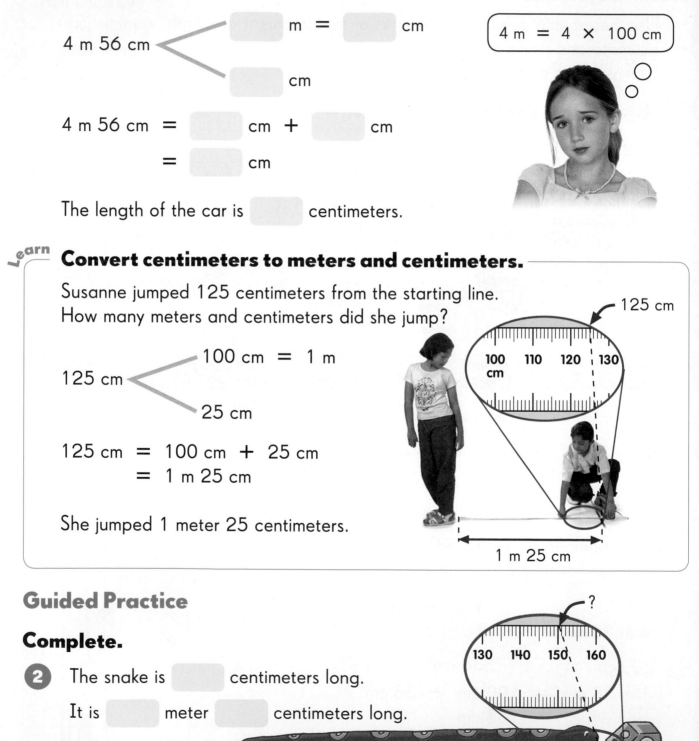

4 m 56 cm ⟨ [＿＿] m = [＿＿] cm

[＿＿] cm

4 m = 4 × 100 cm

4 m 56 cm = [＿＿] cm + [＿＿] cm

= [＿＿] cm

The length of the car is [＿＿] centimeters.

Convert centimeters to meters and centimeters.

Susanne jumped 125 centimeters from the starting line.
How many meters and centimeters did she jump?

125 cm ⟨ 100 cm = 1 m

25 cm

125 cm = 100 cm + 25 cm
= 1 m 25 cm

She jumped 1 meter 25 centimeters.

125 cm

100   110   120   130
cm

1 m 25 cm

Guided Practice

Complete.

2 The snake is [＿＿] centimeters long.

It is [＿＿] meter [＿＿] centimeters long.

?

130   140   150   160

Hands-On Activity

Materials:
- measuring tape
- piece of paper, wadded into a ball

WORKING TOGETHER

STEP 1 Stand behind a starting line and toss the paper ball.

STEP 2 Estimate how far the paper ball is from the starting line.

STEP 3 Measure the distance with the measuring tape.

STEP 4 Fill in the blanks. Then compare your measurements with those of your classmates.

Description	My Estimate	My Measure
Distance from Starting Line	___ m ___ cm	___ m ___ cm

Let's Practice

Convert to centimeters.

1 7 m = [____] cm

2 5 m 92 cm = [____] cm

3 2 m 40 cm = [____] cm

4 3 m 8 cm = [____] cm

Convert to meters and centimeters.

5 800 cm = [____] m [____] cm

6 156 cm = [____] m [____] cm

7 380 cm = [____] m [____] cm

8 909 cm = [____] m [____] cm

ON YOUR OWN

Go to Workbook B: Practice 1, pages 23–26

Lesson 11.2 Kilometers and Meters

Lesson Objectives

- Use kilometer and meter as units of measurement of length.
- Estimate and measure length.
- Convert units of measurement.

Vocabulary
kilometer (km)
distance

Learn Use kilometers to measure length and distance.

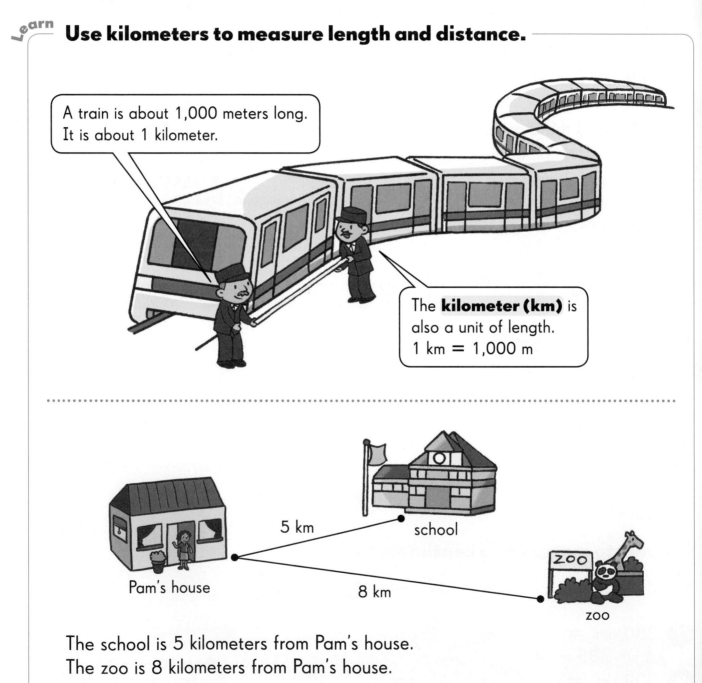

A train is about 1,000 meters long. It is about 1 kilometer.

The **kilometer (km)** is also a unit of length.
1 km = 1,000 m

The school is 5 kilometers from Pam's house.
The zoo is 8 kilometers from Pam's house.

Learn **Convert kilometers and meters to meters.**

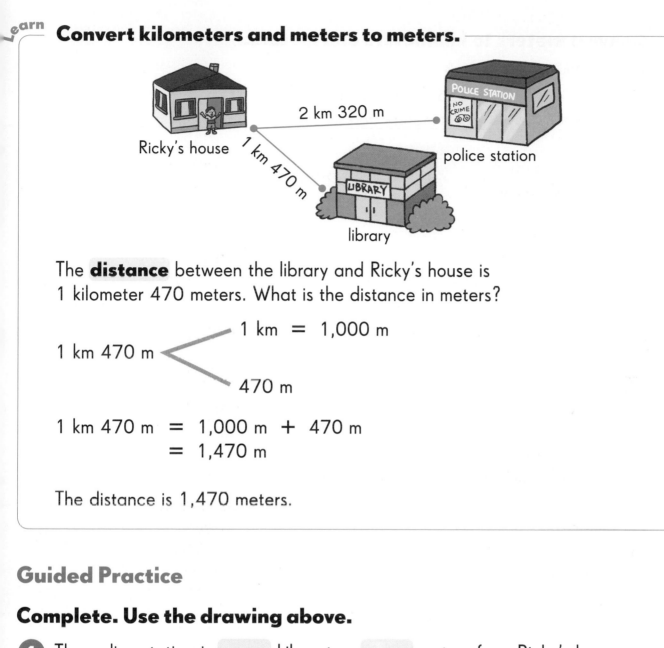

2 km 320 m

Ricky's house

1 km 470 m

police station

library

The **distance** between the library and Ricky's house is
1 kilometer 470 meters. What is the distance in meters?

$$1 \text{ km} = 1{,}000 \text{ m}$$

1 km 470 m

$$470 \text{ m}$$

$$1 \text{ km } 470 \text{ m} = 1{,}000 \text{ m} + 470 \text{ m}$$
$$= 1{,}470 \text{ m}$$

The distance is 1,470 meters.

Guided Practice

Complete. Use the drawing above.

1. The police station is [ ] kilometers [ ] meters from Ricky's house.

   The distance between the police station and Ricky's house is [ ] meters.

Complete.

2. 4 km 235 m

   [ ] km = [ ] m

   [ ] m

   4 km 235 m = [ ] m

   $$4 \text{ km} = 4 \times 1{,}000 \text{ m}$$

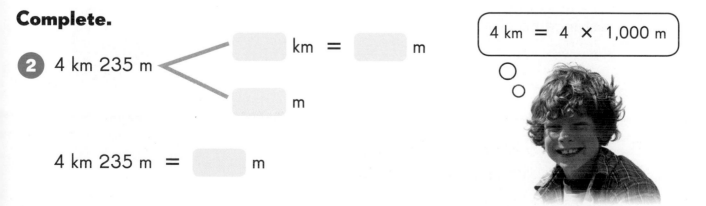

Convert meters to kilometers and meters.

A plane flies 2,790 meters above the ground.
How high is the plane above the ground?
Express your answer in kilometers and meters.

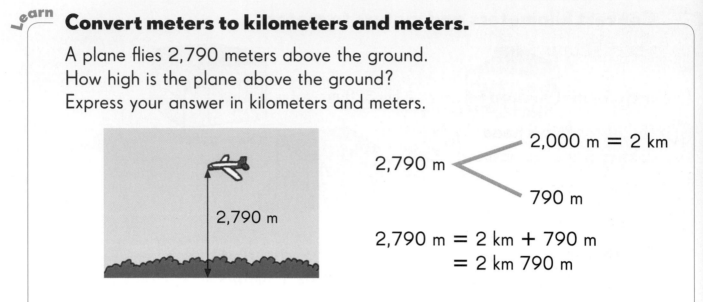

2,790 m
2,000 m = 2 km
790 m

$2{,}790 \text{ m} = 2 \text{ km} + 790 \text{ m}$
$= 2 \text{ km } 790 \text{ m}$

The plane is 2 kilometers 790 meters above the ground.

Guided Practice

Complete.

3 The distance from Zack's home to school
is 5,275 meters.
He bikes to school every morning.
What is the distance he bikes in
kilometers and meters?

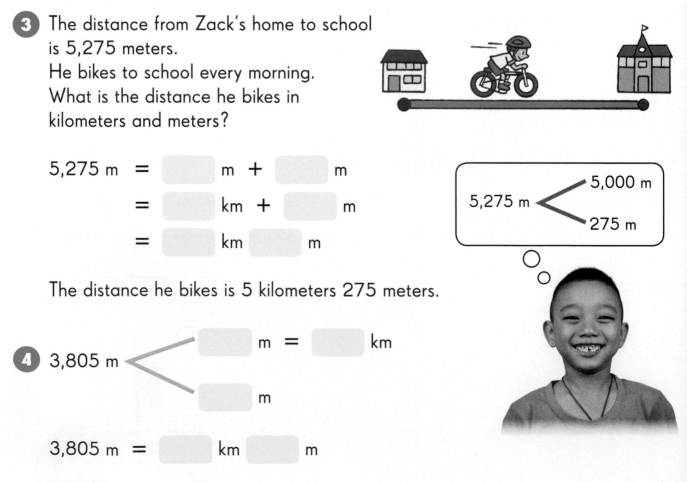

$5{,}275 \text{ m} = \boxed{} \text{ m} + \boxed{} \text{ m}$

$= \boxed{} \text{ km} + \boxed{} \text{ m}$

$= \boxed{} \text{ km} \boxed{} \text{ m}$

5,275 m
5,000 m
275 m

The distance he bikes is 5 kilometers 275 meters.

4 3,805 m
$\boxed{} \text{ m} = \boxed{} \text{ km}$
$\boxed{} \text{ m}$

$3{,}805 \text{ m} = \boxed{} \text{ km} \boxed{} \text{ m}$

Let's Practice

The map is not drawn to scale. Find each distance.

1 The distance between Crystal Lake and the Campsite is about [ ] kilometers.

2 The distance between Trail Head and Crystal Lake is about [ ] kilometers [ ] meters.

3 The distance from the Campsite to Look-Out Station is about [ ] kilometers and [ ] meters.

Campsite

9,700 m

5,600 m

Crystal Lake

5,600 m

Look-Out Station

3,800 m

Trail Head

Convert kilometers and meters to meters.

4 4 km = [ ] m

5 6 km 128 m = [ ] m

6 8 km 700 m = [ ] m

7 2 km 49 m = [ ] m

8 5 km 80 m = [ ] m

9 3 km 7 m = [ ] m

Convert meters to kilometers and meters.

10 5,000 m = [ ] km [ ] m

11 1,465 m = [ ] km [ ] m

12 5,400 m = [ ] km [ ] m

13 2,084 m = [ ] km [ ] m

14 7,090 m = [ ] km [ ] m

15 9,009 m = [ ] km [ ] m

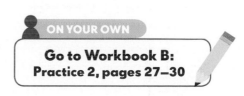

ON YOUR OWN

Go to Workbook B: Practice 2, pages 27–30

Lesson 11.3 Kilograms and Grams

Lesson Objectives

- Read scales in kilograms and grams.
- Estimate and find actual masses of objects by using different scales.
- Convert units of measurement.

Vocabulary
kilogram (kg)
gram (g)

Learn **Use grams to find the mass of items that are less than one kilogram.**

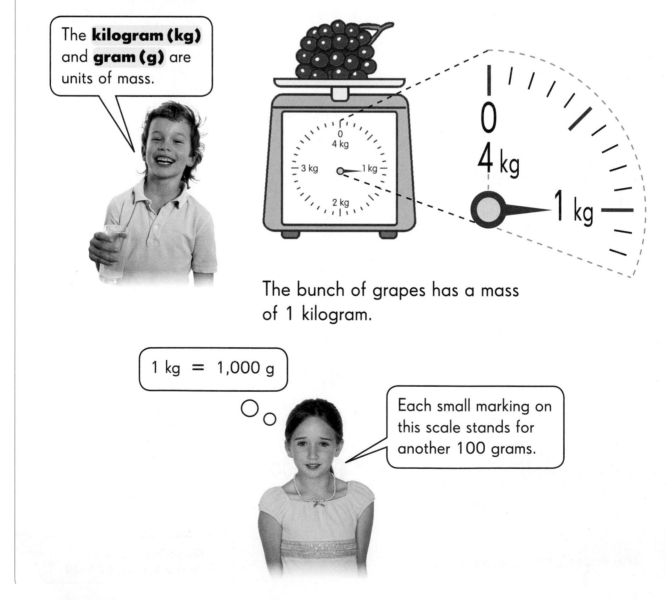

The **kilogram (kg)** and **gram (g)** are units of mass.

The bunch of grapes has a mass of 1 kilogram.

1 kg = 1,000 g

Each small marking on this scale stands for another 100 grams.

Luis uses this scale to find the mass of items that are light.

Use this scale to measure mass 1 kilogram or less. Each small marking stands for another 10 grams.

The pencil case has a mass of 500 grams.

Guided Practice

Complete.

1. The carrots have a mass of 600 grams. What is the mass of the pumpkin?

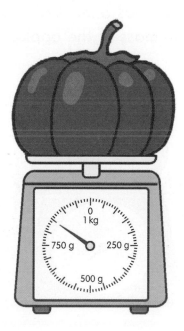

The mass of the pumpkin is _____ grams.

Learn Use kilograms to find the mass of items that are more than one kilogram.

Celia uses this scale to find the mass of items that are heavier.

Use this scale to measure mass 4 kilograms or less. Each small marking stands for another 100 grams.

The mass of the watermelon is 2 kilograms.

· ·

The cabbage has a mass of 1 kilogram 500 grams.
What is the mass of the apples?

The mass of the apples is 2 kilograms 300 grams.

Guided Practice

Read each scale to find the mass.

2

The mass of the apples is

[   ] grams.

3

The mass of the vegetables is

[   ] grams.

4

The mass of the pineapple is

[   ] grams.

5

The mass of the melon is

[   ] grams.

Learn — Convert kilograms and grams to grams.

The mass of a bag of potatoes is 1 kilogram 250 grams.
What is the mass of the bag of potatoes in grams?

1 kg 250 g
— 1 kg = 1,000 g
— 250 g

1 kg 250 g = 1,000 g + 250 g
= 1,250 g

The mass of the bag of potatoes is 1,250 grams.

Guided Practice

Complete.

6 8 kg 405 g

☐ kg = ☐ g

☐ g

8 kg 405 g = ☐ g

8 kg = 8 × 1,000 g

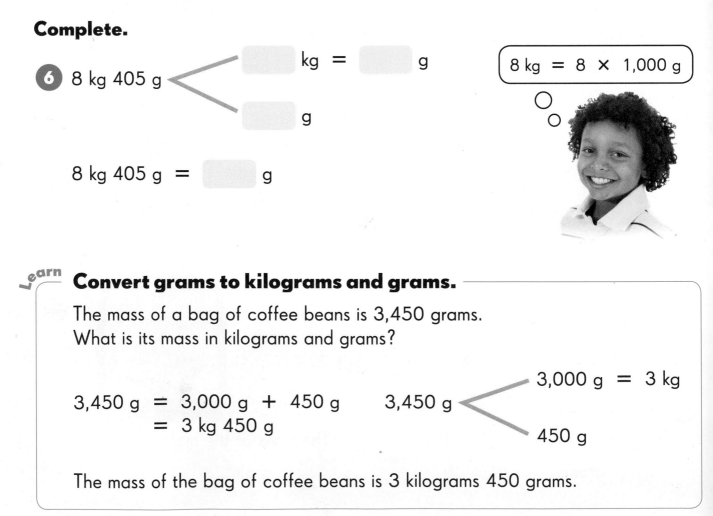

Learn — Convert grams to kilograms and grams.

The mass of a bag of coffee beans is 3,450 grams.
What is its mass in kilograms and grams?

3,450 g = 3,000 g + 450 g   3,450 g
= 3 kg 450 g

3,450 g
— 3,000 g = 3 kg
— 450 g

The mass of the bag of coffee beans is 3 kilograms 450 grams.

Guided Practice

Complete.

7 5,805 g
- ☐ g = ☐ kg
- ☐ g

5,805 g = ☐ kg ☐ g

Let's Practice

Complete.

1

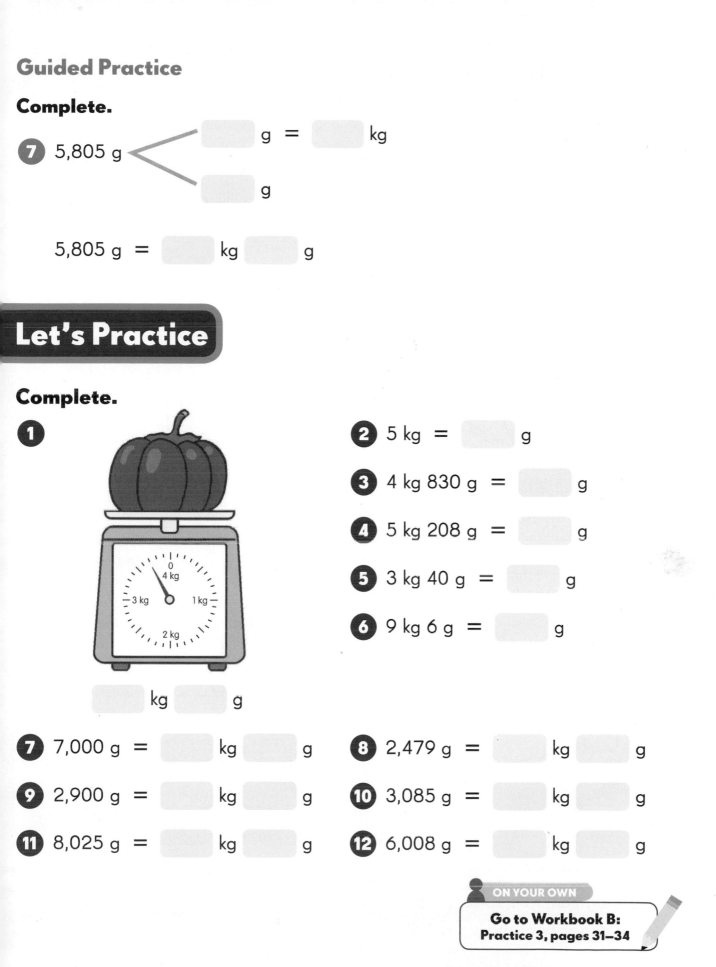

☐ kg ☐ g

2 5 kg = ☐ g

3 4 kg 830 g = ☐ g

4 5 kg 208 g = ☐ g

5 3 kg 40 g = ☐ g

6 9 kg 6 g = ☐ g

7 7,000 g = ☐ kg ☐ g

8 2,479 g = ☐ kg ☐ g

9 2,900 g = ☐ kg ☐ g

10 3,085 g = ☐ kg ☐ g

11 8,025 g = ☐ kg ☐ g

12 6,008 g = ☐ kg ☐ g

ON YOUR OWN

**Go to Workbook B:
Practice 3, pages 31–34**

11.4 Liters and Milliliters

Lesson Objectives

- Estimate and find the volume of liquid in liters and milliliters.
- Find the volume and capacity of a container.
- Convert units of measurement.

Learn **Use liters and milliliters to measure capacity.**

The **liters (L)** and **milliliters (mL)** are units of capacity.

1 L = 1,000 mL

The measuring cup is marked in liters (L) and milliliters (mL).

The jug can hold up to 1 liter of water.
The capacity of the jug is 1 liter.

Capacity is the amount of liquid a container can hold.

Meaning of volume and capacity

How is volume different from capacity?

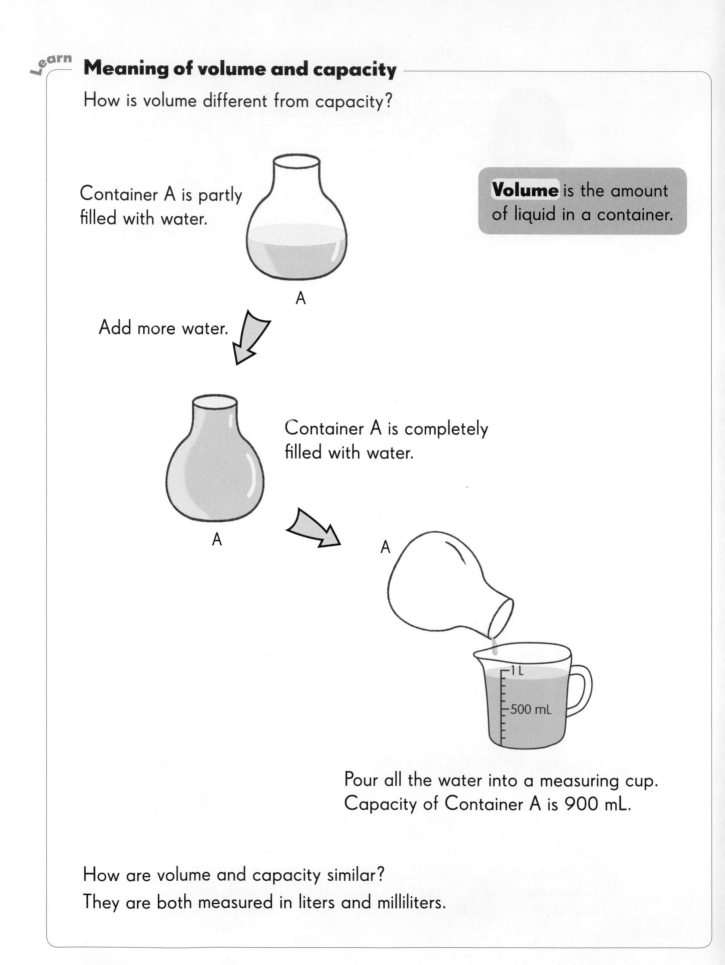

Container A is partly
filled with water.

A

Volume is the amount
of liquid in a container.

Add more water.

Container A is completely
filled with water.

A

A

Pour all the water into a measuring cup.
Capacity of Container A is 900 mL.

How are volume and capacity similar?
They are both measured in liters and milliliters.

Use measuring cups to measure the volume of water.

Each marking on this measuring cup stands for another 100 milliliters.

This cup contains 700 milliliters of water.

Each marking on this measuring cup stands for another 50 milliliters.

This cup contains 400 milliliters of water.

Each marking on this measuring cup stands for another 10 milliliters.

This cup contains 100 milliliters of water.

Guided Practice

Find the volume.

1

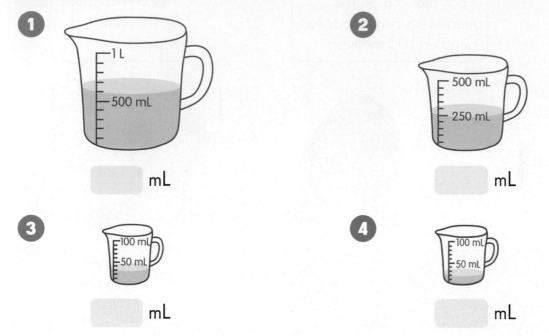

_____ mL

2

_____ mL

3

_____ mL

4

_____ mL

ℓᵉᵃʳⁿ **Use liters and milliliters to measure capacity.**

A water jug is completely filled with water.
The water is emptied into measuring cups.

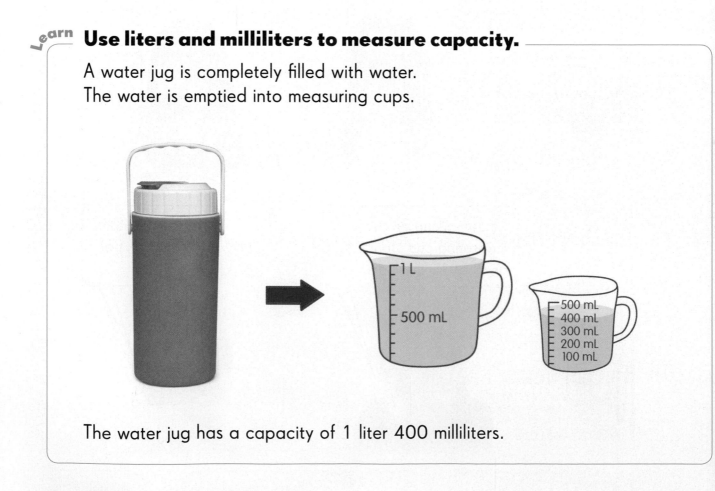

The water jug has a capacity of 1 liter 400 milliliters.

Guided Practice

Find the capacity.

5

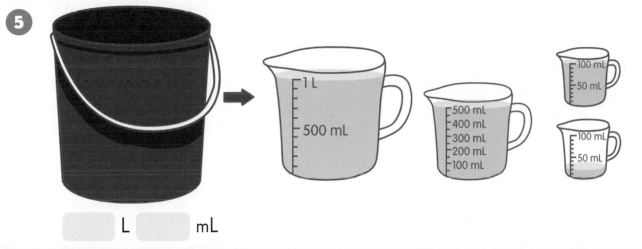

[   ] L [   ] mL

 Hands-On Activity

Materials:
- 4 containers of different sizes
- metric measuring cup

Use four containers of different sizes.
Work in groups of four.

STEP 1 Estimate the capacity of each container in liters and milliliters.

STEP 2 Fill each container completely with water.
Then empty the water into a measuring cup to find its capacity.

STEP 3 Complete a copy of this chart.
Compare your findings with your classmates.

Container	A	B	C	D
Our Estimate				
Actual Capacity				

Learn — **Convert liters and milliliters to milliliters.**

The volume of orange juice in a container is 2 liters 370 milliliters.
What is the volume in milliliters?

2 L 370 mL

- 2 L = 2,000 mL
- 370 mL

2 L 370 mL = 2,000 mL + 370 mL
= 2,370 mL

The volume of orange juice in the container is 2,370 milliliters.

Guided Practice

Complete.

6 7 L 745 mL

☐ L = ☐ mL

☐ mL

7 L 745 mL = ☐ mL

7 L = 7 × 1,000 mL

Learn — **Convert milliliters to liters and milliliters.**

The capacity of a barrel is 8,725 milliliters.
What is the capacity of the barrel in liters and milliliters?

8,725 mL

- 8,000 mL = 8 L
- 725 mL

8,725 mL = 8,000 mL + 725 mL
= 8 L 725 mL

The capacity of the barrel is 8 liters 725 milliliters.

Guided Practice

Complete.

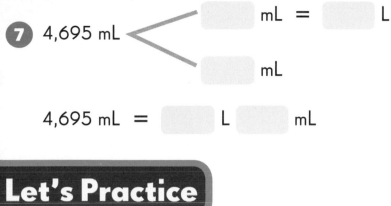

(7) 4,695 mL ⟨ [　] mL = [　] L

[　] mL

4,695 mL = [　] L [　] mL

Let's Practice

Find the capacity of the tank.

1

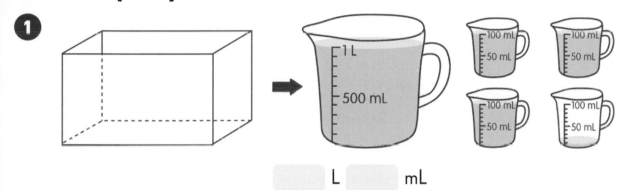

[　] L [　] mL

Complete.

2) 6 L 328 mL = [　] mL   3) 4 L 400 mL = [　] mL

4) 9 L 705 mL = [　] mL   5) 5 L 45 mL = [　] mL

6) 3 L 90 mL = [　] mL   7) 6 L 7 mL = [　] mL

8) 2,000 mL = [　] L [　] mL   9) 5,430 mL = [　] L [　] mL

10) 9,809 mL = [　] L [　] mL   11) 9,045 mL = [　] L [　] mL

12) 3,070 mL = [　] L [　] mL

ON YOUR OWN

**Go to Workbook B:
Practice 4, pages 35–38**

13) 9,008 mL = [　] L [　] mL

Put On Your Thinking Cap!

PROBLEM SOLVING

1 How much oil is in the beaker?
Express your answer in mL.

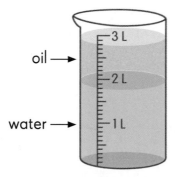

2 Mr. Smith has three coins. One out of the three is a fake coin.
It is lighter than a real coin. With the help of a balance, how
can you tell which is the fake coin?

Explain what happens if you:

a choose the two real coins first.

b choose one real coin and one fake coin first.

3 Show how these two containers can be used to
measure 200 milliliters of water exactly.

1 L   600 mL

ON YOUR OWN

**Go to Workbook B:
Put on Your Thinking Cap!
page 39–40**

Chapter Wrap Up

Study Guide
You have learned...

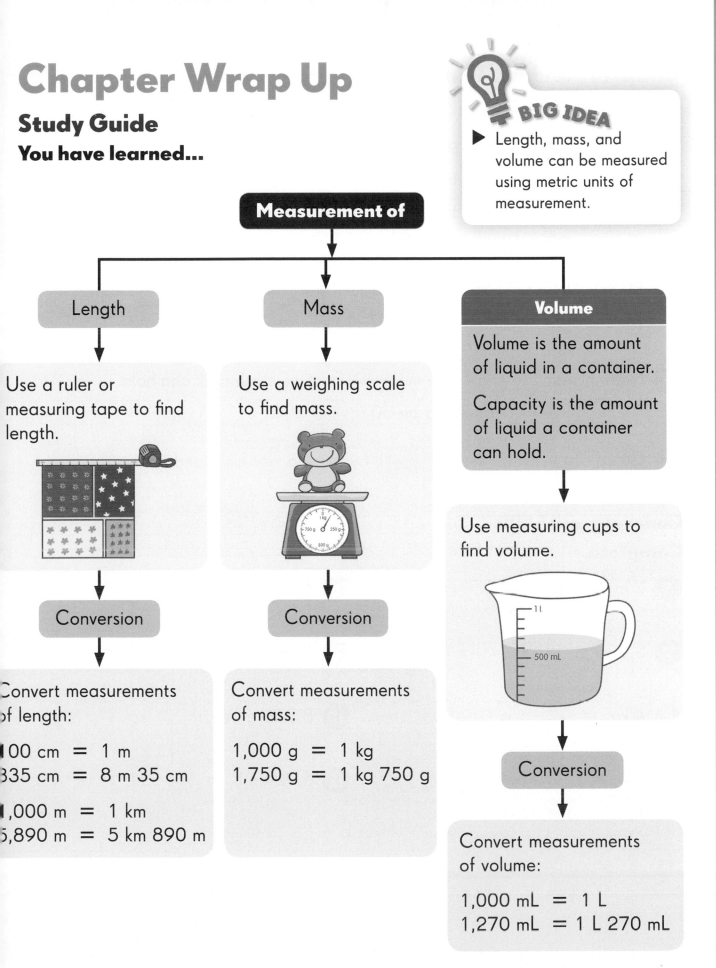

BIG IDEA

► Length, mass, and volume can be measured using metric units of measurement.

Measurement of

Length

Use a ruler or measuring tape to find length.

Conversion

Convert measurements of length:

100 cm = 1 m
835 cm = 8 m 35 cm

1,000 m = 1 km
5,890 m = 5 km 890 m

Mass

Use a weighing scale to find mass.

Conversion

Convert measurements of mass:

1,000 g = 1 kg
1,750 g = 1 kg 750 g

Volume

Volume is the amount of liquid in a container.

Capacity is the amount of liquid a container can hold.

Use measuring cups to find volume.

1 L

500 mL

Conversion

Convert measurements of volume:

1,000 mL = 1 L
1,270 mL = 1 L 270 mL

Chapter Review/Test

Vocabulary
Choose the correct word.

1 Ariel has two pieces of fabric.
The total _____ of the two pieces of fabric is
5 meters 92 centimeters.

kilometers
milliliters
length
mass
liters

2 Mabel will be traveling soon. She is weighing her luggage.
The total _____ of her luggage is 55 kilograms.

3 Nathan wants to know how much water his new fish tank can hold.
He measures its capacity to be 30 _____ 500 _____ .

4 Caleb has to travel several _____ by train to visit his grandparents.

Concepts and Skills
Complete.

5 7 m 69 cm = _____ cm

6 641 cm = _____ m _____ cm

7 8,905 m = _____ km _____ m

8 3 km 509 m = _____ m

9 4 kg = _____ g

10 8,555 g = _____ kg _____ g

11 3 L = _____ mL

12 6,924 mL = _____ L _____ mL

Chapter 12 Real-World Problems: Measurement

Lessons

12.1 Real-World Problems: One-Step Problems

12.2 Real-World Problems: Two-Step Problems

BIG IDEA

▶ Bar models can be used to solve one- and two-step problems on measurements.

Recall Prior Knowledge

Adding, subtracting, multiplying, and dividing

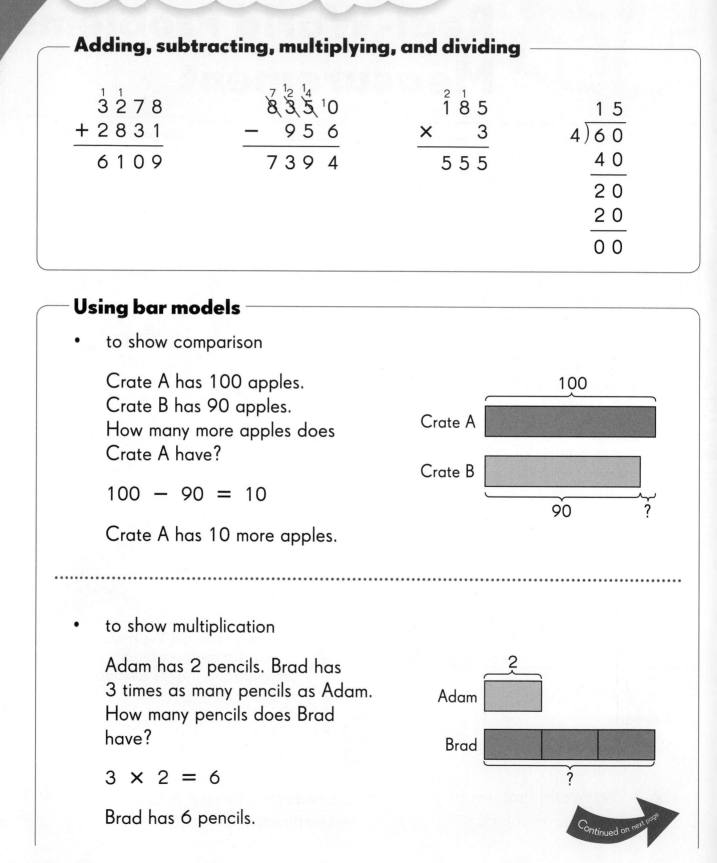

$$\begin{array}{r} \overset{1}{3}\overset{1}{2}78 \\ +\;2831 \\ \hline 6109 \end{array}$$

$$\begin{array}{r} \overset{7}{\cancel{8}}\overset{12}{\cancel{3}}\overset{14}{\cancel{5}}{}^1 0 \\ -\;\;\;956 \\ \hline 7394 \end{array}$$

$$\begin{array}{r} \overset{2}{1}\overset{1}{8}5 \\ \times\;\;\;\;3 \\ \hline 555 \end{array}$$

$$\begin{array}{r} 15 \\ 4\overline{)60} \\ 40 \\ \hline 20 \\ 20 \\ \hline 00 \end{array}$$

Using bar models

- to show comparison

    Crate A has 100 apples.
    Crate B has 90 apples.
    How many more apples does
    Crate A have?

    $100 - 90 = 10$

    Crate A has 10 more apples.

    100

    Crate A

    Crate B

    90   ?

- to show multiplication

    Adam has 2 pencils. Brad has
    3 times as many pencils as Adam.
    How many pencils does Brad
    have?

    $3 \times 2 = 6$

    Brad has 6 pencils.

    2

    Adam

    Brad

    ?

Continued on next page

• to show division

A box has 45 strawberries. Laura shares the strawberries equally among 5 friends. How many strawberries does each person get?

$45 \div 5 = 9$

Each person gets 9 strawberries.

45

?

Tyrone has 24 yogurt bars. He puts them in boxes of 4. How many boxes does he need?

$24 \div 4 = 6$

He needs 6 boxes.

24

4   4

?

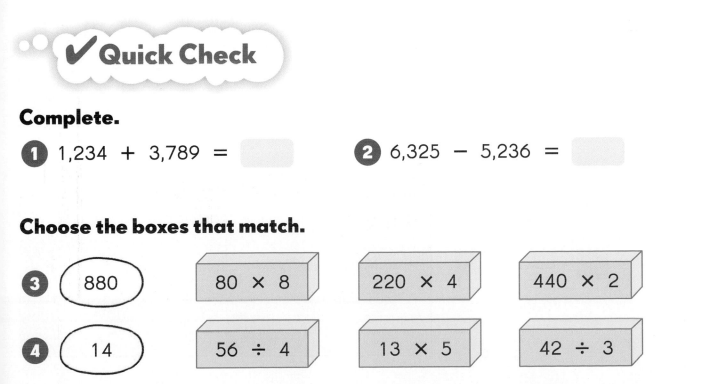

✔ **Quick Check**

Complete.

1 $1,234 + 3,789 =$ ⬚

2 $6,325 - 5,236 =$ ⬚

Choose the boxes that match.

3 (880)   80 × 8   220 × 4   440 × 2

4 (14)   56 ÷ 4   13 × 5   42 ÷ 3

Decide which situation describes the bar models.

5

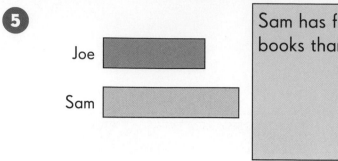

Sam has fewer books than Joe.	Joe has more books than Sam.	Joe has fewer books than Sam.
A	B	C

6

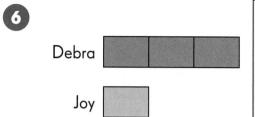

Joy has 3 times as many pencils as Debra.	Debra has 2 times as many pencils as Joy.	Debra has 3 times as many pencils as Joy.
A	B	C

7

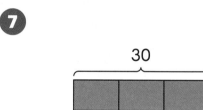

Divide 30 items into 3 equal groups. How many items are in each group?	Divide 30 items into groups of 3. How many groups are there?
A	B

8

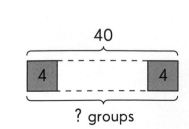

Divide 40 items into 4 equal groups. How many items are in each group?	Divide 40 items into groups of 4. How many groups are there?
A	B

Real-World Problems: One-Step Problems

Lesson Objectives

- Draw bar models to solve one-step measurement problems.
- Choose the operation to solve one-step problems.

Use addition to solve measurement problems.

Keisha ties a package with a string 75 centimeters long.
She ties another package with a string 255 centimeters long.
What is the total length of the two strings she uses?
Give your answer in meters and centimeters.

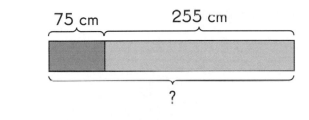

```
  1 1
    7 5
+ 2 5 5
———————
  3 3 0
```

$$75 + 255 = 330$$
$$330 \text{ cm} = 3 \text{ m } 30 \text{ cm}$$

The total length of the two strings is 3 meters 30 centimeters.

100 cm = 1 m
300 cm = 3 m
330 cm = 3 m 30 cm

Guided Practice

Solve.

1 Abel tied a gift box with a ribbon 56 centimeters long.
He tied another gift box with a ribbon 184 centimeters long.
What was the total length of ribbon that he used?
Give your answer in meters and centimeters.

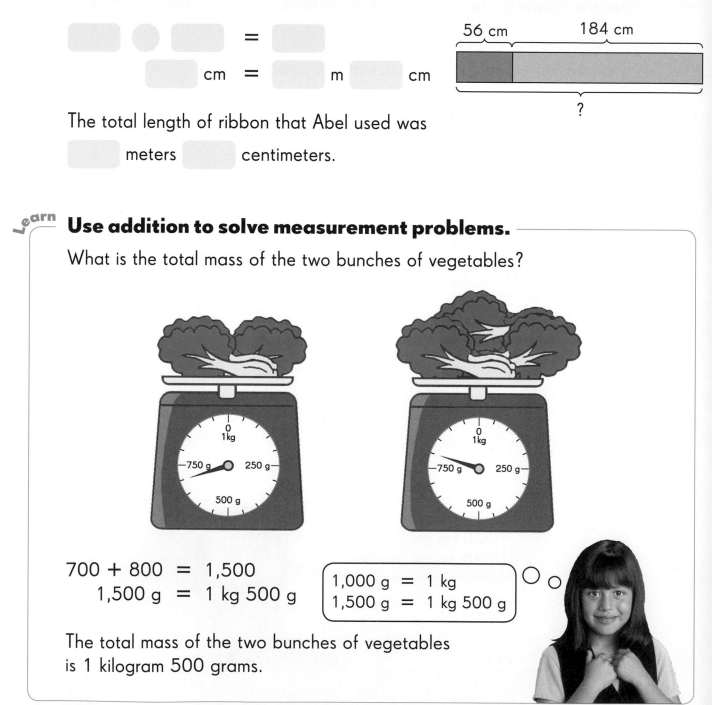

[____] • [____] = [____]

[____] cm = [____] m [____] cm

56 cm   184 cm

?

The total length of ribbon that Abel used was

[____] meters [____] centimeters.

Learn Use addition to solve measurement problems.

What is the total mass of the two bunches of vegetables?

700 + 800 = 1,500
    1,500 g = 1 kg 500 g

1,000 g = 1 kg
1,500 g = 1 kg 500 g

The total mass of the two bunches of vegetables
is 1 kilogram 500 grams.

Guided Practice

Solve.

2 Sonia walks 650 meters to her friend's house.
She takes a longer route home and walks 740 meters.
What is the total distance she walked?
Give your answer in kilometers and meters.

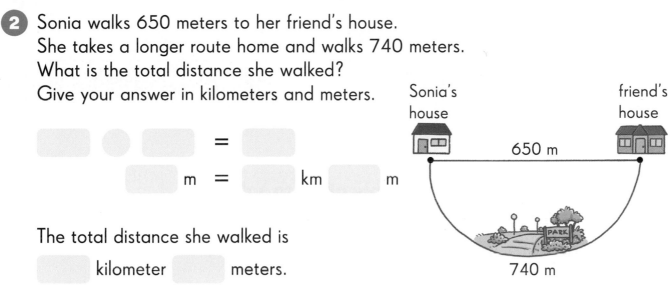

Sonia's house   friend's house
650 m
740 m

$\boxed{} \ \bullet \ \boxed{} \ = \ \boxed{}$

$\boxed{} \ m \ = \ \boxed{} \ km \ \boxed{} \ m$

The total distance she walked is

$\boxed{}$ kilometer $\boxed{}$ meters.

Use subtraction to solve measurement problems.

The distance between Town A and Town B is 420 kilometers.
The distance between Town B and Town C is 28 kilometers.
What is the difference between the two distances?

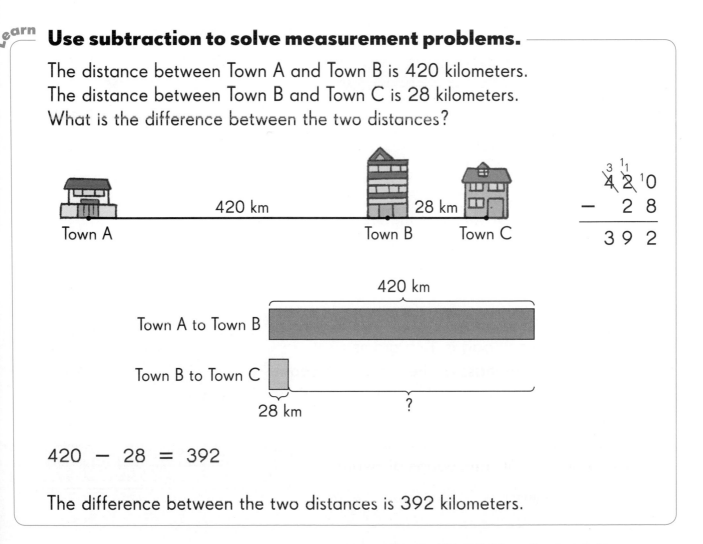

$$
\begin{array}{r}
{}^{3}\cancel{4}\,{}^{1}\cancel{2}\,{}^{1}0 \\
-\quad 2\ 8 \\
\hline
3\ 9\ 2
\end{array}
$$

420 km

Town A to Town B

Town B to Town C

28 km   ?

$420 - 28 = 392$

The difference between the two distances is 392 kilometers.

Guided Practice

3 An inflatable pool contains 356 liters of water.
15 liters of water leaks from it.
Find the volume of water that is left.

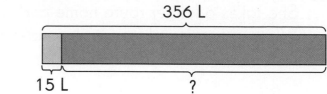

356 L

15 L   ?

▢ ● ▢ = ▢

▢ liters of water is left.

Learn Use bar models and multiplication to solve measurement problems.

Julio has 4 pieces of wire each 178 centimeters long.
What is the total length of wire?
Give your answer in meters and centimeters.

178 cm

?

$$\begin{array}{r} \overset{3\ \ 3}{1\ 7\ 8} \\ \times\quad 4 \\ \hline 7\ 1\ 2 \end{array}$$

4 × 178 = 712
712 cm = 7 m 12 cm

The total length of wire is 7 meters 12 centimeters.

Guided Practice

4 A teacher puts some beans equally into 5 bags.
The mass of each bag is 125 grams.
What is the total mass of the 5 bags of beans?

▢ ● ▢ = ▢

The total mass of the 5 bags of beans
is ▢ grams.

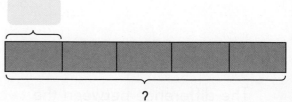

?

Use bar models and division to solve measurement problems.

An oil delivery truck has 96 liters of fuel.
The fuel is pumped equally into 3 tanks.
How many liters of fuel are in each tank?

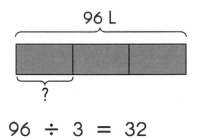

96 L

?

$96 \div 3 = 32$

There are 32 liters of fuel in each tank.

```
      3 2
 3)9 6
   9 0
   ───
     6
     6
   ───
     0
```

Guided Practice

5 Janice cuts a ribbon that is 90 centimeters long into 5 equal pieces. How long is each piece?

[   ] ● [   ] = [   ]

Each piece of ribbon is [   ] centimeters long.

?

Solve.

6 A grocer buys 850 kilograms of granola.
He repacks the granola equally into 5-kilogram bags.
How many bags are there?

[   ] ● [   ] = [   ] tens ● [   ] [   ]

= [   ] tens

= [   ]

| 5 kg | | 5 kg |

?

There are [   ] bags.

Let's Practice

Solve. Draw bar models to help you.

 1 Rose has 1,000 milliliters of milk.
She completely fills some mugs with all the milk.
The capacity of each mug is 250 milliliters.
How many mugs does she use?

2 Ruby buys 81 kilograms of flour for her bakery.
She repacks the flour equally into 9 bags.
How many kilograms of flour are in each bag?

3 A statue of President Lincoln is about 6 meters high.
The Empire State Building is 65 times as tall.
About how tall is the Empire State Building?

6 meters

4 Mr. Mills is 197 centimeters tall.
He is 23 centimeters taller than Mrs. Mills.
How tall is Mrs. Mills?
Give your answer in meters and centimetres.

5 Mrs. Martinelli buys 675 grams of pasta on Monday.
She buys 750 grams of pasta on Tuesday.
What is the total mass of pasta she buys?
Give your answer in kilograms and grams.

ON YOUR OWN

**Go to Workbook B:
Practice 1, pages 41—44**

Lesson 12.2 Real-World Problems: Two-Step Problems

Lesson Objectives

* Draw bar models to solve two-step measurement problems.
* Choose the operations to solve problems.
* Write and solve two-step measurement problems.

Learn Solve measurement problems using two operations.

Sam cuts a string into 5 pieces and has 9 centimeters left.
Each of the 5 pieces of string is 28 centimeters long.

a What is the total length of the 5 pieces of string?

b How much string did Sam start with?
Give your answer in meters and centimeters.

a
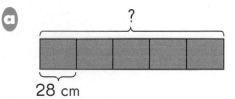

$$\begin{array}{r} \overset{4}{2}\,8 \\ \times \quad 5 \\ \hline 1\,4\,0 \end{array}$$

$$28 \times 5 = 140$$

The total length of the 5 pieces of string is 140 centimeters.

b
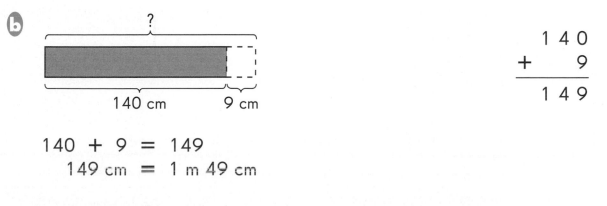

140 cm   9 cm

$$\begin{array}{r} 1\,4\,0 \\ + \quad 9 \\ \hline 1\,4\,9 \end{array}$$

$$140 + 9 = 149$$
$$149 \text{ cm} = 1 \text{ m } 49 \text{ cm}$$

Sam had 1 meter 49 centimeters of string to start with.

Guided Practice

1 Alex and Billy compete in a bike race.
Each of them bikes from Point A to Point B and back again.
The distance between Point A and Point B is 54 meters.
When Alex completes the race, Billy has only biked 36 meters.
How much farther does Billy have to bike to complete the race?

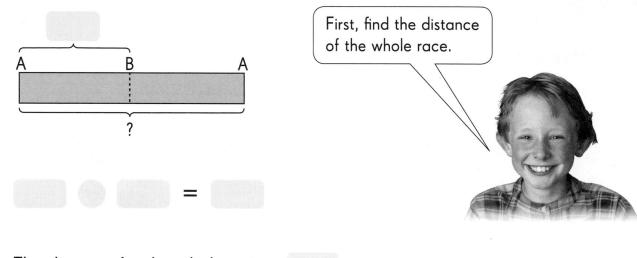

First, find the distance of the whole race.

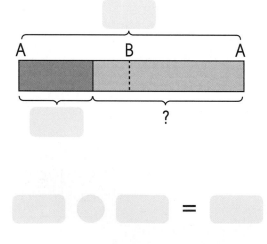

The distance for the whole race is [ ] meters.

Billy has to bike another [ ] meters to complete the race.

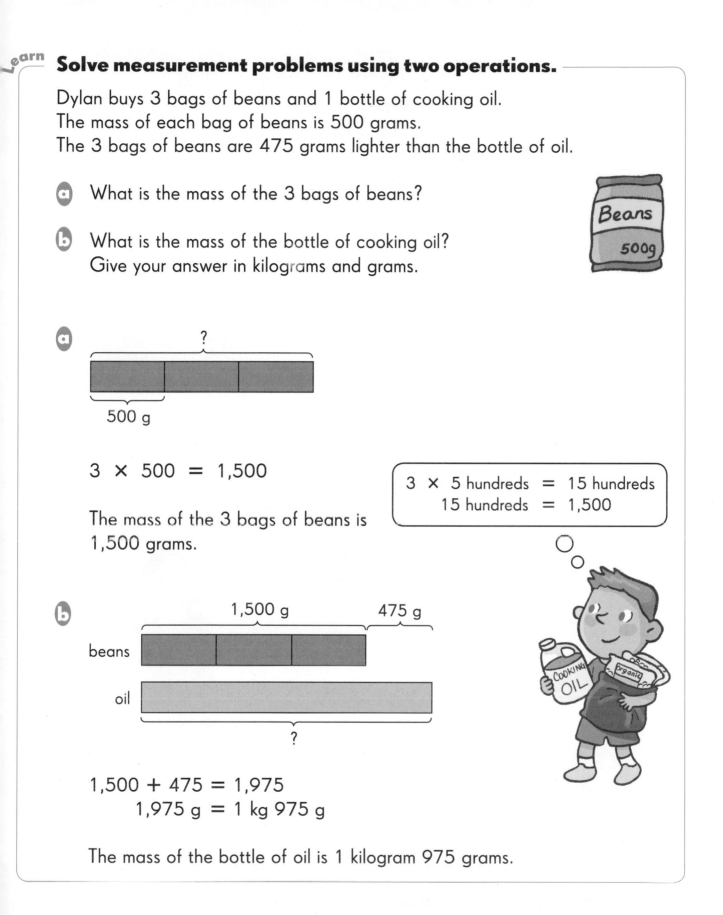

Learn **Solve measurement problems using two operations.**

Dylan buys 3 bags of beans and 1 bottle of cooking oil.
The mass of each bag of beans is 500 grams.
The 3 bags of beans are 475 grams lighter than the bottle of oil.

ⓐ What is the mass of the 3 bags of beans?

ⓑ What is the mass of the bottle of cooking oil?
Give your answer in kilograms and grams.

ⓐ

?

500 g

$3 \times 500 = 1,500$

The mass of the 3 bags of beans is
1,500 grams.

3×5 hundreds $= 15$ hundreds
15 hundreds $= 1,500$

ⓑ

1,500 g   475 g

beans

oil

?

$1,500 + 475 = 1,975$
$1,975$ g $= 1$ kg 975 g

The mass of the bottle of oil is 1 kilogram 975 grams.

Guided Practice

2 Liza has 780 grams of dried peas.
She uses 330 grams to make pea soup.
Then she packs the remaining peas equally into 5 bags.
Find the mass of each bag of peas.

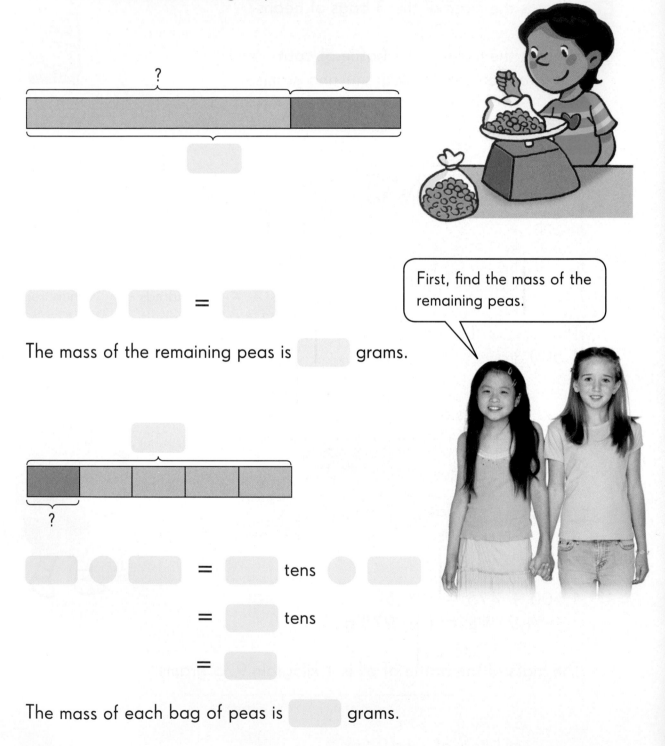

First, find the mass of the remaining peas.

[ ] ● [ ] = [ ]

The mass of the remaining peas is [ ] grams.

[ ] ● [ ] = [ ] tens ● [ ]

= [ ] tens

= [ ]

The mass of each bag of peas is [ ] grams.

Solve measurement problems using two operations.

A water cooler contains 27 liters of water.
A teacher uses all the water to completely fill several
3-liter bottles for a science experiment.

a How many bottles does the teacher fill?

b The teacher uses 5 bottles of water for one experiment.
How many bottles of water are left?

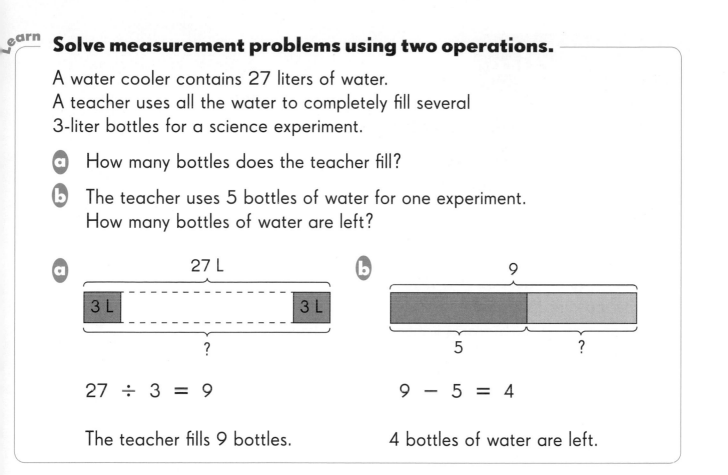

$27 \div 3 = 9$

The teacher fills 9 bottles.

$9 - 5 = 4$

4 bottles of water are left.

Guided Practice

Complete.

3 Ian stacks 5 glasses of juice.
Each glass contains 185 milliliters of juice.

a Find the total volume of juice in the 5 glasses.

b Ian drinks one glass of juice.
How much juice is left?

a ⬜ ● ⬜ = ⬜

The total volume of juice in the 5 glasses

is ⬜ milliliters.

b ⬜ ● ⬜ = ⬜

⬜ milliliters of juice is left.

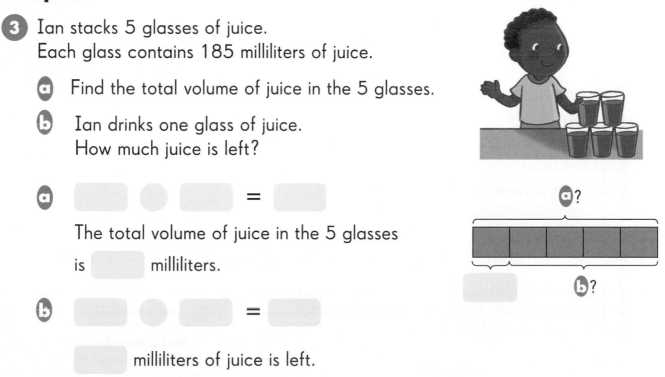

Let's Practice

Solve. Use bar models to help you.

1 Matt has 95 centimeters of rope.
He cuts 14 centimeters from it.
He then cuts the rest into 3 equal pieces.
What is the length of each piece?

2 The mass of Package A is 245 grams.
The mass of Package B is twice as much as Package A.
Package C is 175 grams lighter than Package B.
Find the mass of Package C.

3 A barrel has 49 liters of water.
Erin adds another 14 liters into the barrel.
She then pours all the water equally into 7 pails.
How much water is in each pail?

4 A green ribbon is 4 meters long.
A red ribbon is 6 times as long as the green ribbon.
Martin cuts the red ribbon into 3 equal pieces.
What is the length of each piece of red ribbon?

5 Mrs. Lee buys a bag of beans and a bag of flour.
The bag of beans is 230 grams.
The bag of flour is 4 times as heavy as the bag of beans.
Find the total mass of the flour and the beans.
Give your answer in kilograms and grams.

6 Trent is preparing for an endurance race.
He runs 685 meters, swims 490 meters, and cycles 900 meters.
What is the distance he covers?
Give your answer in kilometers and meters.

ON YOUR OWN

**Go to Workbook B:
Practice 2, pages 45—50**

**Read the real-world problem. Study the bar models.
Then answer the questions.**

There are 3 pitchers of cranberry juice on a table.
Each pitcher has 800 milliliters of juice.
All the juice in the 3 pitchers is poured equally into 8 glasses.
How much juice is in each glass?

Dana draws these bar models to solve the real-world problem.

Total amount of juice

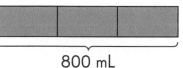

800 mL

Amount of juice in each glass

800 mL

Are the bar models correct? Explain your answer.
If the bar models are not correct, draw the correct bar models.

CRITICAL THINKING SKILLS
Put On Your Thinking Cap!

PROBLEM SOLVING

1. Lucas has a 12-liter pail and a 5-liter pail.
Explain how he can get the following amount
of water using these pails.

   a. 2 liters

   b. 3 liters

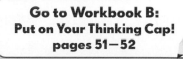

ON YOUR OWN

**Go to Workbook B:
Put on Your Thinking Cap!
pages 51—52**

Chapter Wrap Up

Study Guide
You have learned...

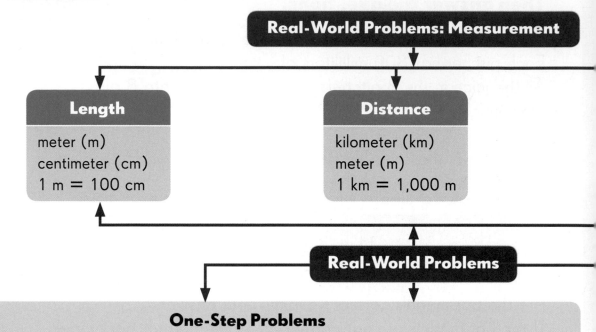

Real-World Problems: Measurement

Length
meter (m)
centimeter (cm)
1 m = 100 cm

Distance
kilometer (km)
meter (m)
1 km = 1,000 m

Real-World Problems

One-Step Problems

Length

Pole A is 134 centimeters long.
Pole B is 103 centimeters long.
Both poles are placed end to end.
What is the total length of both poles?

134 + 103 = 237

The total length of both poles is
237 centimeters.

Distance

The distance between Sam's house and his
school is 455 meters. The distance between
Sam's house and the library is 280 meters.
How much nearer is the library than the
school to Sam's house?

455 − 280 = 175

The library is 175 meters nearer.

Mass

The mass of a block of cheese is 2 kilograms.
Chef Clark buys 16 such blocks of cheese.
What is the mass of cheese Chef Clark buys?

16 × 2 = 32

He buys 32 kilograms of cheese.

Volume

Chloe fills 4 identical tanks completely with
112 liters of water.
What is the volume of water in each tank?

112 ÷ 4 = 28

The volume of water in each tank is 28 liters.

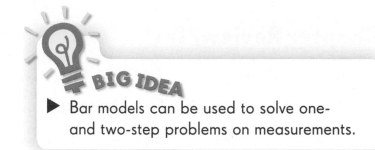

BIG IDEA

▶ Bar models can be used to solve one-
and two-step problems on measurements.

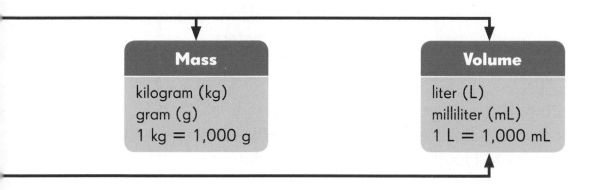

Mass
kilogram (kg) gram (g) 1 kg = 1,000 g

Volume
liter (L) milliliter (mL) 1 L = 1,000 mL

Two-Step Problems

Sally has a length of ribbon 2 meters long. She cuts 6 equal pieces from the ribbon and has 110 centimeters left.
What is the length of each of the 6 pieces of ribbon?

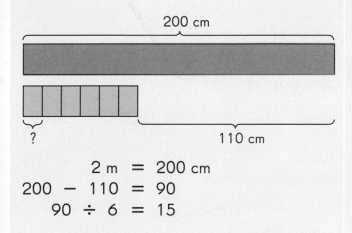

200 cm

? 110 cm

2 m = 200 cm
200 − 110 = 90
90 ÷ 6 = 15

The length of each piece is 15 centimeters.

Joan buys 3 cans of oatmeal and 2 bottles of liquid detergent. The mass of each can of oatmeal is 3 kilograms.
The mass of each bottle of liquid detergent is 500 grams. What is the total mass of the items?

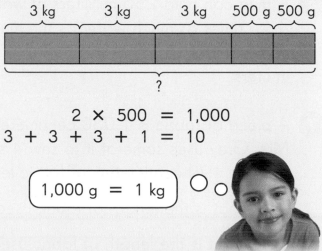

3 kg   3 kg   3 kg   500 g 500 g

?

2 × 500 = 1,000
3 + 3 + 3 + 1 = 10

1,000 g = 1 kg

The total mass is 10 kilograms.

Chapter Review/Test

Problem Solving

Solve. Use bar models to help you.

1 The Benaro family is going camping. They want to place two sleeping bags end to end. The lengths of the sleeping bags are 153 centimeters and 167 centimeters. How long does the tent need to be? Give your answer in meters and centimeters.

2 On a road trip, Mr. Stewart drives 850 kilometers from Chicago to Kansas City. He drives another 1,280 kilometers from Kansas City to Houston. What is the total distance he drives?

3 The mass of a package is 210 grams. What is the mass of 4 similar packages?

4 A pot has 950 milliliters of soup. The chef pours all the soup equally into 5 bowls. How much soup is there in each bowl?

5 Mr. Geller pours 135 liters of water equally into 3-liter pails. How many pails does he fill up?

6 A mug can hold 250 milliliters of water. A pitcher can hold three times as much water as the mug. What is the total capacity of the mug and the pitcher? Give your answer in liters.

7 A piece of fabric is 1,030 centimeters long. Mrs. Grey uses some of it to sew 4 similar table runners. There is 190 centimeters of fabric left.

 What is the length of fabric used by Mrs. Grey?

 What is the length of fabric used for each table runner? Give your answer in meters and centimeters.

13 Bar Graphs and Line Plots

Lessons

13.1 Making Bar Graphs with Scales

13.2 Reading and Interpreting Bar Graphs

13.3 Line Plots

BIG IDEAS

▶ Bar graphs and line plots help to organize data. Bar graphs are used to compare data. Line plots show how data is spread out.

Recall Prior Knowledge

Using a picture graph to represent data

Four friends made some posters.

The picture graph shows the number of posters made by the four friends.

Number of Posters Made

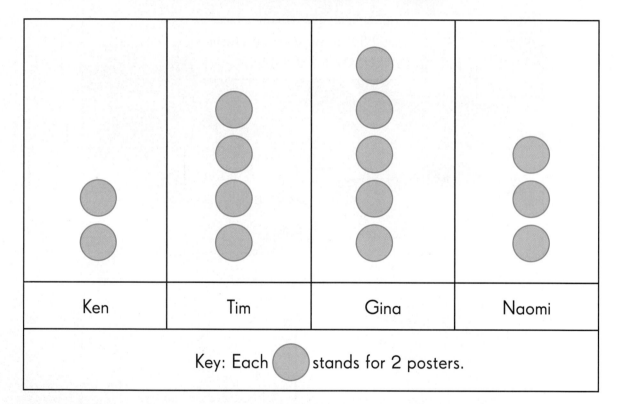

Key: Each ⬤ stands for 2 posters.

A picture graph shows information (data) using pictures and symbols.
The key shows what each symbol, or picture, stands for.

Ken made 4 posters.
Tim made 8 posters.
Gina made 4 more posters than Naomi.
The four friends made 28 posters in all.

Using a bar graph to represent data

The tally chart shows the kinds of fruits in Sara's picnic basket.

Fruits in Sara's Picnic Basket

Kind of Fruit	Tally	Number of Fruits
plum	///	3
pear	////	4
orange	//// //	7

She used the data in the tally chart to draw a bar graph.

Fruits in Sara's Picnic Basket

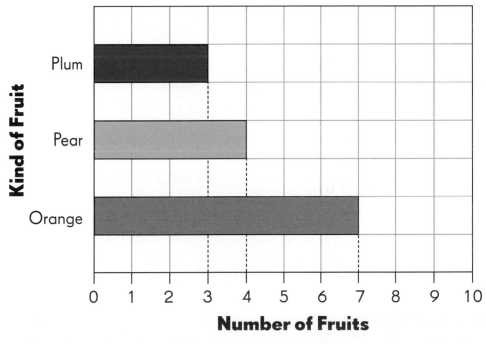

The bar graphs shows that Sara has 4 pears and 3 plums.
She has a total of 14 pieces of fruit in her picnic basket.

✔ Quick Check

Miguel is helping his teacher to find his classmates' favorite colors.
The picture graph shows the number of classmates who like each color.

Favorite Colors

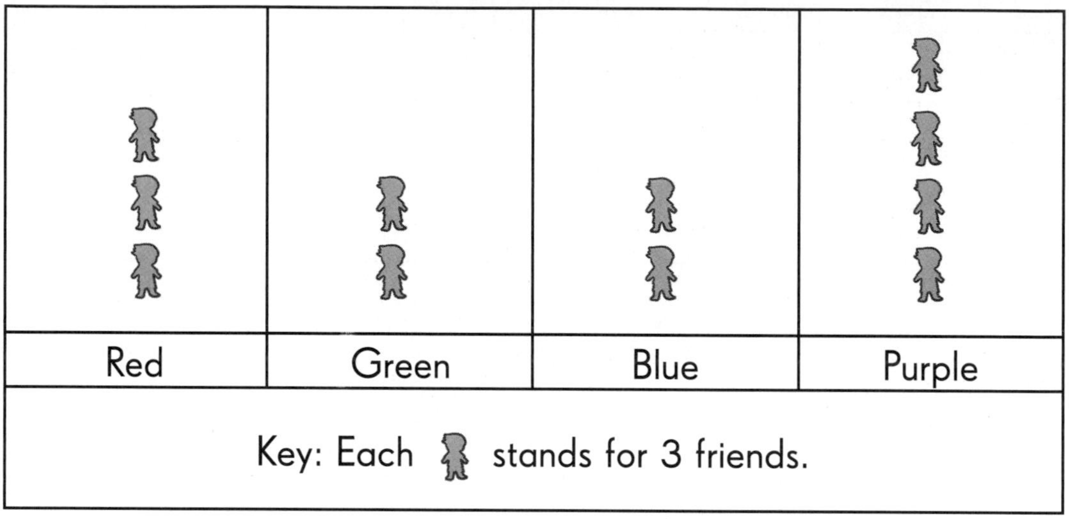

Red	Green	Blue	Purple
3 figures	2 figures	2 figures	4 figures

Key: Each 🧍 stands for 3 friends.

Complete. Use the picture graph to help you.

1 _____ is the color chosen most often.

2 There are _____ classmates who like purple.

3 The number of classmates who like _____ is the same as those who like _____ .

4 Miguel has _____ classmates in all.

The tally chart shows the kinds and number of animals that are found at a zoo.

Complete the tally chart.

5

Animals in the Zoo

Kind of Animal	Tally	Number of Animals
Polar Bear	//	
Elephant	////	
Penguin	̶H̶H̶T̶ ///	
Dolphin	̶H̶H̶T̶	

Complete the bar graph. Use the data in the tally chart.

6

Animals in the Zoo

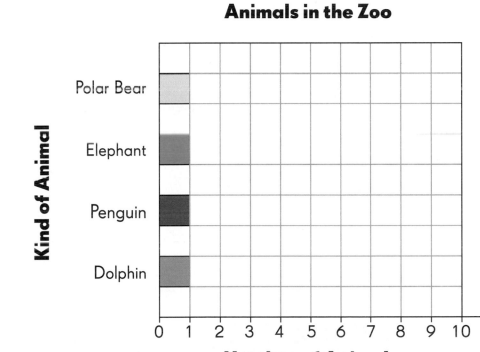

Read and interpret the bar graph.

7 There are ____ more penguins than elephants.

8 There are ____ fewer polar bears than dolphins.

9 There are ____ elephants and polar bears in the zoo.

Lesson 13.1 Making Bar Graphs with Scales

Vocabulary

vertical

horizontal

axis

scale

Lesson Objective

*   Make bar graphs with scales using data in picture graphs and tally charts.

Learn **Make graphs using data from picture graphs.**

Four friends went for a nature walk.
The picture graph shows the number of butterflies that each friend saw on the walk.

A picture graph is useful for comparing data.

Butterflies Seen

Sam	🦋 🦋 🦋 🦋	4
Jamal	🦋 🦋 🦋 🦋 🦋 🦋 🦋 🦋 🦋 🦋	10
Karen	🦋 🦋 🦋 🦋 🦋 🦋 🦋 🦋	8
Roger	🦋 🦋 🦋 🦋 🦋 🦋	6
Key: Each 🦋 stands for 1 butterfly.		

Butterflies Seen

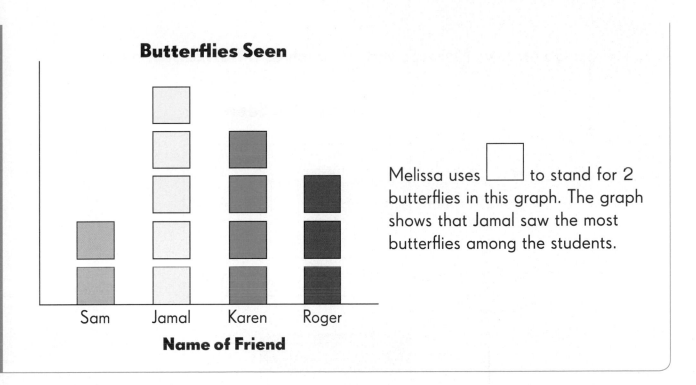

Name of Friend

Melissa uses ☐ to stand for 2 butterflies in this graph. The graph shows that Jamal saw the most butterflies among the students.

Continued on next page

Use vertical and horizontal bar graphs to represent data.

Melissa uses the data in the picture graph to make a **vertical** bar graph. A **scale** shows the value of the bars. In this graph, the vertical **axis** or grid line is marked 0, 2, 4, 6, 8, 10, and 12. These markings represent the scale.

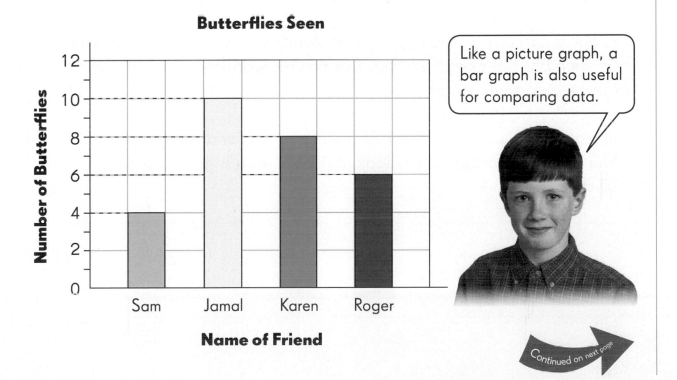

Like a picture graph, a bar graph is also useful for comparing data.

Then Linda redraws Melissa's vertical graph as a **horizontal** graph.

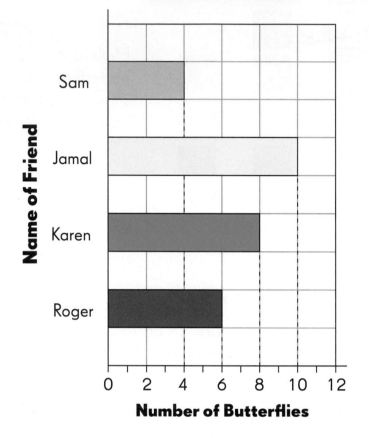

Butterflies Seen

A bar graph uses vertical or horizontal bars to show data. The length of each bar represents a value. This can be read from the scale marked on the axis of the graph.

Linda's graph uses a scale of 2. It starts with 0 and skips in twos. The greatest number on the scale is 12 because it needs to include all the data.

Guided Practice

The bar graph shows the data in the tally chart.

Our Model Cars

Name	Tally	Number of Model Cars
Ken	⊦⊦⊦⊦ I	6
Tasha	⊦⊦⊦⊦ III	8
Bryan	⊦⊦⊦⊦ ⊦⊦⊦⊦ II	12
Pat	II	2

Find the missing data.

1

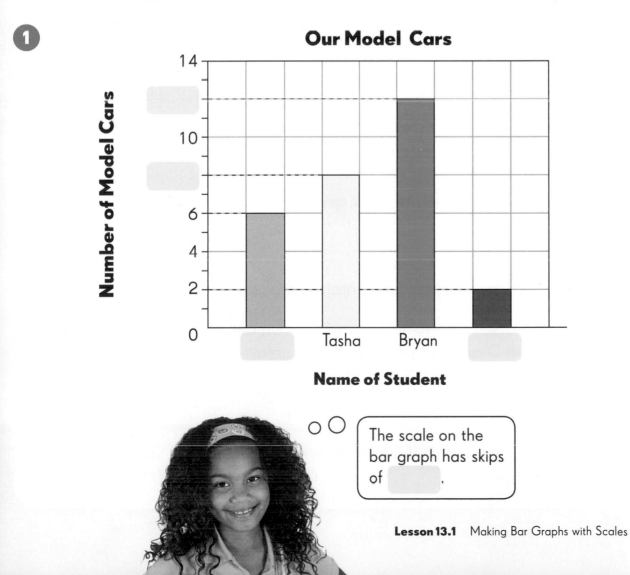

Our Model Cars

The scale on the bar graph has skips of _____.

Math Journal

King Elementary School has a field day each year. Groups of students take part in the field day. The table shows the number of medals won by each group.

Medals Won

Group	Number of Medals
Evergreen	10
Birch	14
Maple	18
Gum	12
Bay	16

WORKING TOGETHER

Make a bar graph that displays the data in the table.

Follow the steps to make your graph.

STEP 1 Use grid paper.
Give the bar graph a title.
Label the vertical and horizontal axes of the graph.

STEP 2 Choose a suitable scale to show the number of medals won.
Start with 0 and then complete the scale.

STEP 3 Draw the bars.
Choose a different color for each bar.

STEP 4 Check the length of the bars against the data to be sure the lengths are correct.

Answer each question.

1 How did you decide on a scale for your graph? Explain your answer.

2 What is the greatest number for your scale? Explain why.

3 Only groups that won 10 or more medals are shown in the table on page 88. In all, 100 medals were won. How many medals are not shown in the table? Explain your answer.

Hands-On Activity

WORKING TOGETHER

Divide the class into groups.
Conduct a survey within each group to find the total number of letters found in each classmate's whole name. (This includes the family name.)

Tally the results and record the findings below.

Letters in Each Classmate's Whole Name

Name of Student	Tally	Number of Letters

On a grid paper, make a bar graph that displays the above data effectively.

Ask your classmates questions based on your bar graph.

Justin and his friends are folding paper objects.

The number of each type of paper object made is shown below.

 18 paper airplanes

15 paper balls

21 paper boats

12 paper cranes

6 paper frogs

Use a copy of the bar graph.

Help Justin show the number of paper objects on the graph.

1

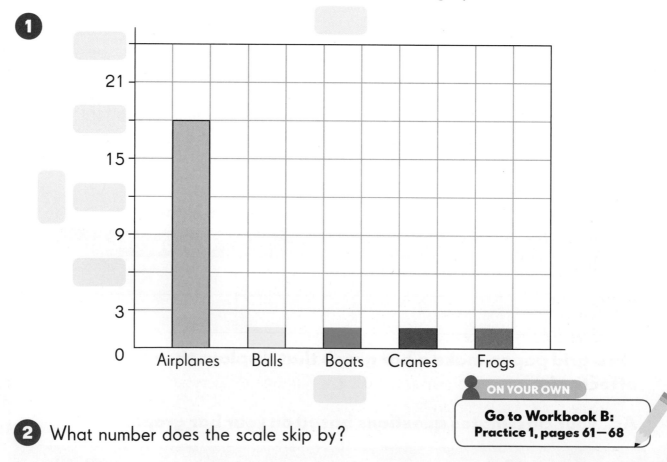

2 What number does the scale skip by?

ON YOUR OWN

**Go to Workbook B:
Practice 1, pages 61—68**

Lesson 13.2 Reading and Interpreting Bar Graphs

Lesson Objectives

- Read and interpret data from bar graphs.
- Solve problems using bar graphs.

Learn Read and interpret bar graphs to solve problems.

Tricia sold tickets from Monday to Friday last week.
She drew a bar graph to show the number of tickets she sold each day.

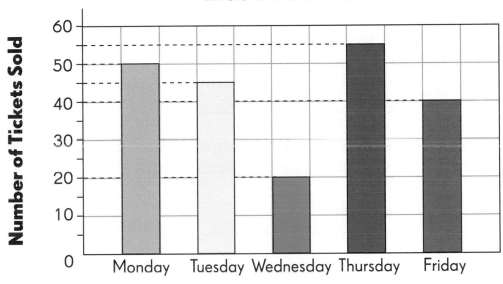

Tricia's Ticket Sales

a How many tickets did Tricia sell on Monday?
Tricia sold 50 tickets on Monday.

b On which day did Tricia sell 45 tickets?
She sold 45 tickets on Tuesday.

c On which day did she sell the least number of tickets?
She sold the least on Wednesday.

Continued on next page

d How many fewer tickets did she sell on Monday than on Thursday?
55 tickets were sold on Thursday.
50 tickets were sold on Monday.
Subtract to compare.
55 − 50 = 5
She sold 5 fewer tickets on Monday.

e On which day did she sell twice as many tickets as on another day?
She sold twice as many tickets on Friday as on Wednesday.

40 tickets were sold on Friday, and 20 tickets were sold on Wednesday. 20 is 40 two times.

Guided Practice

Edwin owns an art store. He draws a bar graph to show the number of each kind of product in his shop.

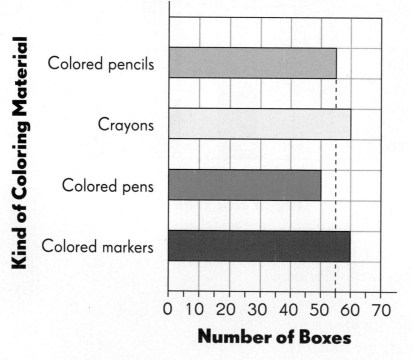

Coloring Materials in Edwin's Art Store

Kind of Coloring Material

Colored pencils
Crayons
Colored pens
Colored markers

0 10 20 30 40 50 60 70

Number of Boxes

Answer each question.

1 How many boxes of colored pencils are there?

2 There are 50 boxes of one kind of product. Which product is it?

3 There are [   ] more boxes of crayons than colored pencils.

4 The art store has the same number of boxes of [   ] as [   ].

5 The art store has 10 fewer boxes of [   ] than colored markers.

The bar graph below shows the number of adults and children who visited a zoo from Monday to Sunday.

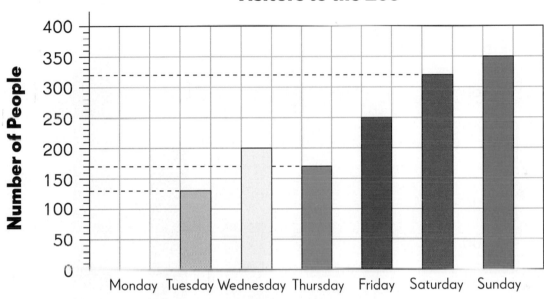

Visitors to the Zoo

Number of People

Day of the Week

Use the bar graph to answer the questions.

6 How many people visited the zoo on Wednesday? [   ] people

7 On which day did 170 people visit the zoo? [   ]

8 Which day had the most visitors? Give a reason for this. [   ]

9 On which day did no one visit the zoo? Give a reason for this. [   ]

10 On which day were there 150 more people than on Thursday? [   ]

11 On which day were there 120 fewer people than on Friday? [   ]

12 On Sunday, 125 adults visited the zoo.
How many children visited the zoo that day? [   ] children

Let's Explore!

WORK IN PAIRS

The bar graph shows the number of books children borrowed from the library over five days.

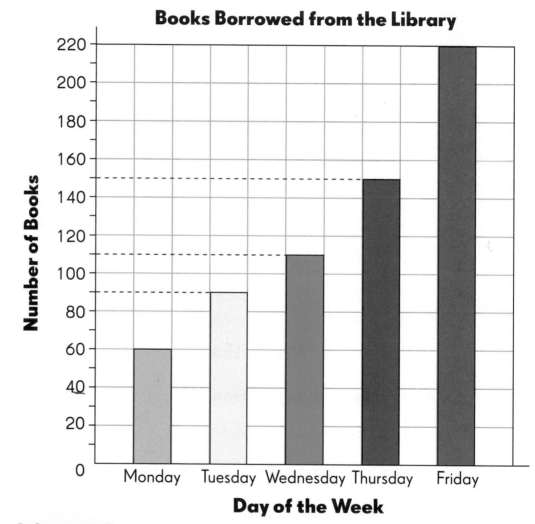

Books Borrowed from the Library

Number of Books

Day of the Week

Read the graph.
Write three questions about the information you can find from the graph.
Use the words given to help you get started.

How many books	more than	fewer than	twice as
many as	the least	the most	on which day

Let's Practice

The bar graph shows the number of pages read in a day by Rachel and her friends.

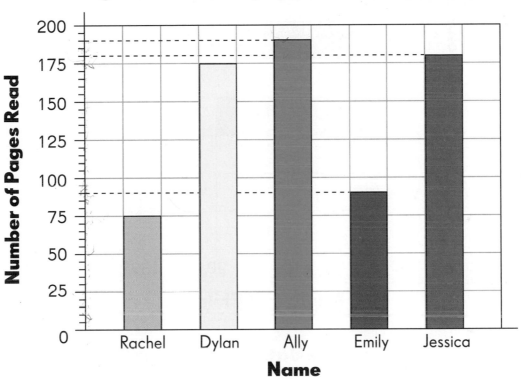

Pages Read in a Day by Rachel and Her Friends

Use the bar graph to answer the questions.

1 How many pages did Ally read?   pages

2 Who read 90 pages?

3 Who read the most pages?

4 Who read the fewest pages? How much did she read?

5 How many more pages did Ally read than Rachel?   more

6 Who read twice as many pages as Emily?

7 Jessica wants to read twice as many pages as Dylan. How many more pages must she read?   more

The bar graph shows the favorite colors of a group of children.

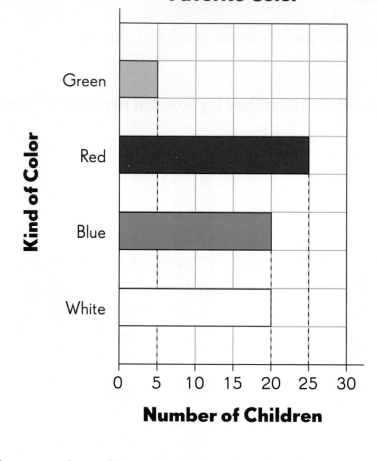

Favorite Color

Answer each question. Use the data in the bar graph.

8 How many more children like white than green?   children

9 How many children like green or white?   children

10 8 children who chose red were boys.
How many girls chose red?   girls

11 10 children changed their mind and chose green instead of blue.
How many children like green now?   children

ON YOUR OWN

Go to Workbook B:
Practice 2, pages 69–74

 Line Plots

Lesson Objective

- Make a line plot to represent data.

Vocabulary
line plot
survey

Learn

Use line plots to show how often something happens.

Rick surveys 8 of his friends to find the number of books read in January.
The table shows the results of the **survey**.

Number of Books Read in January

Name of Friend	Number of Books	Name of Friend	Number of Books
Tom	2	Alice	4
Kevin	3	Alex	1
Robin	1	Allie	2
Suki	4	Mark	2

Rick recorded his data in a tally chart.

Number of Books Read in January

Number of Books	Tally	Number of Friends
1	//	2
2	///	3
3	/	1
4	//	2

Continued on next page

Rick draws a number line to make a **line plot**. The line plot shows the results of his survey.

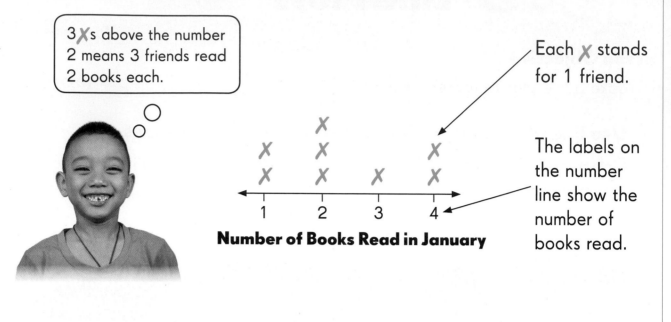

3 X s above the number 2 means 3 friends read 2 books each.

Each X stands for 1 friend.

The labels on the number line show the number of books read.

Number of Books Read in January

Three friends read 2 books each in January.
Two friends read the most number of books.
The least number of friends read 3 books.
Two friends read 4 books each and two friends read 1 book each.
Three friends read more than 2 books each.

Guided Practice

Sara surveyed the families in her neighborhood to find the number of pets they have. The table shows the results of her survey.

Number of Pets in Each Family

Family	A	B	C	D	E	F	G	H	I	J
Number of Pets	5	2	1	2	0	3	2	3	2	2

Complete the tally chart. Then answer the question.

1

Number of Pets in Each Family

Number of Pets	Tally	Number of Families
0	/	
1		
2		
3	//	
4		
5		

2 How many families did Sara survey? [ ] families

Sara made a line plot of the data.

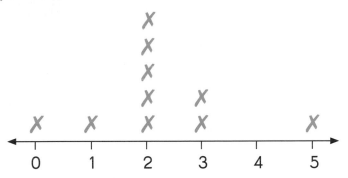

Number of Pets in Each Family

Complete the sentences. Use the data in the line plot.

3 Each X stands for 1 [ ] .

4 The labels on the number line stand for the number of [ ] .

5 The greatest number of families had [ ] pets.

6 No family had [ ] pets.

7 [ ] families had more than 2 pets.

Use line plots to organize data.

Martha conducted a survey. She wanted to find out the number of hours her classmates spent on homework each day. She recorded her data in a table.

Number of Hours Spent on Homework

Number of Hours	Number of Classmates
1	2
2	3
3	5
4	2

A line plot is an easy way to organize data. It makes it easy to see how the data is grouped, compared, and spread.

Then she displayed her data in a line plot.

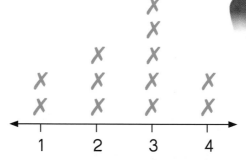

Number of Hours Spent on Homework

Martha found that five of her classmates spent 3 hours on their homework each day.

Five classmates spent less than 3 hours on their homework. Martha surveyed a total of 12 classmates.

The greatest number of hours spent on homework is 4. The same number of classmates spent the least and greatest number of hours on their homework.

Guided Practice

A carnival recorded the number of games won
by each player at one booth.
Numbers of games won — 3, 5, 2, 1, 3, 1, 3, 3, 3, 2, 2, 1, 1, 1, 2, 4, 4, 3.

Complete the table.

Number of Games Won

Number of Games Won	Number of People
1	
	4
3	
4	
	1

8 **Show the data in a line plot. Remember to give your line plot a title.**

Answer each question. Use the data in your line plot.

9 How many people won exactly 2 games?   people

10 How many people won more than 1 game?   people

11 How many people were surveyed in all?   people

12 What is the most frequent number of games won?   games

13   as many people won 2 games as the number of people who won 4 games.

14 Three times as many people won   games as the number of people who won   games.

Hands-On Activity

Conduct a survey to find the number of fruits third graders eat in a week.

1 Use the tally chart to record your findings.

Number of ⬚	Tally	Number of ⬚
⬚	⬚	⬚
⬚	⬚	⬚
⬚	⬚	⬚
⬚	⬚	⬚

2 Then show the data in a line plot.
Remember to give it a title.

3 Write 3 statements about the data shown in the line plot.

What does each ✗ stands for? What do the numbers on the number line stand for?

What is the greatest number of fruits eaten in a week? What is the least number of fruits eaten in a week?

Let's Practice

Solve.

The tally chart shows the number of football games a group of people watched in a season.

Complete the tally chart.

1

Number of Football Games Watched

Number of Football Games	Tally	Number of People
0	~~////~~	5
1	///	
2	////	
3	/	
4	//	

2 Show the data in a line plot. Remember to give it a title.

Answer each question. Use the data in your line plot.

3 How many people watched three or more football games? _____ people

4 How many people did not watch any football games? _____ people

5 **a** Did more people watch 2 football games or 4 football games in a season? _____ football games

b How many more? _____ more

6 What was the most common number of football games watched?
_____ football games

Kim conducted a survey to find the number of paintbrushes her friends use for an art lesson. The table shows the results of her survey.

Number of Paintbrushes Used for Art Lesson

Name of Friend	Number of Paintbrushes
Renee	3
Lynn	5
Sam	2
Joy	2
Debra	2
Joe	5

7 **Show the data on a line plot.**
Remember to give it a title.

Answer each question. Use your line plot to help you.

8 Which numbers will she mark on the horizontal line of the line plot?

9 What do the ✗s on the line plot stand for?

10 How many ✗s are marked on the line plot?

11 How many friends use 5 paintbrushes? _____ friends

12 How many paintbrushes do most friends use?

_____ paintbrushes

13 **a** Look at the tally chart. Find the total number of paintbrushes used by Kim's friends. _____ paintbrushes

b If each paintbrush costs $2, how much was spent in all? $ _____

ON YOUR OWN

Go to Workbook B:
Practice 3, pages 75–82

Put On Your Thinking Cap!

PROBLEM SOLVING

Study the information.

> Mary Lou noticed that 18 classmates are wearing yellow shirts. There were 7 more classmates wearing red shirts than blue shirts. There were 10 fewer classmates wearing blue shirts than yellow shirts.

Read bar graphs A, B, and C carefully. Which of the bar graphs shows **all** the given information **correctly**? Explain your answer.

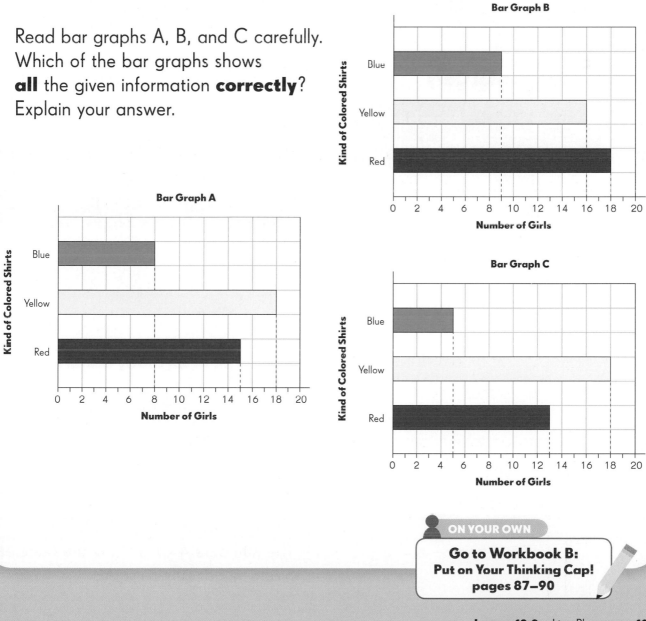

ON YOUR OWN

**Go to Workbook B:
Put on Your Thinking Cap!
pages 87–90**

Chapter Wrap Up

Study Guide
You have learned...

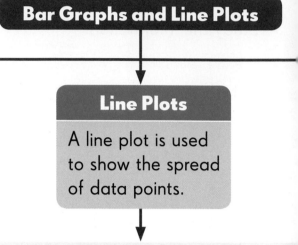

Bar Graphs and Line Plots

Tally Chart

A tally chart is used to record and organize data. A tally mark on the chart stands for 1 of something.

Line Plots

A line plot is used to show the spread of data points.

Our Model Cars

Name	Tally	Number of Model cars
Ken	ℋℋ I	6
Tasha	III	3
Bryan	ℋℋ IIII	9
Pat	III	3

Number of birthday cards received – 4, 5, 5, 6, 6, 6

Number of Birthday Cards Received

Number of Birthday Cards	Number of Friends
4	1
5	2
6	3

Number of Birthday Cards Received

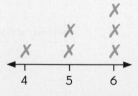

Number of Birthday Cards

Each X stands for 1 friend.
The numbers 4 to 6 show the number of birthday cards received.

BIG IDEAS

▶ Bar graphs and line plots help to organize data. Bar graphs are used to compare data. Line plots show how data is spread out.

Bar Graph

A bar graph uses bars to show data. The scales show the value of the bars.

Favorite Fruits

Favorite Fruit	apple	peach	orange	pear
Number of Children	10	15	25	20

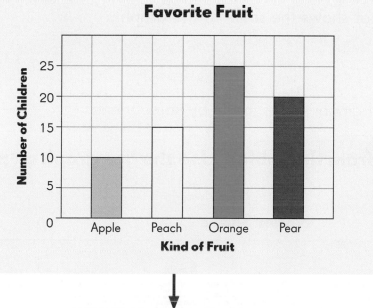

Read and interpret data.

Chapter Review/Test

Vocabulary

Fill in the blanks. Use the words in the box.

| line plot |
| survey |
| bar graph |
| key |
| scale |
| tally chart |
| picture graph |
| vertical |
| horizontal |
| axis |

1 TV stations conduct a _____ when they want to find out all the shows that students watch.

2 The numbers running along an axis of a bar graph are called the _____ .

3 A _____ uses pictures or symbols and a _____ to show what these symbols stand for.

4 A _____ is useful for showing the spread of data.

5 A _____ uses vertical or horizontal bars to show data.

6 An easy way to record data during a survey is to use a _____ .

7 A bar graph can be drawn as a _____ or _____ bar graph.

8 An _____ is a grid line that shows the scale of the graph.

Concepts and Skills

The table shows the number of ginger snaps made by some friends.

What number is missing from the table? Use the bar graph on page 109 to help you.

9

Ginger Snaps

Name of Girl	Molly	Sally	Kelly	Nelly	Ally
Number of Ginger Snaps	20	50	40		60

Use the data in the table to help you.
Use a copy of the bar graph and complete it.

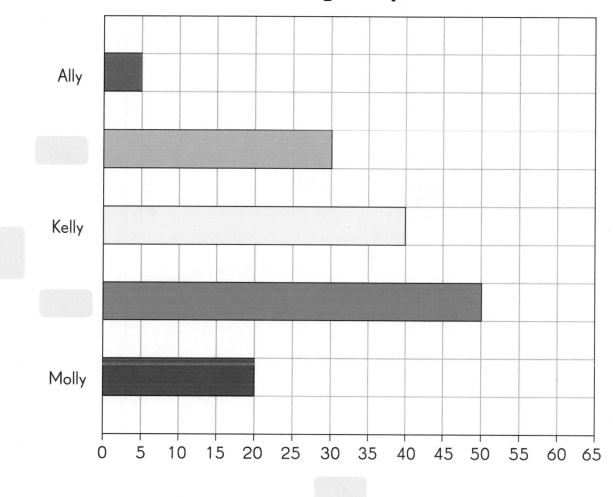

Ginger Snaps

Ally

Kelly

Molly

0 5 10 15 20 25 30 35 40 45 50 55 60 65

Answer each question. Use the data in your bar graph.

10 Who made twice as many ginger snaps as Nelly?

11 Who made 10 fewer ginger snaps than Ally?

Abigail organized a class party.
There was a treasure hunt to find the number of balloons
hidden in the cafeteria. Different numbers of balloons are found
by different children.
Number of balloons found — 0, 3, 3, 1, 1, 1, 5, 4, 1, 1, 2,
5, 4, 4, 2, 5, 4, 2, 2, 5, 5.

12 **Show the data in line plot.**
Remember to give your line plot a title.

Fill in the blanks.
Use the data in the line plot to help you.

13 Each X stands for   .

14   children have the greatest number of balloons.

15 The least number of balloons found is   .

16   children found more than 2 balloons.

17   children took part in the treasure hunt.

The line plot shows the number of field goals that were scored by football players last season.

Study the line plot and fill in the blanks.

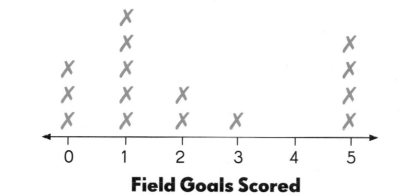

Field Goals Scored

Fill in the blanks. Use the data in the line plot.

18 Each ✗ stands for 1 _____ .

19 _____ players scored 5 field goals.

20 _____ as many football players scored 2 field goals as 3 field goals.

21 _____ times as many football players scored 0 field goals as 3 field goals.

14 Fractions

What fraction of the squares on the quilt has a heart on it?

Lessons

BIG IDEA

▶ Fractions can be used to describe parts of a region or parts of a set.

Recall Prior Knowledge

Understanding fractions

A fraction names equal parts of a whole

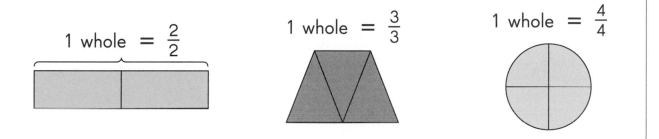

1 whole $= \frac{2}{2}$

1 whole $= \frac{3}{3}$

1 whole $= \frac{4}{4}$

Identifying unit fractions and non-unit fractions

A unit fraction names one of the equal parts of a whole

$\frac{1}{3}$ is a unit fraction.

$\frac{1}{3}$
$\frac{1}{3}$
$\frac{1}{3}$

A non-unit fraction names more than one equal part of a whole

$\frac{3}{4}$ is a non-unit fraction.

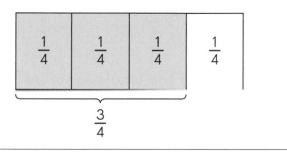

$\frac{3}{4}$

Making one whole with unit fractions

$\frac{1}{2} + \frac{1}{2} = \frac{2}{2}$

$\phantom{\frac{1}{2} + \frac{1}{2}} = 1$

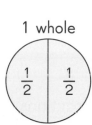

1 whole

Comparing and ordering unit fractions

Compare

$\frac{1}{2}$ is greater than $\frac{1}{3}$. $\frac{1}{2} > \frac{1}{3}$

$\frac{1}{4}$ is less than $\frac{1}{3}$. $\frac{1}{4} < \frac{1}{3}$

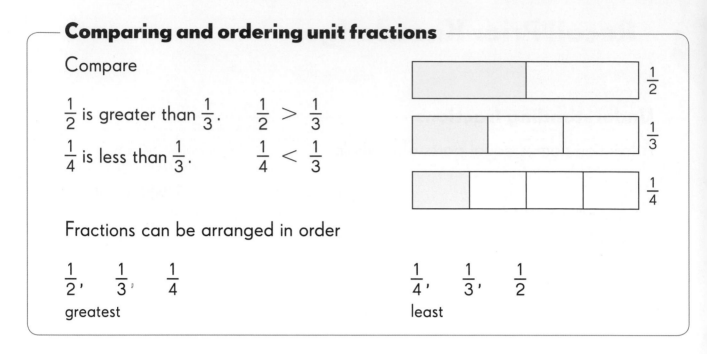

Fractions can be arranged in order

$\frac{1}{2}$, $\frac{1}{3}$, $\frac{1}{4}$ $\frac{1}{4}$, $\frac{1}{3}$, $\frac{1}{2}$

greatest   least

Like fractions

Like fractions are fractions whose wholes are divided into the same number of parts

The whole is divided into 3 parts.

Fraction of the whole in yellow is $\frac{1}{3}$.

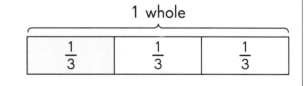

The whole is divided into 3 parts.

Fraction of the whole in yellow is $\frac{2}{3}$.

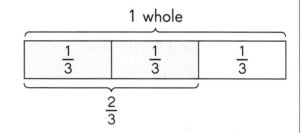

The whole is divided into 3 parts.

Fraction of the whole in yellow is $\frac{3}{3} = 1$.

$\frac{1}{3}$, $\frac{2}{3}$, and $\frac{3}{3}$ are like fractions.

Adding and subtracting like fractions

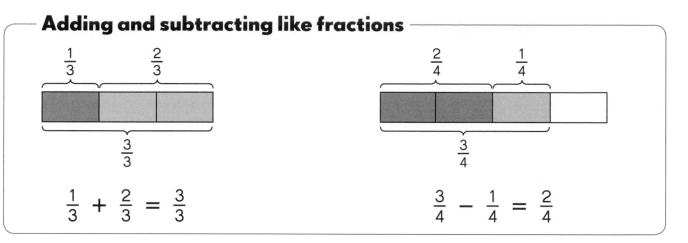

$$\frac{1}{3} + \frac{2}{3} = \frac{3}{3}$$

$$\frac{3}{4} - \frac{1}{4} = \frac{2}{4}$$

Reading a number line

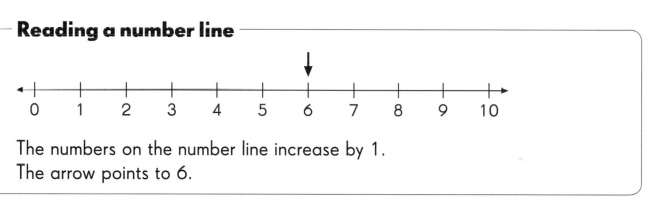

The numbers on the number line increase by 1.
The arrow points to 6.

✔ Quick Check

Match the unit fractions with their correct model and fractional names.

1

Models	Unit Fractions	Fractional Names

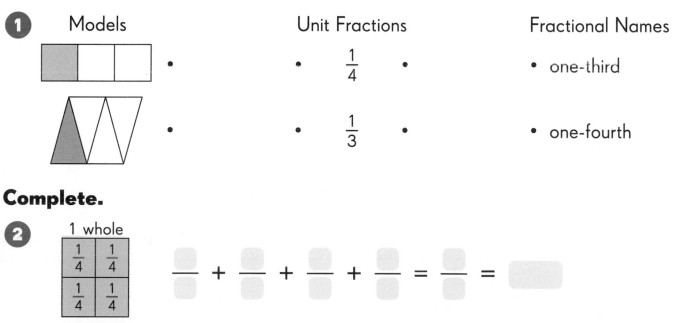

Models

Unit Fractions
- $\frac{1}{4}$ •
- $\frac{1}{3}$ •

Fractional Names
- one-third
- one-fourth

Complete.

2

1 whole

$\frac{1}{4}$	$\frac{1}{4}$
$\frac{1}{4}$	$\frac{1}{4}$

$$\frac{\square}{\square} + \frac{\square}{\square} + \frac{\square}{\square} + \frac{\square}{\square} = \frac{\square}{\square} = \boxed{}$$

Compare the fractions. Choose > or <.

3 $\frac{1}{4}$ is ⬤ $\frac{1}{2}$.

4 $\frac{1}{2}$ is ⬤ $\frac{1}{3}$.

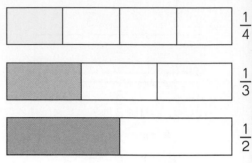

Order the fractions $\frac{1}{4}$, $\frac{1}{2}$, and $\frac{1}{3}$ from greatest to least.

5 ▢ , ▢ , ▢
greatest

Find the like fractions.

6 $\frac{2}{3}$, $\frac{3}{4}$, $\frac{1}{2}$, $\frac{1}{3}$, $\frac{3}{3}$

7 $\frac{2}{4}$, $\frac{1}{4}$, $\frac{1}{2}$, $\frac{2}{3}$, $\frac{3}{4}$

Complete the models. Then add.

8

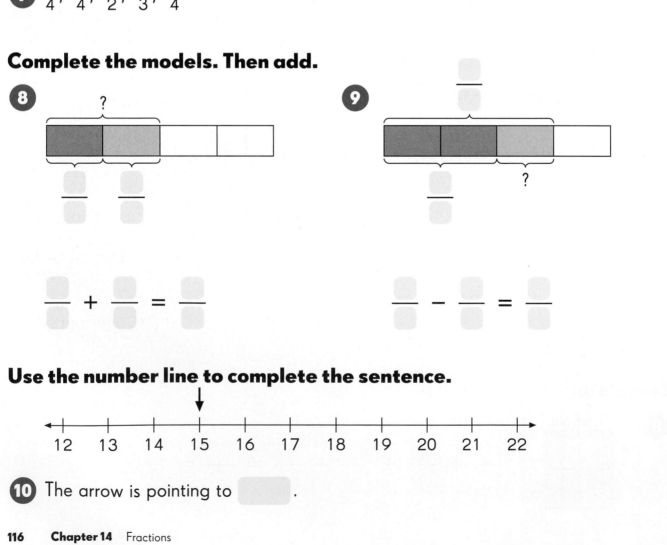

$\frac{\square}{\square} + \frac{\square}{\square} = \frac{\square}{\square}$

9

$\frac{\square}{\square} - \frac{\square}{\square} = \frac{\square}{\square}$

Use the number line to complete the sentence.

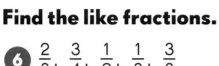

10 The arrow is pointing to ▢ .

14.1 Understanding Fractions

Lesson Objectives

- Read, write, and identify fractions of wholes with more than 4 parts.
- Identify numerator and denominator.

Learn Make one whole with more than 4 equal parts.

Divide a rectangular cake into 5 equal parts.

This **whole** is made up of 5 **equal parts**.

$\frac{1}{5}$ is 1 out of the 5 equal parts.

$\frac{5}{5}$ is a whole.

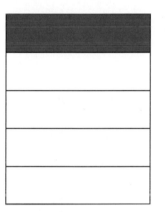

Read and write $\frac{1}{5}$ as one-fifth. How do you read and write other unit fractions?

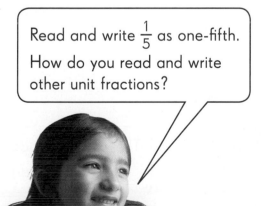

Fraction	Read as
$\frac{1}{6}$	one-sixth
$\frac{1}{7}$	one-seventh
$\frac{1}{8}$	one-eighth
$\frac{1}{9}$	one-ninth
$\frac{1}{10}$	one-tenth
$\frac{1}{11}$	one-eleventh
$\frac{1}{12}$	one-twelfth

Guided Practice

Complete.

1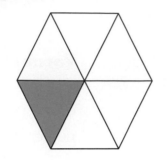

The whole is divided into ☐ equal parts.

☐/☐ of the whole is shaded.

☐ - ☐ of the whole is shaded.

 Learn **Use models to show non-unit fractions.**

The model shows a whole with 5 equal parts.

2 parts are red and 3 parts are yellow.
What fraction of the whole is red?

Number of red parts = 2
Number of parts altogether = 5

Fraction of the whole in red is $\frac{2}{5}$.

Fraction of the whole in yellow is $\frac{3}{5}$.

$\frac{2}{5}$ and $\frac{3}{5}$ together make 1 whole.

Read and write,
$\frac{2}{5}$ as two-fifths,
$\frac{3}{5}$ as three-fifths.

Guided Practice

Find the fraction of the whole that is shaded.

2

☐/6 of the circle is shaded.

The whole is made up of ☐ equal parts.

Write in words.

3 $\frac{4}{6}$ [   ]

4 $\frac{5}{12}$ [   ]

5 $\frac{1}{9}$ [   ]

6 $\frac{4}{10}$ [   ]

Complete.

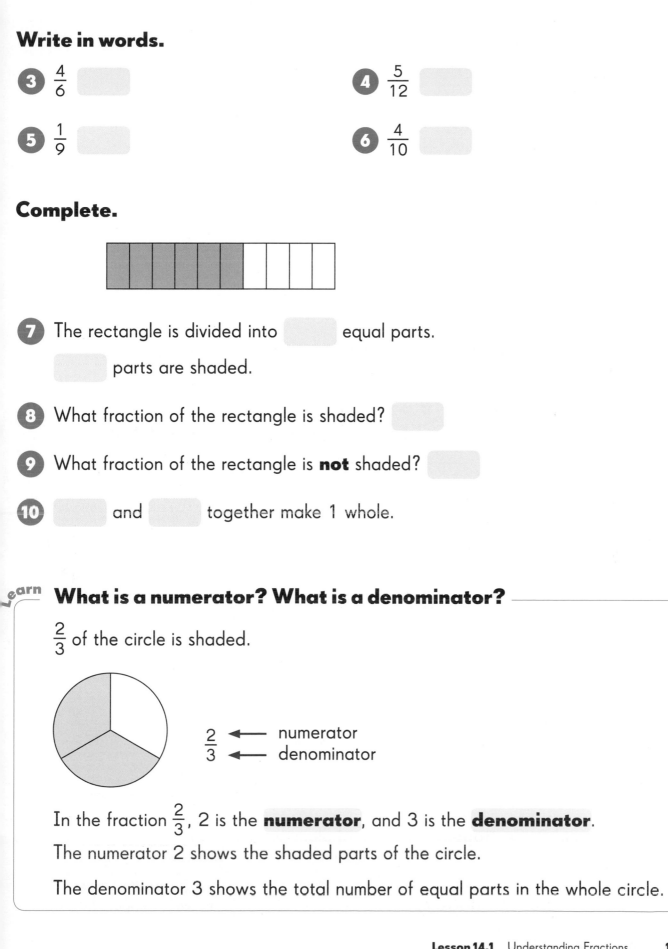

7 The rectangle is divided into [   ] equal parts.

[   ] parts are shaded.

8 What fraction of the rectangle is shaded? [   ]

9 What fraction of the rectangle is **not** shaded? [   ]

10 [   ] and [   ] together make 1 whole.

Learn What is a numerator? What is a denominator?

$\frac{2}{3}$ of the circle is shaded.

$\frac{2}{3}$ ← numerator
← denominator

In the fraction $\frac{2}{3}$, 2 is the **numerator**, and 3 is the **denominator**.

The numerator 2 shows the shaded parts of the circle.

The denominator 3 shows the total number of equal parts in the whole circle.

Guided Practice

Complete.

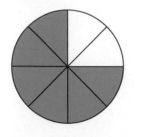

11 [   ] of the circle is shaded.

12 The numerator of the fraction is [   ] .

13 The denominator of the fraction is [   ] .

Let's Practice

What fraction is shaded? Choose the correct answers.

1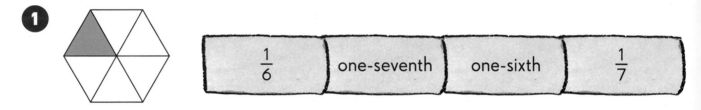

$\frac{1}{6}$ one-seventh   one-sixth $\frac{1}{7}$

Complete.

Jane wants to make a number train with 10 🔲 . She starts by connecting 7 🔲 .

2 She needs to connect [   ] more 🔲 to complete the train.

3 What fraction of the number train has she already connected? [   ]

4 What fraction of the cubes has she not yet connected? [   ]

5 [   ] and [   ] together make 1 whole.

ON YOUR OWN

Go to Workbook B:
Practice 1, pages 91–92

Lesson 14.2 Understanding Equivalent Fractions

Lesson Objectives

- Use models to identify equivalent fractions.
- Use a number line to identify equivalent fractions.

Vocabulary
equivalent fractions

number line

What are equivalent fractions?

Look at the fraction strips.

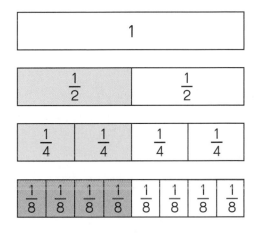

1	One whole
$\frac{1}{2}$ $\frac{1}{2}$	1 out of 2 equal parts $= \frac{1}{2}$
$\frac{1}{4}$ $\frac{1}{4}$ $\frac{1}{4}$ $\frac{1}{4}$	2 out of 4 equal parts $= \frac{2}{4}$
$\frac{1}{8}$ $\frac{1}{8}$ $\frac{1}{8}$ $\frac{1}{8}$ $\frac{1}{8}$ $\frac{1}{8}$ $\frac{1}{8}$ $\frac{1}{8}$	4 out of 8 equal parts $= \frac{4}{8}$

The fractions $\frac{1}{2}$, $\frac{2}{4}$, and $\frac{4}{8}$ have different numerators and denominators.

But $\frac{1}{2}$ is equal to $\frac{2}{4}$.

$\frac{1}{2}$ is also equal to $\frac{4}{8}$.

$\frac{1}{2}$, $\frac{2}{4}$, and $\frac{4}{8}$ are called **equivalent fractions**.

$\frac{1}{2}$, $\frac{2}{4}$, and $\frac{4}{8}$ name the same parts of a whole.

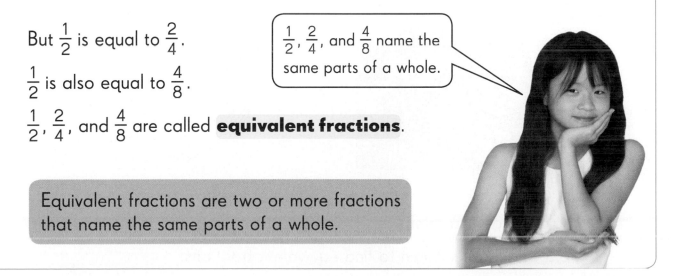

Equivalent fractions are two or more fractions that name the same parts of a whole.

Hands-On Activity

WORK IN PAIRS

Materials:
• 3 paper strips of the same size

STEP 1 Cut out three paper strips.
Fold the first strip into three equal parts.
Then unfold the strip and draw lines along the folds to divide the strip into three equal parts.

STEP 2 Shade one part of the strip.
You get the shaded fraction $\frac{1}{3}$.

STEP 3 Refold the strip. Then fold it into half.
You will find that $\frac{2}{6}$ is an equivalent fraction of $\frac{1}{3}$.

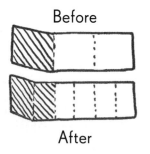

Before

After

STEP 4 Make shaded fractions for $\frac{1}{4}$ and $\frac{3}{4}$ with the remaining paper strips.
Fold these strips again to find equivalent fractions.

Guided Practice

Find the equivalent fractions.

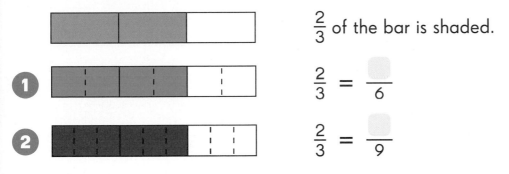

$\frac{2}{3}$ of the bar is shaded.

1 $\frac{2}{3} = \frac{\boxed{}}{6}$

2 $\frac{2}{3} = \frac{\boxed{}}{9}$

Find the missing numerators and denominators.

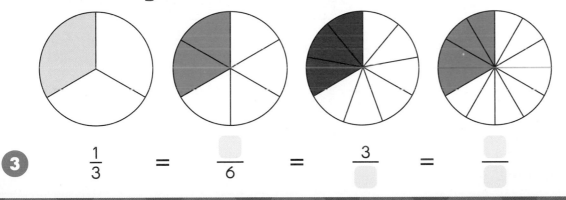

3 $\frac{1}{3} = \frac{\boxed{}}{6} = \frac{3}{\boxed{}} = \frac{\boxed{}}{\boxed{}}$

 Hands-On Activity

> All three rectangles should be of same width and height.

Use grid paper.

STEP 1 Draw a rectangle that has 1 row and 4 columns. Shade the first column.

STEP 2 Then draw a rectangle that has 1 row and 8 columns. Shade the first 2 columns.

STEP 3 Finally, draw a rectangle that has 1 row and 12 columns. Shade the first 3 columns.

What do you notice about the shaded parts?
What fraction of each rectangle is shaded?

Use a number line to find equivalent fractions.

Look at the **number lines**.

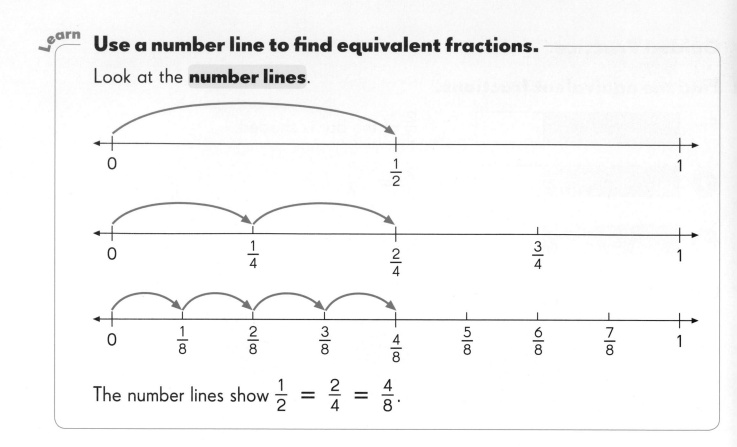

The number lines show $\frac{1}{2} = \frac{2}{4} = \frac{4}{8}$.

Guided Practice

Copy the number lines on grid paper.

Fill in the missing fractions on the number lines.

Use the number lines to find the equivalent fractions.

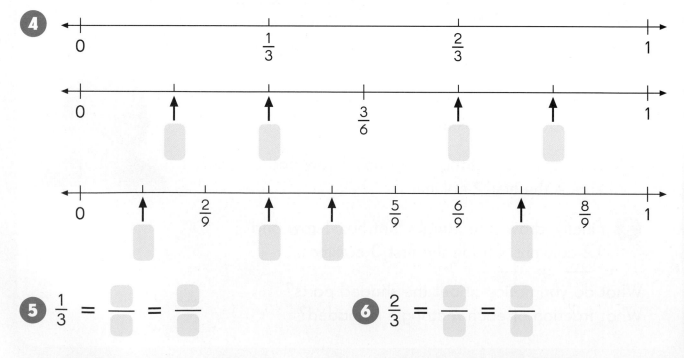

4

5 $\frac{1}{3} = \frac{\Box}{\Box} = \frac{\Box}{\Box}$

6 $\frac{2}{3} = \frac{\Box}{\Box} = \frac{\Box}{\Box}$

Let's Practice

Find equivalent fractions of $\frac{2}{5}$.

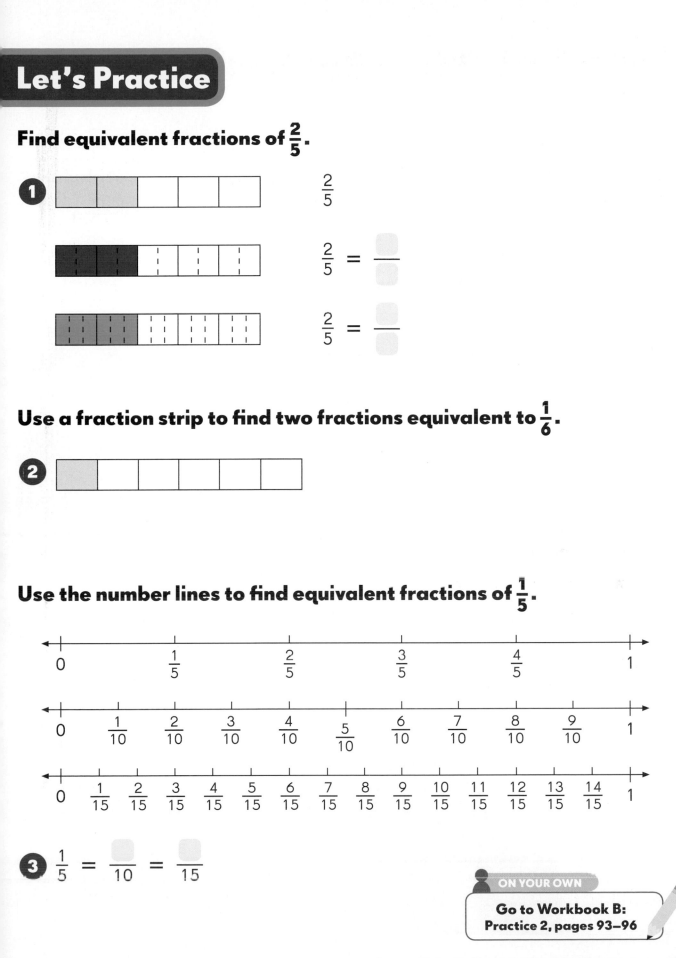

1

$\frac{2}{5}$

$\frac{2}{5} = \dfrac{}{}$

$\frac{2}{5} = \dfrac{}{}$

Use a fraction strip to find two fractions equivalent to $\frac{1}{6}$.

2

Use the number lines to find equivalent fractions of $\frac{1}{5}$.

3 $\frac{1}{5} = \dfrac{}{10} = \dfrac{}{15}$

ON YOUR OWN

Go to Workbook B:
Practice 2, pages 93–96

14.3 More Equivalent Fractions

Lesson Objectives

- Use multiplication and division to find equivalent fractions.
- Write fractions in simplest form.

Vocabulary
simplest form

Learn Use multiplication to find equivalent fractions.

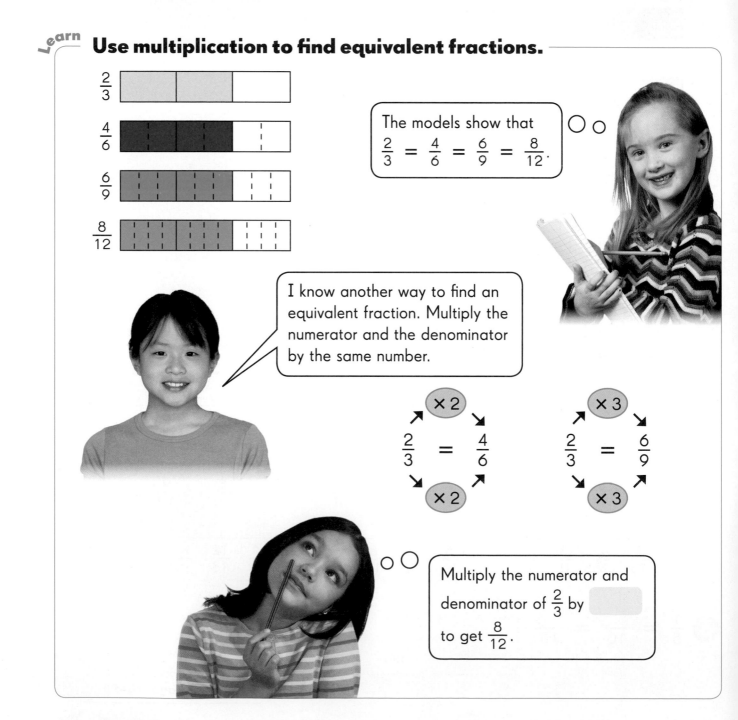

$\frac{2}{3}$

$\frac{4}{6}$

$\frac{6}{9}$

$\frac{8}{12}$

The models show that $\frac{2}{3} = \frac{4}{6} = \frac{6}{9} = \frac{8}{12}$.

I know another way to find an equivalent fraction. Multiply the numerator and the denominator by the same number.

$\frac{2}{3} = \frac{4}{6}$ (×2, ×2)

$\frac{2}{3} = \frac{6}{9}$ (×3, ×3)

Multiply the numerator and denominator of $\frac{2}{3}$ by ___ to get $\frac{8}{12}$.

Guided Practice

Use models and multiplication to find equivalent fractions.

1 models

2 multiplication

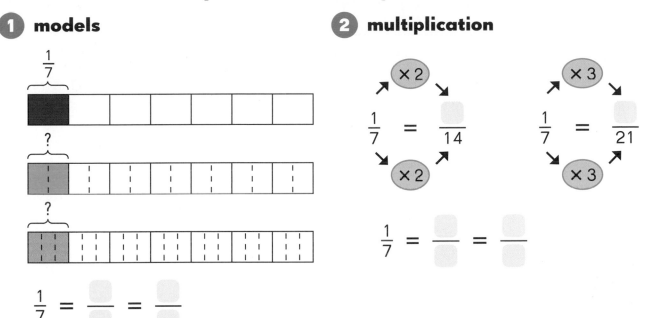

$$\frac{1}{7} = \frac{}{} = \frac{}{}$$

Use division to find a fraction in simplest form.

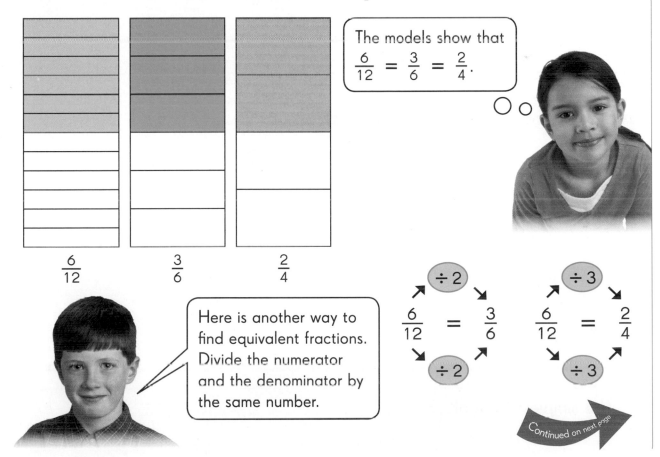

The models show that $\frac{6}{12} = \frac{3}{6} = \frac{2}{4}$.

$$\frac{6}{12} \qquad \frac{3}{6} \qquad \frac{2}{4}$$

Here is another way to find equivalent fractions. Divide the numerator and the denominator by the same number.

Continued on next page

Is $\frac{2}{4}$ the simplest fraction equivalent to $\frac{6}{12}$?

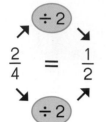

$$\frac{2}{4} = \frac{1}{2}$$

No, you can divide the numerator and denominator of $\frac{2}{4}$ by the same number further.

$\frac{1}{2}$ is the **simplest form** of $\frac{2}{4}$.

The simplest fraction equivalent to $\frac{6}{12}$ is $\frac{1}{2}$.

Use division to find a fraction in its simplest form.

Guided Practice

Divide to find the equivalent fractions of $\frac{4}{12}$.

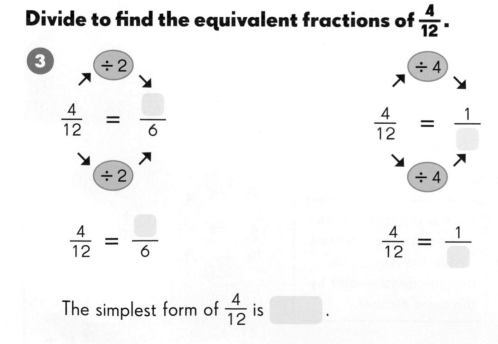

3

$$\frac{4}{12} = \frac{\square}{6}$$

$$\frac{4}{12} = \frac{\square}{6}$$

$$\frac{4}{12} = \frac{1}{\square}$$

$$\frac{4}{12} = \frac{1}{\square}$$

The simplest form of $\frac{4}{12}$ is ____.

Let's Practice

Find the equivalent fraction.

1

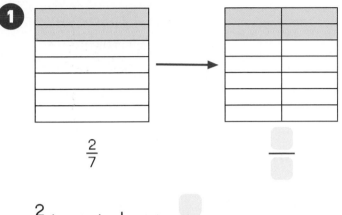

$\frac{2}{7}$

$\frac{\square}{\square}$

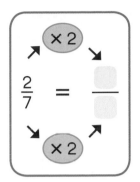

$\frac{2}{7}$ is equivalent to $\frac{\square}{\square}$.

Use models and division.

2

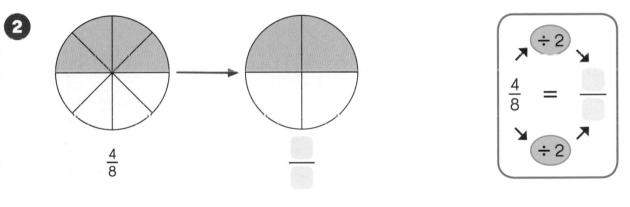

$\frac{4}{8}$

$\frac{\square}{\square}$

$\frac{4}{8}$ is equivalent to $\boxed{}$.

Find the first eight fractions equivalent to $\frac{5}{6}$.

3 $\frac{5}{6} = \frac{\square}{\square} = \frac{\square}{\square} = \frac{\square}{\square} = \frac{\square}{\square} = \frac{\square}{\square} = \frac{\square}{\square} = \frac{\square}{\square} = \frac{\square}{\square}$

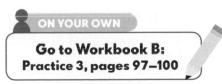

ON YOUR OWN

Go to Workbook B:
Practice 3, pages 97–100

Lesson 14.4 Comparing Fractions

Lesson Objectives

- Compare and order fractions.
- Show fractions as points or distances on a number line.
- Compare and order fractions using benchmark fractions.

Vocabulary
benchmark
like fractions
unlike fractions

Learn Compare fractions using pictures and number lines.

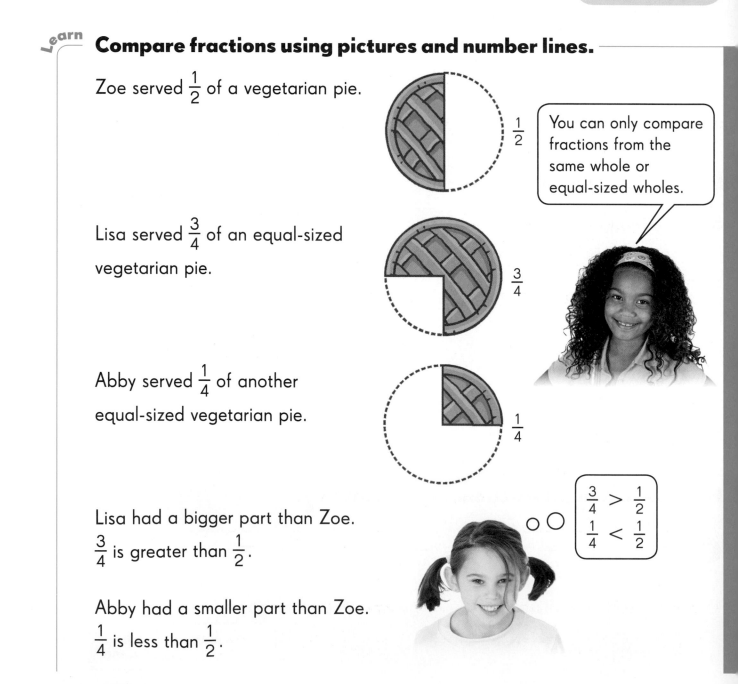

Zoe served $\frac{1}{2}$ of a vegetarian pie.

$\frac{1}{2}$

You can only compare fractions from the same whole or equal-sized wholes.

Lisa served $\frac{3}{4}$ of an equal-sized vegetarian pie.

$\frac{3}{4}$

Abby served $\frac{1}{4}$ of another equal-sized vegetarian pie.

$\frac{1}{4}$

$$\frac{3}{4} > \frac{1}{2}$$
$$\frac{1}{4} < \frac{1}{2}$$

Lisa had a bigger part than Zoe.
$\frac{3}{4}$ is greater than $\frac{1}{2}$.

Abby had a smaller part than Zoe.
$\frac{1}{4}$ is less than $\frac{1}{2}$.

The number lines show $\frac{1}{2}$, $\frac{1}{4}$, and $\frac{3}{4}$.

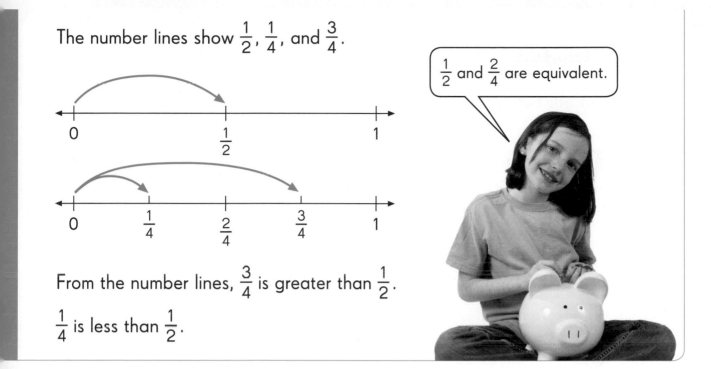

$\frac{1}{2}$ and $\frac{2}{4}$ are equivalent.

From the number lines, $\frac{3}{4}$ is greater than $\frac{1}{2}$.

$\frac{1}{4}$ is less than $\frac{1}{2}$.

Guided Practice

Compare the fractions.

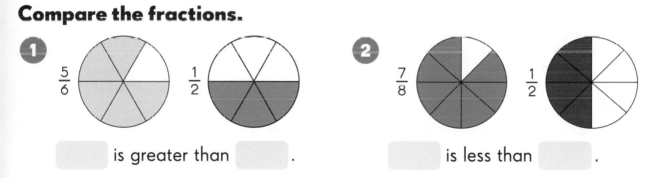

1 $\frac{5}{6}$ $\frac{1}{2}$

     is greater than   .

2 $\frac{7}{8}$ $\frac{1}{2}$

     is less than   .

Copy the number lines on grid paper.

Mark and label the fractions $\frac{1}{3}$, $\frac{2}{3}$, $\frac{1}{4}$, and $\frac{3}{4}$ on the appropriate number line.

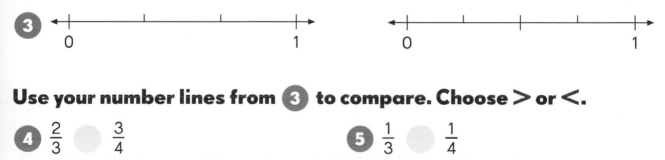

3 0   1   0   1

Use your number lines from **3** to compare. Choose > or <.

4 $\frac{2}{3}$ ⬤ $\frac{3}{4}$

5 $\frac{1}{3}$ ⬤ $\frac{1}{4}$

Hands-On Activity

 Cut out two paper strips of the same size.

 STEP 1 Fold the first strip in half.

 STEP 2 Unfold the strip.
Use a colored pencil to draw a line along the fold.

 STEP 3 Refold the strip.
Then fold it in half twice.

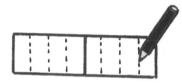

 STEP 4 Unfold the strip.
Use a different color to draw lines along the new folds.

 STEP 5 Shade to show a fraction greater than $\frac{1}{2}$.

The shaded fraction is $\frac{}{}$.

 STEP 6 Now fold the second strip in half and repeat **STEP 2** to **STEP 4**.

STEP 7 Shade a fraction that is less than $\frac{1}{2}$.

The shaded fraction is $\frac{}{}$.

Use models to compare like fractions.

Gina, Heather, and Rita each have an equal-sized paper plate for a craft project.

Each girl divides her plate into eight equal parts.

Gina decorates $\frac{3}{8}$ of her plate.

Heather decorates $\frac{5}{8}$ of her plate.

Rita decorates $\frac{8}{8}$ of her plate.

Who decorates the most?
Who decorates the least?

Like fractions have the same denominator. So you only compare the numerators.

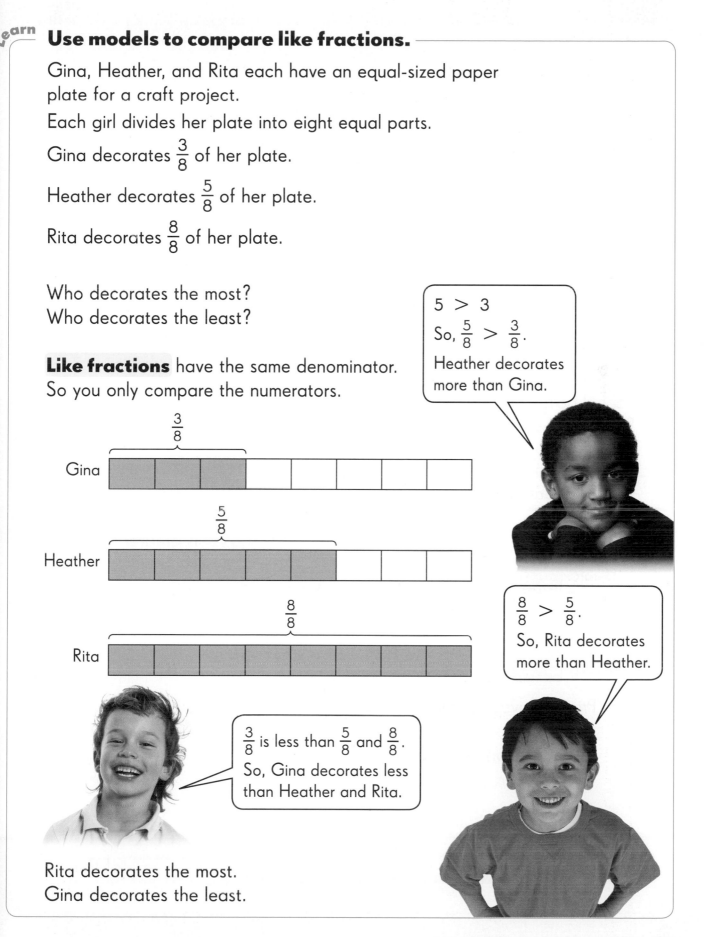

$5 > 3$
So, $\frac{5}{8} > \frac{3}{8}$.
Heather decorates more than Gina.

$\frac{8}{8} > \frac{5}{8}$.
So, Rita decorates more than Heather.

$\frac{3}{8}$ is less than $\frac{5}{8}$ and $\frac{8}{8}$.
So, Gina decorates less than Heather and Rita.

Rita decorates the most.
Gina decorates the least.

Guided Practice

Complete.

6 Danny and Keith buy an equal-sized pizza each.

Danny eats $\frac{2}{5}$ of his pizza, and Keith eats $\frac{4}{5}$ of his.

Who eats less?

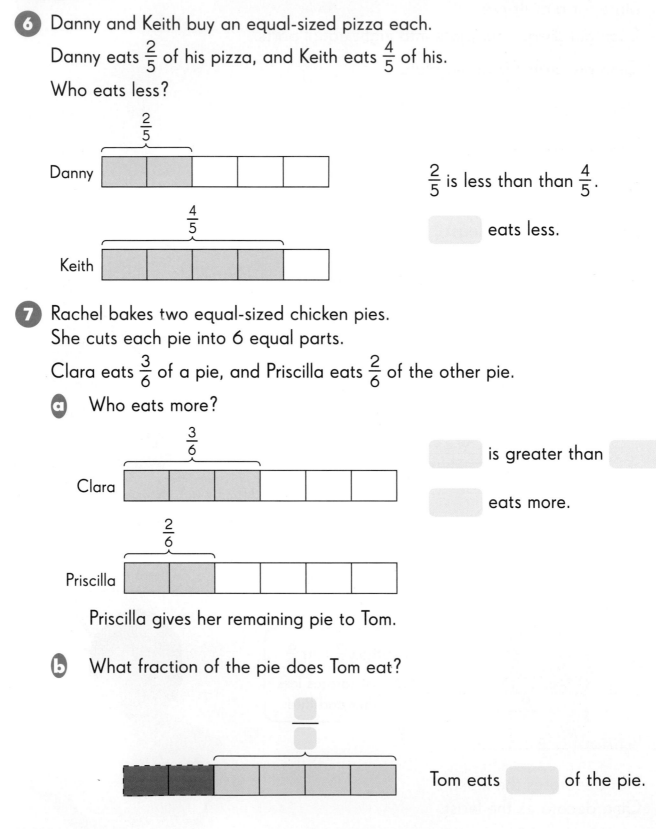

$\frac{2}{5}$ is less than than $\frac{4}{5}$.

[   ] eats less.

7 Rachel bakes two equal-sized chicken pies.
She cuts each pie into 6 equal parts.

Clara eats $\frac{3}{6}$ of a pie, and Priscilla eats $\frac{2}{6}$ of the other pie.

a Who eats more?

[   ] is greater than [   ].

[   ] eats more.

Priscilla gives her remaining pie to Tom.

b What fraction of the pie does Tom eat?

Tom eats [   ] of the pie.

c Who eats the most?

[ ] is greater than [ ] and [ ] .

[ ] eats the most.

d Who eats the least?

[ ] eats the least.

Use models to order like fractions.

Order the fractions from greatest to least.

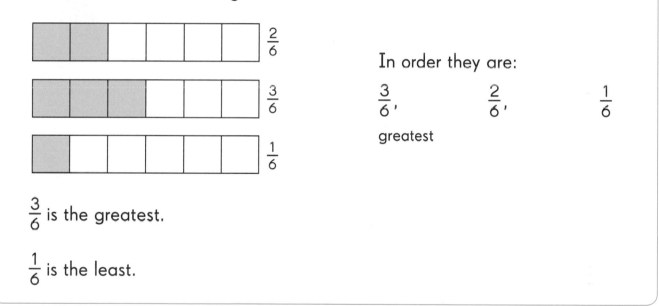

$\frac{2}{6}$

$\frac{3}{6}$

$\frac{1}{6}$

In order they are:

$\frac{3}{6}$, $\frac{2}{6}$, $\frac{1}{6}$

greatest

$\frac{3}{6}$ is the greatest.

$\frac{1}{6}$ is the least.

Guided Practice

Order the fractions from least to greatest.

8

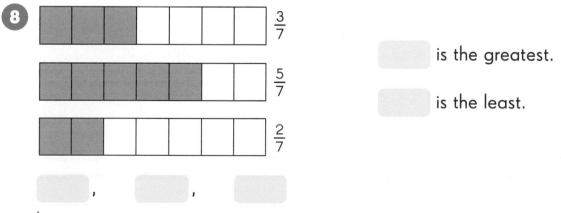

$\frac{3}{7}$

$\frac{5}{7}$

$\frac{2}{7}$

[ ] is the greatest.

[ ] is the least.

[ ] , [ ] , [ ]

least

Compare unlike fractions with the same numerator.

Which is greater, $\frac{3}{5}$ or $\frac{3}{6}$?

$\frac{3}{5}$

$\frac{3}{6}$

> The fractions have the same numerator, so compare the denominators.

$\frac{3}{5}$ is greater than $\frac{3}{6}$.

The greater fraction is the one with the smaller denominator.

....

Which fraction is less, $\frac{2}{10}$ or $\frac{2}{7}$?

$\frac{2}{10}$

$\frac{2}{7}$

$\frac{2}{10}$ is less than $\frac{2}{7}$.

The smaller fraction is the one with the greater denominator.
Fractions with different denominators are **unlike fractions**.

Guided Practice

Complete.

9 Which is less, $\frac{3}{8}$ or $\frac{3}{5}$?

$\frac{3}{8}$

$\frac{3}{5}$

[   ] is less than [   ].

10 Which is greater, $\frac{1}{3}$ or $\frac{1}{7}$?

[   ] is greater than [   ].

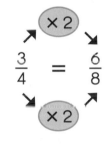

Compare unlike fractions.

Pie A and Pie B are vegetarian pies of the same size.

Mrs. Jones cut $\frac{3}{4}$ of Pie A for Sue.

She cut $\frac{7}{8}$ of Pie B for Tim.

Who got a larger piece?
Who got a smaller piece?

> Remember, you can only compare fractions from the same whole or equal-sized wholes.

Pie A

Pie B

> $\frac{3}{4}$ and $\frac{7}{8}$ are unlike fractions with different numerators.

Pie A: $\frac{1}{4}$ $\frac{1}{4}$ $\frac{1}{4}$ $\frac{1}{4}$

Pie B: $\frac{1}{8}$ $\frac{1}{8}$ $\frac{1}{8}$ $\frac{1}{8}$ $\frac{1}{8}$ $\frac{1}{8}$ $\frac{1}{8}$ $\frac{1}{8}$

You can use multiplication to rewrite unlike fractions as like fractions.

First, find an equivalent fraction of $\frac{3}{4}$ that

has the same denominator as $\frac{7}{8}$.

$$\frac{3}{4} = \frac{6}{8} \quad \times 2$$

Now, the fractions $\frac{6}{8}$ and $\frac{7}{8}$ have a common denominator.

Compare the fractions.

> When the denominators are the same, compare the numerators.

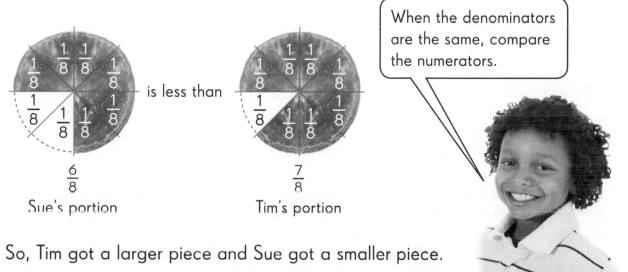

$\frac{6}{8}$ ... is less than ... $\frac{7}{8}$

Sue's portion

Tim's portion

So, Tim got a larger piece and Sue got a smaller piece.

Guided Practice

Find an equivalent fraction. Then compare.

11 Which is greater, $\frac{1}{2}$ or $\frac{4}{10}$?

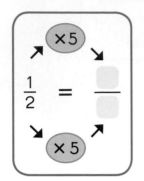

_____ is greater than _____.

---

^{Learn} **Compare unlike fractions.**

You can use division to rewrite unlike fractions as like fractions.

Which is less, $\frac{3}{12}$ or $\frac{2}{4}$?

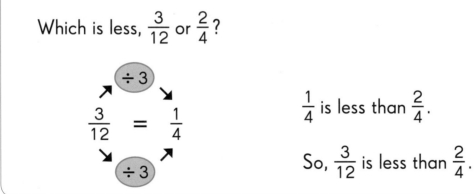

$\frac{1}{4}$ is less than $\frac{2}{4}$.

So, $\frac{3}{12}$ is less than $\frac{2}{4}$.

Guided Practice

Find an equivalent fraction. Then compare.

12 Which is greater, $\frac{8}{12}$ or $\frac{1}{3}$?

_____ is greater than _____.

Compare more unlike fractions.

Which is greater, $\frac{3}{4}$ or $\frac{1}{6}$?

$\frac{3}{4} = \frac{9}{12}$

$\frac{1}{6} = \frac{2}{12}$

$\frac{9}{12}$ is greater than $\frac{2}{12}$.

So, $\frac{3}{4}$ is greater than $\frac{1}{6}$.

$\frac{3}{4} \xrightarrow{\times 3} \frac{9}{12} \xrightarrow{\times 3}$ = $\frac{9}{12}$ $\frac{1}{6} \xrightarrow{\times 2} \frac{2}{12} \xrightarrow{\times 2}$ = $\frac{2}{12}$

Compare the fractions $\frac{3}{4}$ and $\frac{1}{6}$ with the **benchmark** $\frac{1}{2}$.

Fractions less than $\frac{1}{2}$ Fractions greater than $\frac{1}{2}$

0        $\frac{1}{2}$ 1

$\frac{1}{2} = \frac{2}{4} = \frac{3}{6}$

0    $\frac{1}{4}$ $\frac{2}{4}$ $\frac{3}{4}$ 1

0   $\frac{1}{6}$ $\frac{2}{6}$ $\frac{3}{6}$ $\frac{4}{6}$ $\frac{5}{6}$ 1

$\frac{3}{4} > \frac{1}{2}$

$\frac{1}{6} < \frac{1}{2}$

So, $\frac{3}{4} > \frac{1}{6}$.

When you compare fractions with $\frac{1}{2}$ like this, you are using $\frac{1}{2}$ as a **benchmark**.

It is easy to use a benchmark to compare fractions.

The common benchmarks for comparing fractions are 0, $\frac{1}{2}$, and 1.

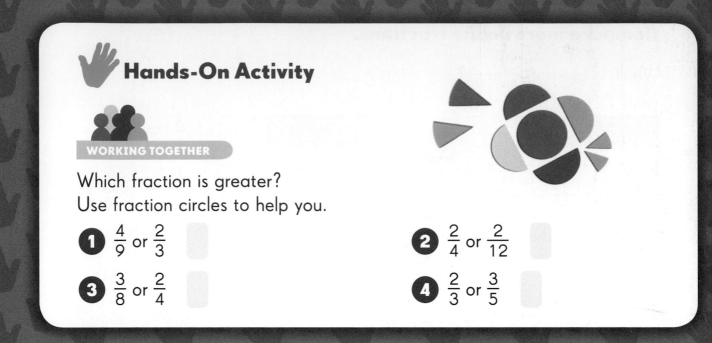

Hands-On Activity

WORKING TOGETHER

Which fraction is greater?
Use fraction circles to help you.

1 $\frac{4}{9}$ or $\frac{2}{3}$

2 $\frac{2}{4}$ or $\frac{2}{12}$

3 $\frac{3}{8}$ or $\frac{2}{4}$

4 $\frac{2}{3}$ or $\frac{3}{5}$

Guided Practice

Compare.

13 Which is less, $\frac{2}{3}$ or $\frac{7}{9}$?

$$\frac{2}{3} = \frac{}{9}$$

14 Which is greater, $\frac{5}{6}$ or $\frac{3}{4}$?

$$\frac{5}{6} = \frac{}{12} \qquad \frac{3}{4} = \frac{}{12}$$

Use the number lines to compare fractions with $\frac{1}{2}$.

15 Which is greater, $\frac{5}{6}$ or $\frac{3}{8}$?

Fractions less than $\frac{1}{2}$ Fractions greater than $\frac{1}{2}$

Compare the fractions to find which is greater than or less than $\frac{1}{2}$.

16 Which is greater, $\frac{2}{5}$ or $\frac{5}{8}$?

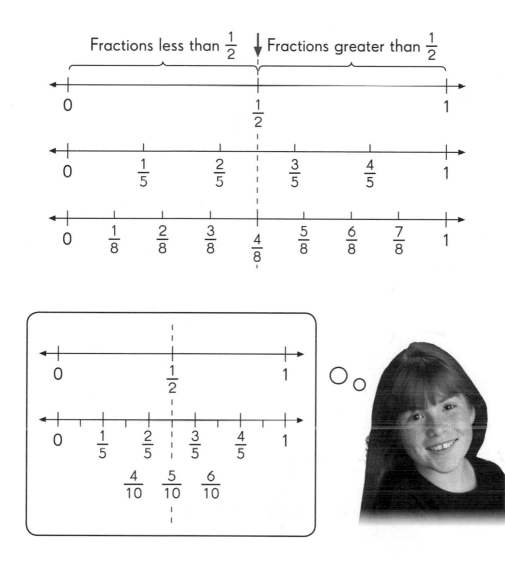

Do these.

Use benchmarks and number lines to help you.

17 Write three fractions, two of which are less than than $\frac{3}{4}$.

18 Write three fractions, two of which are greater than $\frac{1}{2}$.

Learn **Compare and order unlike fractions.**

Method 1.   Use a number line.

Order $\frac{1}{2}$, $\frac{5}{6}$ and $\frac{1}{12}$ from least to greatest.

$$\boxed{\frac{1}{2} \;=\; \frac{3}{6} \;=\; \frac{6}{12}}$$

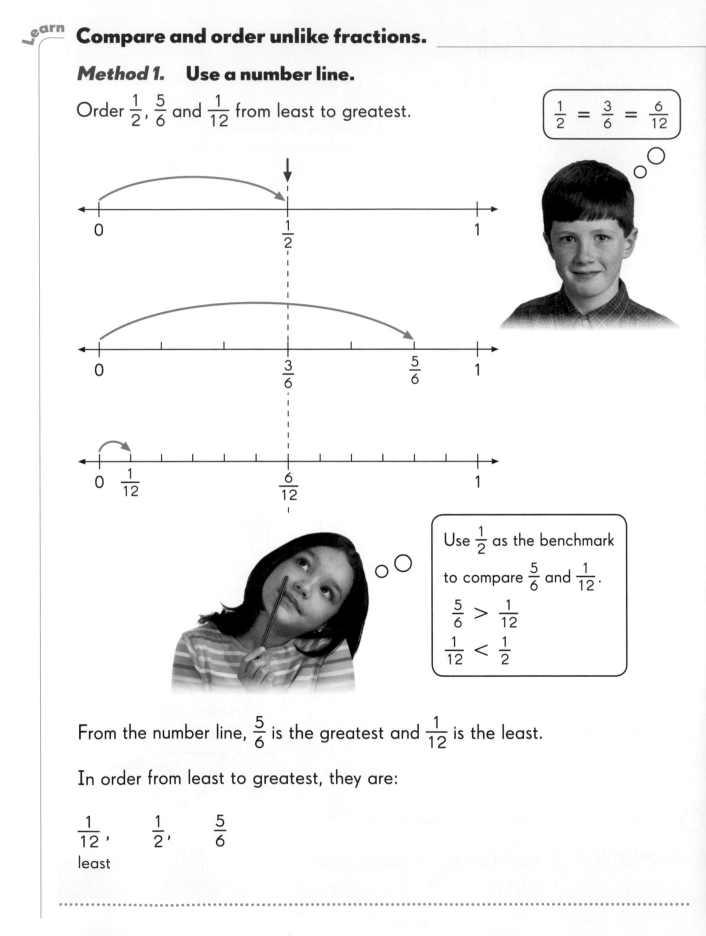

Use $\frac{1}{2}$ as the benchmark to compare $\frac{5}{6}$ and $\frac{1}{12}$.

$$\frac{5}{6} > \frac{1}{12}$$
$$\frac{1}{12} < \frac{1}{2}$$

From the number line, $\frac{5}{6}$ is the greatest and $\frac{1}{12}$ is the least.

In order from least to greatest, they are:

$\frac{1}{12}$, $\frac{1}{2}$, $\frac{5}{6}$

least

Method 2. Use models.

Compare $\frac{5}{6}$ and $\frac{1}{12}$ with $\frac{1}{2}$.

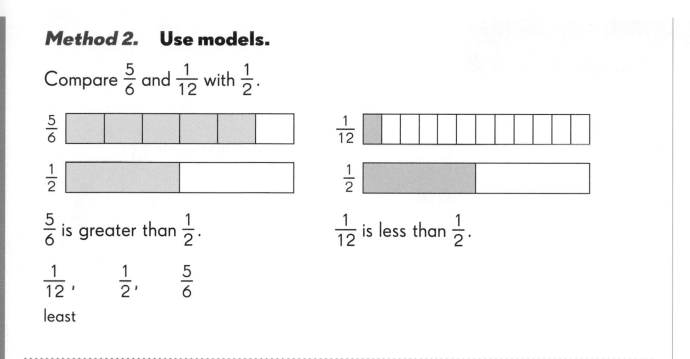

$\frac{5}{6}$ is greater than $\frac{1}{2}$.

$\frac{1}{12}$ is less than $\frac{1}{2}$.

$\frac{1}{12}$, $\frac{1}{2}$, $\frac{5}{6}$

least

Method 3. Use multiplication and division.

Express each fraction with a denominator 12.

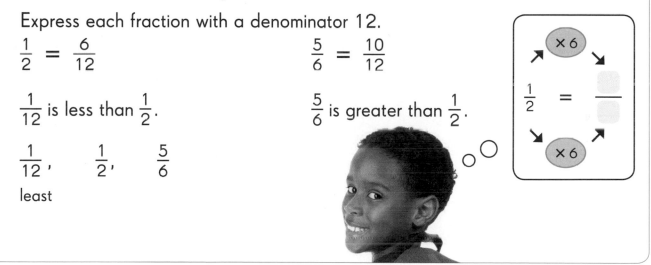

$\frac{1}{2} = \frac{6}{12}$ $\frac{5}{6} = \frac{10}{12}$

$\frac{1}{12}$ is less than $\frac{1}{2}$.

$\frac{5}{6}$ is greater than $\frac{1}{2}$.

$\frac{1}{12}$, $\frac{1}{2}$, $\frac{5}{6}$

least

Guided Practice

Order the fractions from least to greatest.

19 $\frac{7}{8}$, $\frac{1}{4}$, $\frac{1}{2}$

20 $\frac{7}{8}$, $\frac{5}{7}$, $\frac{1}{2}$

Order the fractions from greatest to least.

21 $\frac{1}{2}$, $\frac{9}{10}$, $\frac{2}{5}$

22 $\frac{2}{3}$, $\frac{1}{2}$, $\frac{5}{6}$

Let's Practice

Compare.

1 Which is greater, $\frac{3}{8}$ or $\frac{1}{2}$?

2 Which is less, $\frac{1}{2}$ or $\frac{7}{10}$?

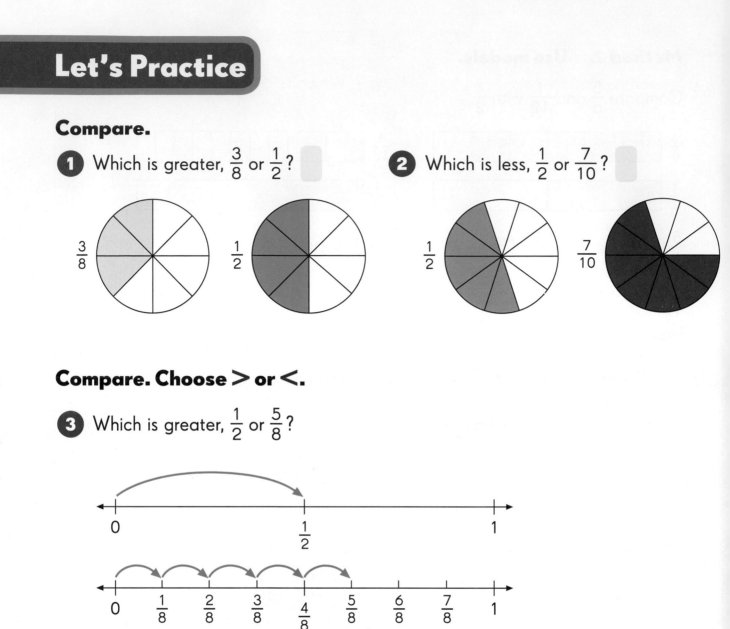

Compare. Choose > or <.

3 Which is greater, $\frac{1}{2}$ or $\frac{5}{8}$?

$\frac{1}{2}$ ⚫ $\frac{5}{8}$

Complete the sentences.

4 More than $\frac{1}{2}$ of the pattern is colored ____.

5 $\frac{1}{4}$ of the pattern is colored ____.

Compare.

6 Which is less, $\frac{3}{10}$ or $\frac{3}{5}$?

7 Which is greater, $\frac{1}{3}$ or $\frac{2}{5}$?

Order the fractions from least to greatest.

8 $\frac{5}{12}$, $\frac{5}{6}$, $\frac{1}{2}$

9 $\frac{3}{4}$, $\frac{7}{12}$, $\frac{2}{3}$

Order the fractions from greatest to least.

10 $\frac{1}{6}$, $\frac{4}{9}$, $\frac{7}{12}$

ON YOUR OWN

**Go to Workbook B:
Practice 4, pages 101–106**

Let's Explore!

Alex, Ben, and Connor each have an equal-sized fraction strip.

Alex's fraction is greater than Ben's and Connor's.
Ben's fraction is less than Connor's.

Alex	
Ben	
Connor	

Look at Alex's fraction strip.
Trace and cut Ben's and Connor's strips on a piece of paper.
Then divide each bar into a different number of equal parts by folding.

1 What could Ben's and Connor's fractions be?
Shade the parts of each bar to show possible answers.

2 Write the fractions and check your answers.

Continued on next page

3 Are there any other possible answers? If so, what are they?

Copy the number line on grid paper.

Compare fractions with common benchmarks of 0, $\frac{1}{2}$, and 1.

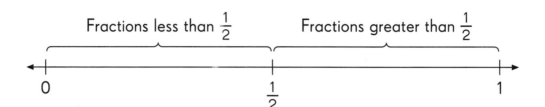

The clues are as follows:

$\frac{2}{11}$ is closer to 0 than to $\frac{1}{2}$.

$\frac{8}{9}$ is closer to 1 than to $\frac{1}{2}$.

$\frac{5}{12}$ is closer to $\frac{1}{2}$ than to 0, but is less than $\frac{1}{2}$.

$\frac{4}{7}$ is closer to $\frac{1}{2}$ than to 1, but is greater than $\frac{1}{2}$.

4 Explore and order these fractions using these benchmarks. Start with the least.

5 Name another fraction closer to 0 than to $\frac{1}{2}$.

6 Name another fraction closer to $\frac{1}{2}$ than to 0, but less than $\frac{1}{2}$.

7 Name another fraction closer to $\frac{1}{2}$ than to 1, but greater than $\frac{1}{2}$.

8 Name another fraction closer to 1 than to $\frac{1}{2}$.

Math Journal

Solve.

Matthew, Jacob, and Ethan each have an equal-sized fraction strip.
Matthew folded his fraction strip into 8 equal parts and shaded 7 parts.
The fraction he shaded is greater than Jacob's and Ethan's.
Jacob's fraction is less than Ethan's.
How would you fold and shade Jacob's and Ethan's fraction strip?

First, I fold Jacob's strip into half and
shade one part.

I must shade a fraction less than $\frac{7}{8}$.

I check my answer: $\frac{1}{2} = \frac{4}{8}$.

So, $\frac{1}{2}$ is less than $\frac{7}{8}$.

1 Now, list all the steps to your answers on a piece
of paper to compare the fractions $\frac{1}{2}$, $\frac{4}{6}$, and $\frac{7}{8}$.

2 Which halves can be compared?
Explain your answer.

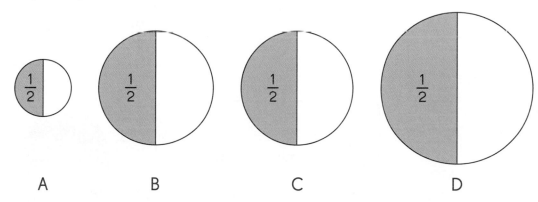

A   B   C   D

14.5 Adding and Subtracting Like Fractions

Lesson Objectives

- Add two or three like fractions with sums to 1.
- Subtract a like fraction from another like fraction or one whole.

Learn **Add like fractions.**

Jerome ate $\frac{1}{7}$ of an omelet.

His brother Randy ate $\frac{5}{7}$ of it.

What fraction of the omelet did they eat altogether?

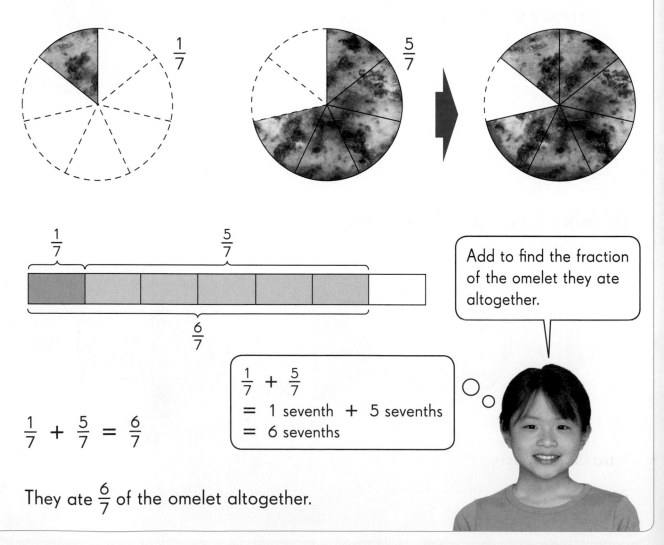

$\frac{1}{7} + \frac{5}{7}$
= 1 seventh + 5 sevenths
= 6 sevenths

Add to find the fraction of the omelet they ate altogether.

$\frac{1}{7} + \frac{5}{7} = \frac{6}{7}$

They ate $\frac{6}{7}$ of the omelet altogether.

Guided Practice

Complete.

1 Add $\frac{2}{6}$ and $\frac{3}{6}$.

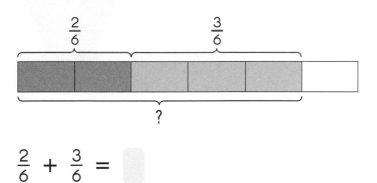

$$\frac{2}{6} + \frac{3}{6} = \boxed{}$$

Subtract like fractions.

Yvonne hiked $\frac{2}{7}$ of a forest trail before lunch.

She hiked again after lunch.

By the end of the day, she had hiked $\frac{6}{7}$ of the trail.

What fraction of the trail did Yvonne hike after lunch?

$$\frac{6}{7} - \frac{2}{7} = \frac{4}{7}$$

Subtract to find the fraction of the trail Yvonne hiked after lunch.

$$\frac{6}{7} - \frac{2}{7}$$
$$= 6 \text{ sevenths } - 2 \text{ sevenths}$$
$$= 4 \text{ sevenths}$$

Yvonne hiked $\frac{4}{7}$ of the forest trail after lunch.

2 $1 - \frac{3}{5} = ?$

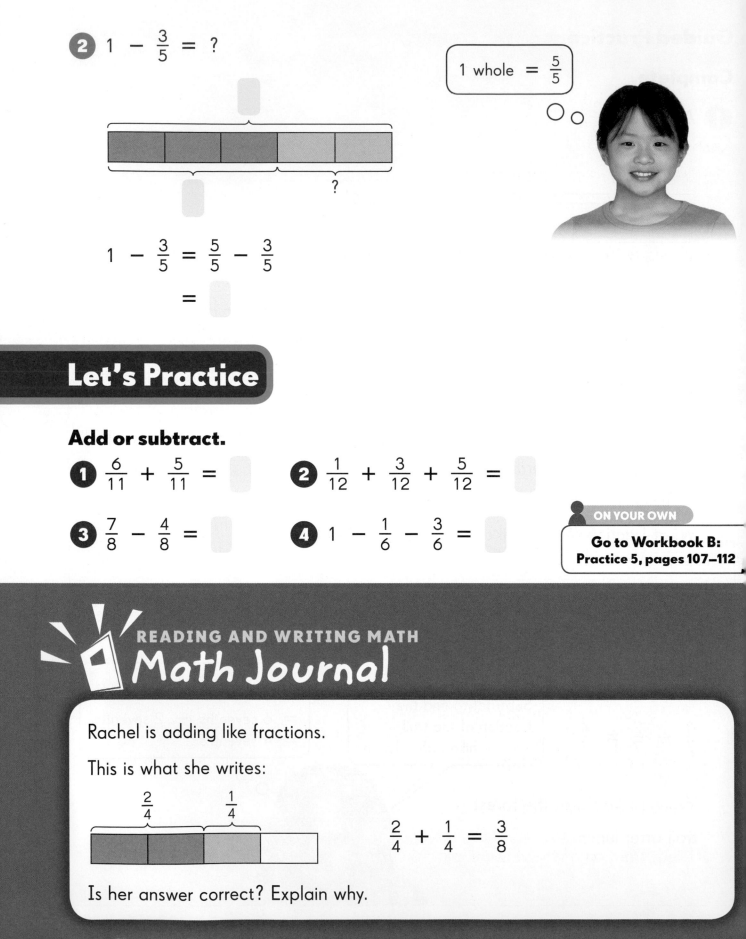

1 whole $= \frac{5}{5}$

$$1 - \frac{3}{5} = \frac{5}{5} - \frac{3}{5}$$

$$=$$

Let's Practice

Add or subtract.

1 $\frac{6}{11} + \frac{5}{11} = $

2 $\frac{1}{12} + \frac{3}{12} + \frac{5}{12} = $

3 $\frac{7}{8} - \frac{4}{8} = $

4 $1 - \frac{1}{6} - \frac{3}{6} = $

ON YOUR OWN

Go to Workbook B: Practice 5, pages 107–112

READING AND WRITING MATH
Math Journal

Rachel is adding like fractions.

This is what she writes:

$\frac{2}{4}$ $\frac{1}{4}$

$$\frac{2}{4} + \frac{1}{4} = \frac{3}{8}$$

Is her answer correct? Explain why.

Lesson 14.6 Fraction of a Set

Lesson Objectives

• Read, write, and identify fractions of a set.
• Find the number of items in a fraction of a set.

Learn **Use pictures to show fractions as part of a set of objects.**

There are 4 apples.
3 out of the 4 apples are red.

$\dfrac{3}{4}$ ← red apples
$\phantom{\dfrac{3}{4}}$ ← total number of apples

What fraction of the apples are red?
$\dfrac{3}{4}$ of the apples are red.

Guided Practice

Find the fractions of a set.

There are 10 flowers.

1 What fraction of the flowers are red?

2 What fraction of the flowers are purple?

3 What fraction of the flowers are yellow?

4 What fraction of the flowers are not red?

Find the fraction of a part of objects.

Here is a set of 12 apples.
The set of apples is divided into 4 equal groups.
3 out of 4 groups of apples are red.

$\frac{3}{4}$ is 3 out of 4 equal groups.

What fraction of the apples is red?

$\frac{3}{4}$ of the apples are red.

Guided Practice

Complete.

5 The set of ducks is divided into _____ equal groups.

6 What fraction of the ducks are yellow?

_____ of the ducks are yellow.

7 What fraction of the ducks are purple?

_____ of the ducks are purple.

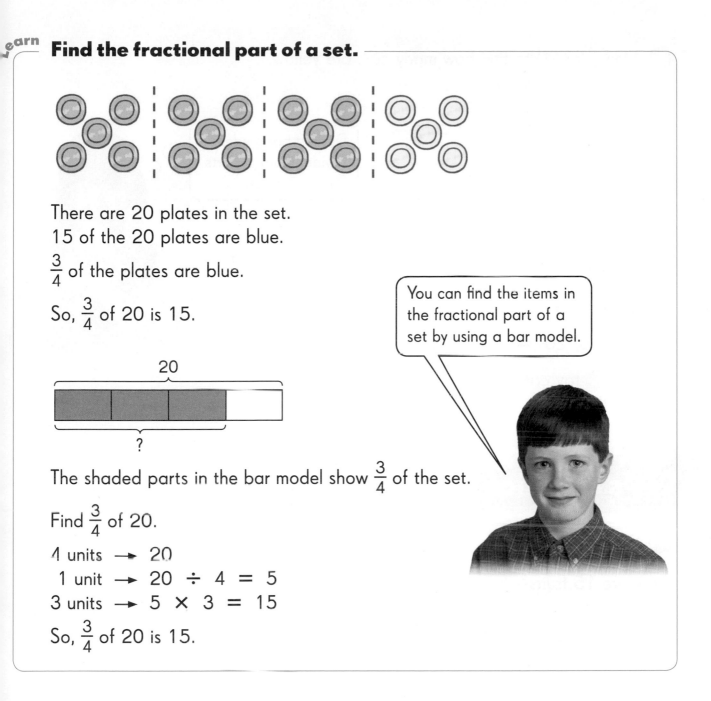

Find the fractional part of a set.

There are 20 plates in the set.
15 of the 20 plates are blue.
$\frac{3}{4}$ of the plates are blue.

So, $\frac{3}{4}$ of 20 is 15.

20

?

The shaded parts in the bar model show $\frac{3}{4}$ of the set.

Find $\frac{3}{4}$ of 20.

4 units ⟶ 20
1 unit ⟶ 20 ÷ 4 = 5
3 units ⟶ 5 × 3 = 15

So, $\frac{3}{4}$ of 20 is 15.

> You can find the items in the fractional part of a set by using a bar model.

Guided Practice

Complete.

8 John has 20 toy cars.
$\frac{3}{5}$ of the toy cars are yellow.
How many toy cars are yellow?

[ ] toy cars are yellow.

9 Find $\frac{3}{5}$ of 20 to find how many cars are yellow.

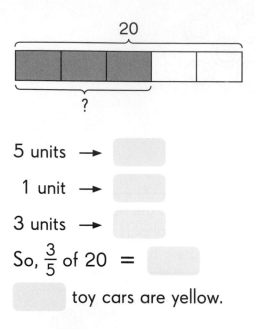

20

?

Draw a bar model.
Divide it into 5 parts.
Shade 3 parts.

5 units ⟶ ▢

1 unit ⟶ ▢

3 units ⟶ ▢

So, $\frac{3}{5}$ of 20 = ▢

▢ toy cars are yellow.

Let's Practice

Solve.

There are 15 fruits.

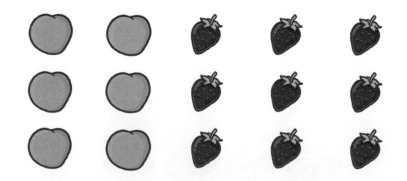

1 What fraction of the fruits are peaches? ▢

2 What fraction of the fruits are strawberries? ▢

Complete.

3 Which of the following sets shows the fraction $\frac{3}{4}$?

 ▢

▢

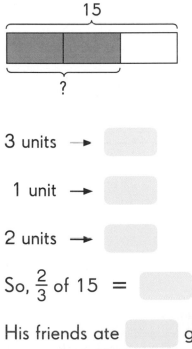 ▢

▢

4 Jerry has 15 granola bars.

$\frac{2}{3}$ of them were eaten by his friends.

How many granola bars did his friends eat?

Find $\frac{2}{3}$ of 15 to find how many granola bars

his friends ate.

15

?

3 units ⟶ ▢

1 unit ⟶ ▢

2 units ⟶ ▢

So, $\frac{2}{3}$ of 15 = ▢

His friends ate ▢ granola bars.

Go to Workbook B:
Practice 6, pages 113–116

CRITICAL THINKING SKILLS
Put On Your Thinking Cap!

PROBLEM SOLVING

1 The model shows $\frac{3}{4}$.

How much of the shading must be erased so that the remaining shaded part is $\frac{3}{8}$ of the strip?

> Try drawing the model in another way.

2 Gary, Joey, and Kylie share a vegetarian pizza.
The pizza is divided into 9 equal slices.

Gary ate $\frac{2}{9}$ of the pizza.

Joey ate more pizza than Kylie.
Together they finished the whole pizza.

What are some possible fractions that show the part of the pizza that Joey and Kylie each ate?

What is the greatest possible fraction that describes the part of the pizza that Kylie eats?

> Try drawing a model first.

ON YOUR OWN

**Go to Workbook B:
Put on Your Thinking Cap!
pages 117–118**

Chapter Wrap Up

Study Guide
You have learned...

💡 **BIG IDEA**

▶ Fractions can be used to describe parts of a region or parts of a set.

Understanding fractions, numerator, and denominator:

Unit fractions

$\frac{1}{6}$ is one-sixth $\frac{1}{7}$ is one-seventh $\frac{1}{8}$ is one-eighth

$\frac{1}{9}$ is one-ninth $\frac{1}{10}$ is one-tenth $\frac{1}{11}$ is one-eleventh

$\frac{1}{12}$ is one-twelfth

Identifying fractions to make a whole

$\frac{2}{5}$ and $\frac{3}{5}$ make 1 whole.

Numerator and Denominator

$\frac{2}{4}$ ← Numerator: Number of equal parts shaded.
　　← Denominator: Number of equal parts the whole is divided into.

Equivalent fractions:

Using a model

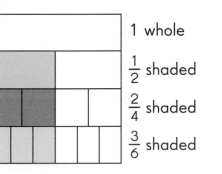

1 whole
$\frac{1}{2}$ shaded
$\frac{2}{4}$ shaded
$\frac{3}{6}$ shaded

Using a number line

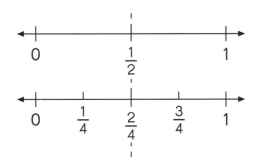

Continued on next page

Using multiplication and division

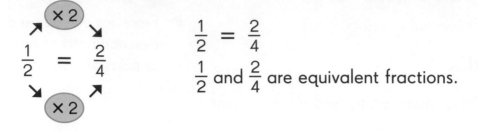

$$\frac{1}{2} = \frac{2}{4}$$

$\frac{1}{2}$ and $\frac{2}{4}$ are equivalent fractions.

Comparing and ordering fractions:

Like fractions are fractions with the same denominators and unlike fractions are fractions with different denominators.

Comparing like fractions

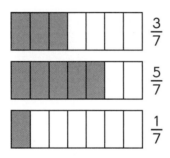 $\frac{3}{7}$

$\frac{5}{7}$

$\frac{1}{7}$

$\frac{5}{7}$ is the greatest.

$\frac{1}{7}$ is the least.

$\frac{5}{7}$, $\frac{3}{7}$, $\frac{1}{7}$

greatest

> When the denominators are the same, compare the numerators.

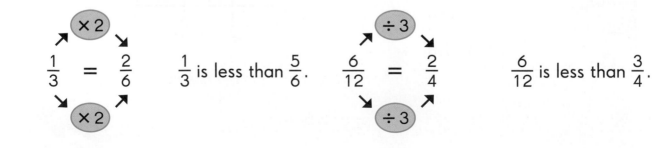

Comparing unlike fractions with the same numerator

$\frac{1}{5}$

$\frac{1}{9}$

$\frac{1}{7}$

$\frac{1}{9}$ is less than $\frac{1}{7}$.

$\frac{1}{5}$ is greater than $\frac{1}{9}$.

Using multiplication and division to compare

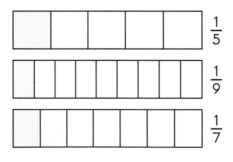

$\frac{1}{3} = \frac{2}{6}$

$\frac{1}{3}$ is less than $\frac{5}{6}$.

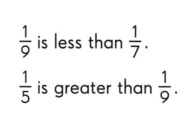

$\frac{6}{12} = \frac{2}{4}$

$\frac{6}{12}$ is less than $\frac{3}{4}$.

Using number lines and a benchmark of $\frac{1}{2}$

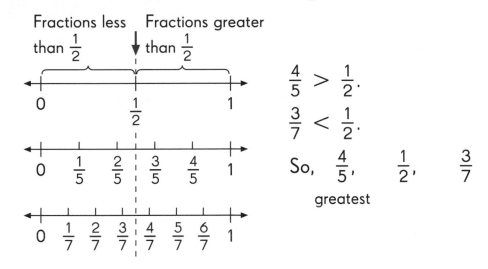

$\frac{4}{5} > \frac{1}{2}$.

$\frac{3}{7} < \frac{1}{2}$.

So, $\frac{4}{5}$, $\frac{1}{2}$, $\frac{3}{7}$

greatest

....

Adding and subtracting like fractions:

$\frac{1}{7} + \frac{5}{7} = \frac{6}{7}$

$\frac{6}{7} - \frac{2}{7} = \frac{4}{7}$

....

Finding fractions of a set using models

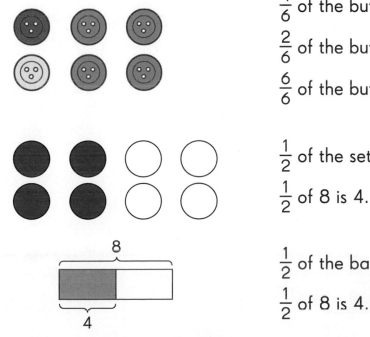

$\frac{4}{6}$ of the buttons are blue.

$\frac{2}{6}$ of the buttons are not blue.

$\frac{6}{6}$ of the buttons are round.

$\frac{1}{2}$ of the set of circles is red.

$\frac{1}{2}$ of 8 is 4.

$\frac{1}{2}$ of the bar model is shaded.

$\frac{1}{2}$ of 8 is 4.

Chapter Review/Test

Vocabulary
Choose the correct word.

1 In the fraction $\frac{4}{5}$, 4 is the [____], and 5 is the [____].

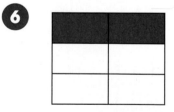

2 $\frac{1}{3}$ and $\frac{2}{3}$ make a [____].

3 $\frac{1}{3}$ and $\frac{3}{9}$ are [____].

4 $\frac{2}{8}$ and $\frac{3}{12}$ are equivalent to $\frac{1}{4}$ in [____].

5 [____] have the same denominators and [____] have different denominators.

> denominator
> simplest form
> numerator
> whole
> equivalent fractions
> like fractions
> unlike fractions

Concept and Skills
Match the fraction names to the models.

6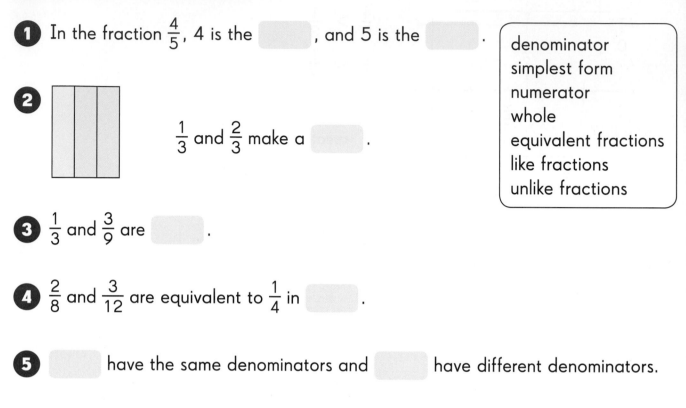

[____]

7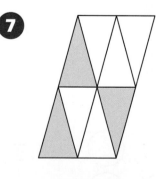

> two-sixths
> three-eighths
> six-twelfths

[____]

8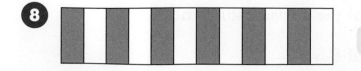

[____]

Complete.

9

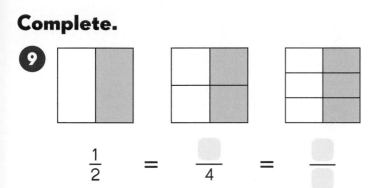

$$\frac{1}{2} \quad = \quad \frac{\boxed{}}{4} \quad = \quad \frac{\boxed{}}{\boxed{}}$$

Find equivalent fractions.

10 $\dfrac{3}{4} = \dfrac{\boxed{}}{8} = \dfrac{\boxed{}}{12}$

11 $\dfrac{2}{3} = \dfrac{\boxed{}}{6} = \dfrac{\boxed{}}{9}$

Simplify the fraction.

12 $\dfrac{8}{12} = \dfrac{\boxed{}}{\boxed{}} = \dfrac{\boxed{}}{\boxed{}}$

Compare fractions.

13 $\dfrac{2}{3}$ and $\dfrac{2}{4}$

 $\boxed{}$ is greater than $\boxed{}$.

14 $\dfrac{1}{3}$ and $\dfrac{1}{4}$

 $\boxed{}$ is less than $\boxed{}$.

Find equivalent fractions. Then, order the fractions from least to greatest.

15 $\dfrac{1}{2} = \boxed{}$ $\dfrac{2}{3} = \boxed{}$ $\dfrac{1}{4} = \boxed{}$

$\boxed{}$, $\boxed{}$, $\boxed{}$
least

Which is the greater fraction? Use $\dfrac{1}{2}$ as a benchmark.

16 $\dfrac{2}{3}, \dfrac{1}{8}$

17 $\dfrac{3}{4}, \dfrac{5}{6}$

Add or subtract.

18 $\frac{3}{8} + \frac{2}{8} =$ ▢

19 $\frac{1}{6} +$ ▢ $= 1$

20 $\frac{5}{6} - \frac{2}{6} =$ ▢

21 $1 - \frac{1}{9} - \frac{5}{9} =$ ▢

Problem Solving
Solve.

22 The difference between my numerator and denominator is 3.
My denominator is the greatest odd number that is less than 10.
What fraction am I?

$$\frac{7}{10}, \quad \frac{4}{7}, \quad \frac{6}{9}, \quad \frac{9}{12}$$

23 Vanessa has 18 cookies.
She eats 3 of them.
What fraction of cookies does she have left?

24 Rebecca reads $\frac{1}{6}$ of a book in the morning.

She reads $\frac{3}{6}$ of the book in the afternoon.

What fraction of the book does she read?

25 Andrea is decorating a paper quilt.

She colors $\frac{2}{5}$ of the squares red.

She colors $\frac{1}{5}$ of them blue.

The rest of the squares will be gold.
What fraction of the quilt will be gold?

15 Customary Length, Weight, and Capacity

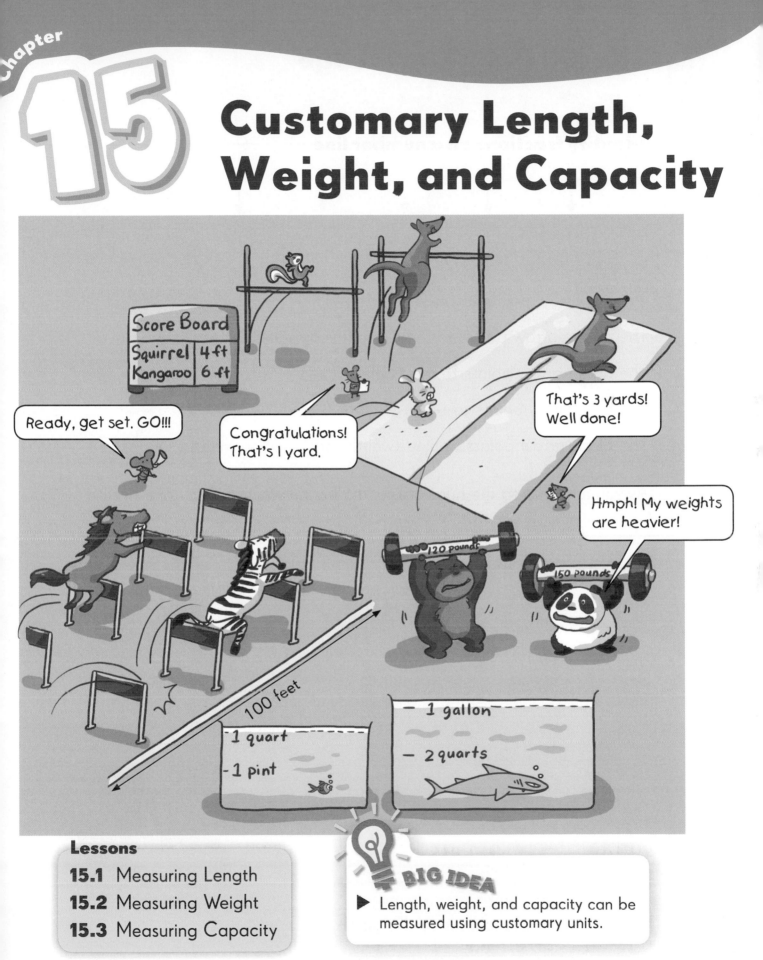

Lessons

15.1 Measuring Length

15.2 Measuring Weight

15.3 Measuring Capacity

BIG IDEA

▶ Length, weight, and capacity can be measured using customary units.

Recall Prior Knowledge

Identify fractions on a number line

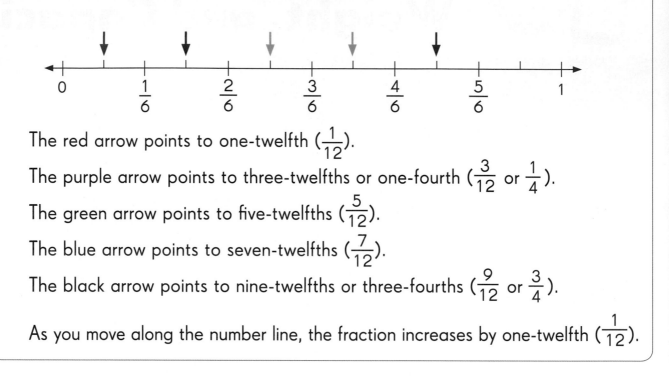

The red arrow points to one-twelfth ($\frac{1}{12}$).

The purple arrow points to three-twelfths or one-fourth ($\frac{3}{12}$ or $\frac{1}{4}$).

The green arrow points to five-twelfths ($\frac{5}{12}$).

The blue arrow points to seven-twelfths ($\frac{7}{12}$).

The black arrow points to nine-twelfths or three-fourths ($\frac{9}{12}$ or $\frac{3}{4}$).

As you move along the number line, the fraction increases by one-twelfth ($\frac{1}{12}$).

Adding like fractions

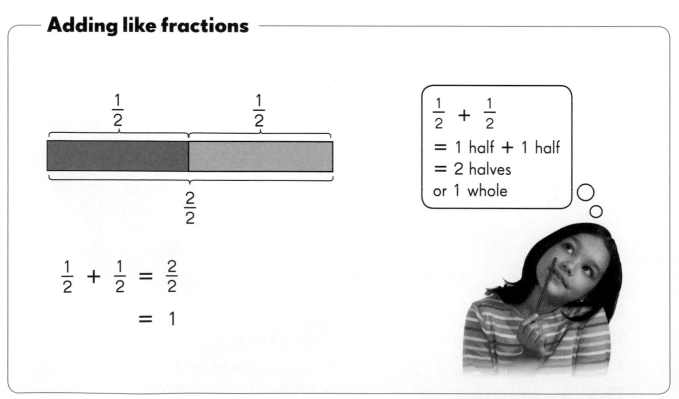

$$\frac{1}{2} + \frac{1}{2} = \frac{2}{2}$$
$$= 1$$

$\frac{1}{2} + \frac{1}{2}$
= 1 half + 1 half
= 2 halves
or 1 whole

Measuring length in feet (ft) and inches (in.)

Both feet (ft) and inches (in.) are customary units of length.

1 foot (ft) = 12 inches (in.)

Feet are used to measure longer lengths.
Inches are used to measure shorter lengths.
Inch-rulers are used for measuring customary lengths.

The arrow points to 1 inch (in.).

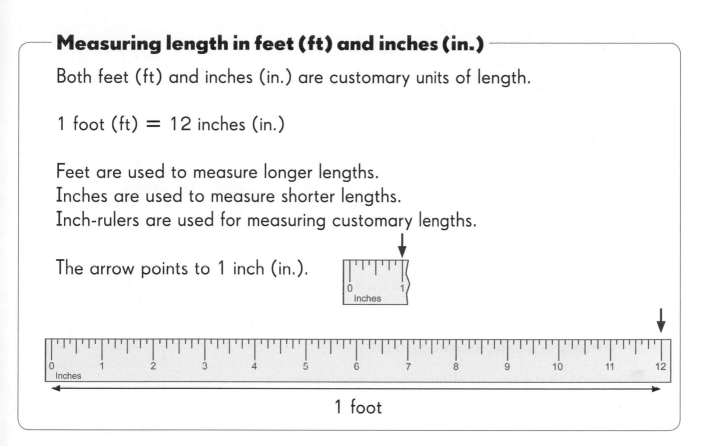

1 foot

Comparing lengths using feet (ft) and inches (in.)

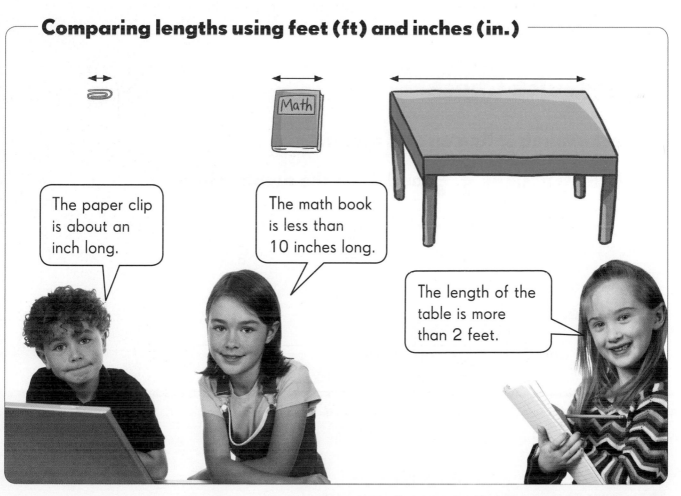

The paper clip is about an inch long.

The math book is less than 10 inches long.

The length of the table is more than 2 feet.

Using tools to measure mass

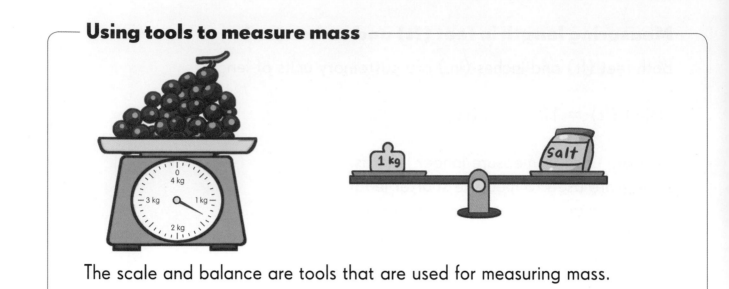

The scale and balance are tools that are used for measuring mass.

Defining volume and capacity

Volume is the amount of liquid in a container.
Capacity is the amount of liquid a container can hold.

Larger containers have a greater capacity than smaller containers.

✔ Quick Check

Copy the number line on grid paper.

Mark the fractions $\frac{3}{8}$, $\frac{5}{8}$, and $\frac{7}{8}$ on the number line.

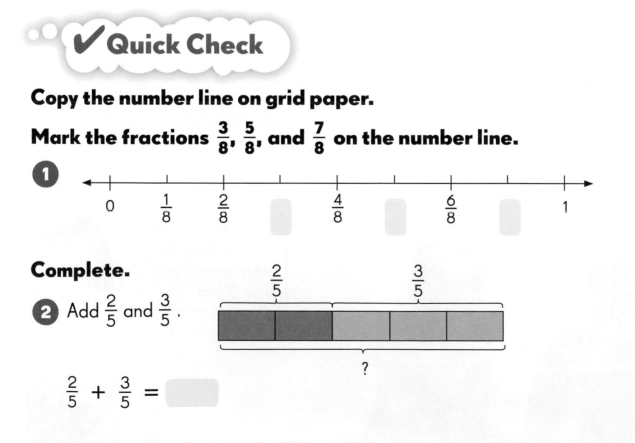

1

$0 \quad \frac{1}{8} \quad \frac{2}{8} \quad \quad \frac{4}{8} \quad \quad \frac{6}{8} \quad \quad 1$

Complete.

2 Add $\frac{2}{5}$ and $\frac{3}{5}$.

$\frac{2}{5} \qquad \frac{3}{5}$

?

$\frac{2}{5} + \frac{3}{5} = $ ⬚

Complete. Use shorter or longer.

 Feet are used to measure [____] lengths.

 Inches are used to measure [____] lengths.

Name two objects for each measure.

5 about one inch long [____]

6 more than one foot long [____]

7 less than one foot long [____]

Choose the correct unit of measure for each. Use inches or feet .

8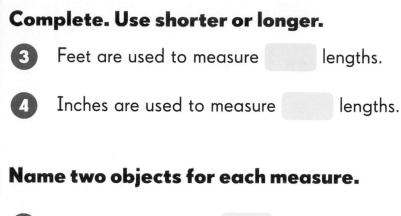
[____]

9
[____]

Fill in the blanks.

 You use a [____] for measuring mass.

11 Container [____] has a greater capacity.

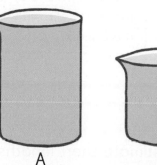 
A   B

Lesson 15.1 Measuring Length

Lesson Objectives

- Use inch, foot, yard, and mile as units of measurement for lengths.
- Estimate and measure given lengths.
- Use referents to estimate lengths.

Vocabulary

inch (in.)

half-inch

foot (ft)

yard (yd)

mile (mi)

Learn Estimate and measure length to the nearest inch (in.).

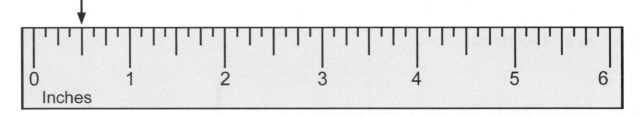

This is an **inch** ruler.
There are 8 divisions in each inch.
The halfway mark between two inch marks is $\frac{1}{2}$ inch.

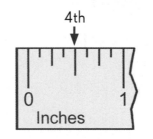

The fourth division-marking is the $\frac{1}{2}$ inch mark.

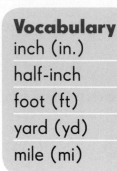

Sally wants to measure the length of these objects.

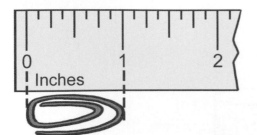

Line up one end of the paper clip with the 0 mark.

The length of the paper clip is 1 inch.
You can use this paper clip to estimate short lengths in inches.

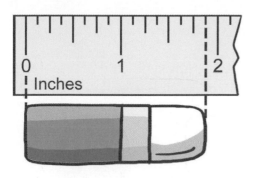

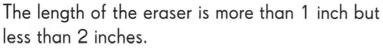

The length of the eraser is 2 inches measured to the nearest inch.

The length of the eraser is more than 1 inch but less than 2 inches.
It is nearer to 2 inches than to 1 inch.
So, the length of the eraser is about 2 inches.

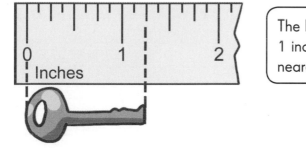

The length of the key is 1 inch, measured to the nearest inch.

The length of the key is more than 1 inch but less than 2 inches.
It is nearer to 1 inch than to 2 inches.
So, the length of the key is about 1 inch.

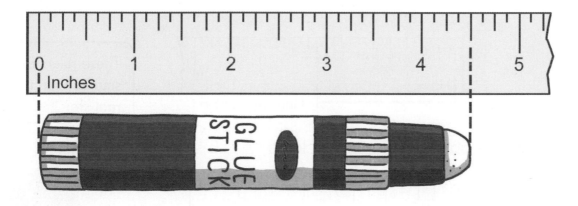

The length of the glue stick is more than 4 inches but less than 5 inches.
It is 4 inches and $\frac{1}{2}$ inch long.
So, the length of the glue stick is about 5 inches.

Guided Practice

Complete.

Estimate the length of the stapler mentally.

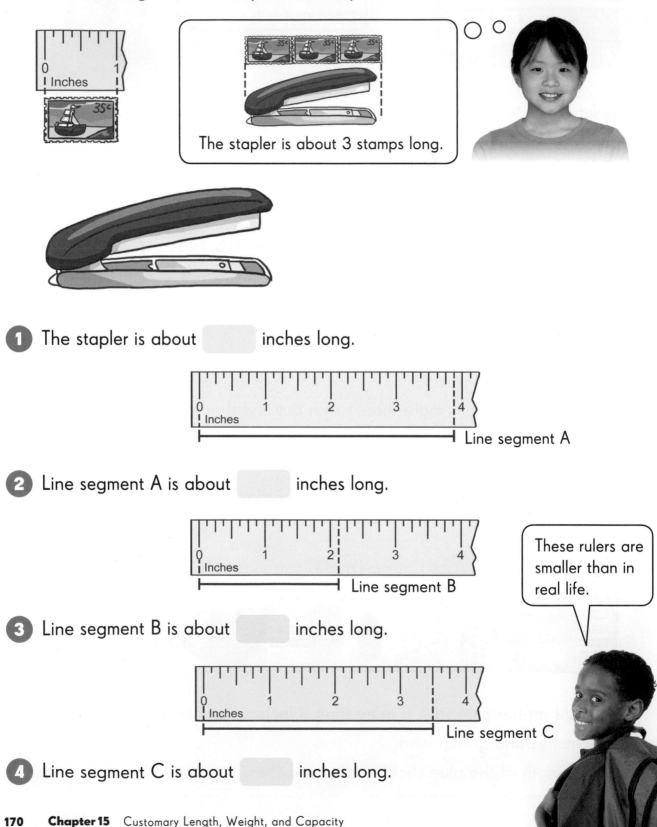

The stapler is about 3 stamps long.

1 The stapler is about ⬚ inches long.

2 Line segment A is about ⬚ inches long.

Line segment A

These rulers are smaller than in real life.

3 Line segment B is about ⬚ inches long.

Line segment B

4 Line segment C is about ⬚ inches long.

Line segment C

Estimate and measure length to the nearest **half-inch.**

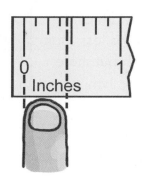

The width of the finger is about $\frac{1}{2}$ inch.
You can use the width of a finger to estimate
short lengths.

This is an eraser.
Now measure the eraser with a ruler.

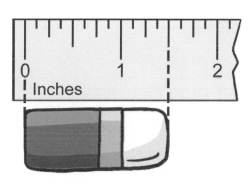

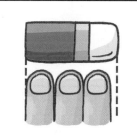

The eraser is about
3 finger widths long.

The length of the eraser is $1\frac{1}{2}$ inches to the nearest half-inch.

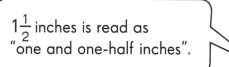

$1\frac{1}{2}$ inches is read as
"one and one-half inches".

$1\frac{1}{2}$ is a mixed number. It means a half more than one.

It is halfway between 1 and 2.

$2\frac{1}{2}$ means a half more than two. $2\frac{1}{2}$ is halfway between 2 and 3.

How do you read these mixed numbers? What do they mean?
$3\frac{1}{2}$: three and one-half $4\frac{1}{2}$: four and one-half

Continued on next page

Gita wants to measure the width and length of a pencil.

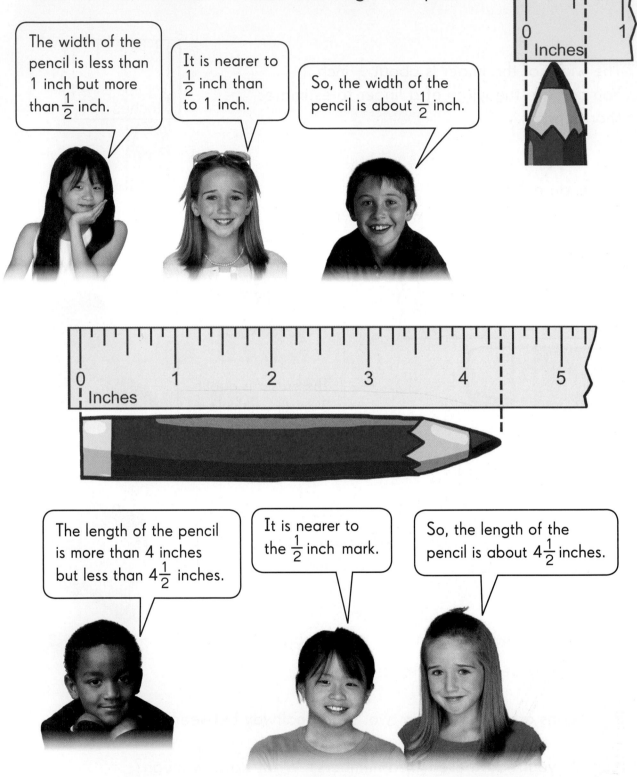

The width of the pencil is less than 1 inch but more than $\frac{1}{2}$ inch.

It is nearer to $\frac{1}{2}$ inch than to 1 inch.

So, the width of the pencil is about $\frac{1}{2}$ inch.

The length of the pencil is more than 4 inches but less than $4\frac{1}{2}$ inches.

It is nearer to the $\frac{1}{2}$ inch mark.

So, the length of the pencil is about $4\frac{1}{2}$ inches.

The width of the pencil is $\frac{1}{2}$ inch, measured to the nearest $\frac{1}{2}$ inch.

The length of the pencil is $4\frac{1}{2}$ inches, measured to the nearest half-inch.

Gita also wants to estimate the length of 3 ribbons.

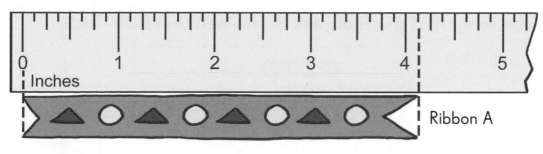

Ribbon A

Ribbon A is more than 4 inches but less than $4\frac{1}{2}$ inches long.

It is nearer to 4 inches than to $4\frac{1}{2}$ inches.

So, the length of Ribbon A is 4 inches to the the nearest half-inch.

Ribbon B

Ribbon B is more than $2\frac{1}{2}$ inches but less than 3 inches long.

It is nearer to 3 inches than to $2\frac{1}{2}$ inches.

So, the length of Ribbon B is 3 inches to the nearest half-inch.

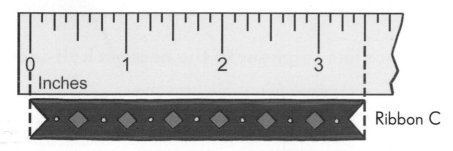

Ribbon C

Ribbon C is more than 3 inches but less than 4 inches long.

It is $3\frac{1}{2}$ inches long.

So, the length of Ribbon C is $3\frac{1}{2}$ inches to the nearest half-inch.

The lengths of Ribbon A, Ribbon B, and Ribbon C are measured to the nearest half-inch.

Guided Practice

Estimate the length of each object to the nearest half-inch.

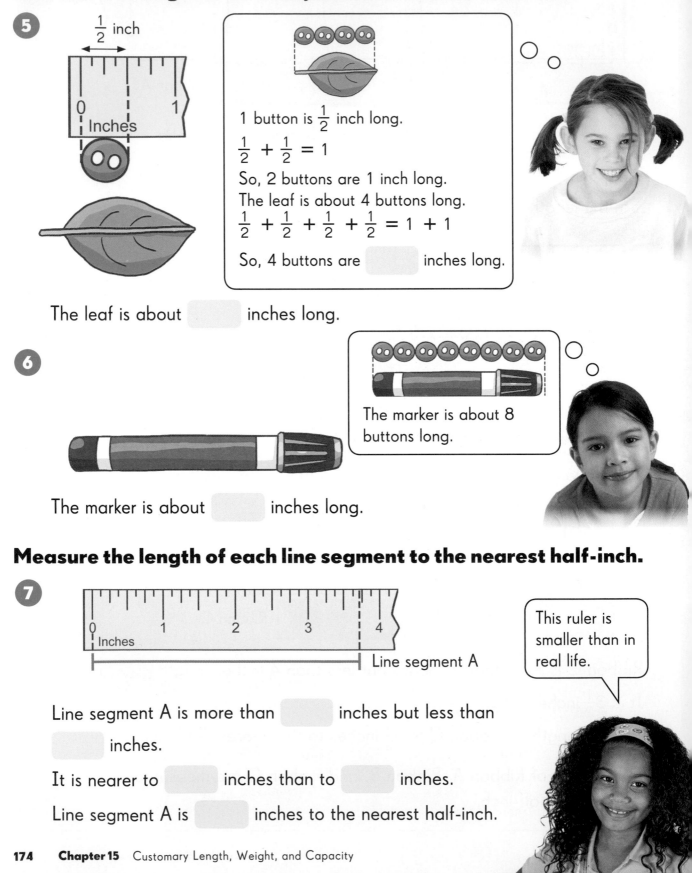

5 $\frac{1}{2}$ inch

0   1
Inches

1 button is $\frac{1}{2}$ inch long.

$\frac{1}{2} + \frac{1}{2} = 1$

So, 2 buttons are 1 inch long.
The leaf is about 4 buttons long.

$\frac{1}{2} + \frac{1}{2} + \frac{1}{2} + \frac{1}{2} = 1 + 1$

So, 4 buttons are [ ] inches long.

The leaf is about [ ] inches long.

6

The marker is about 8 buttons long.

The marker is about [ ] inches long.

Measure the length of each line segment to the nearest half-inch.

7

0   1   2   3   4
Inches

Line segment A

This ruler is smaller than in real life.

Line segment A is more than [ ] inches but less than [ ] inches.

It is nearer to [ ] inches than to [ ] inches.

Line segment A is [ ] inches to the nearest half-inch.

8

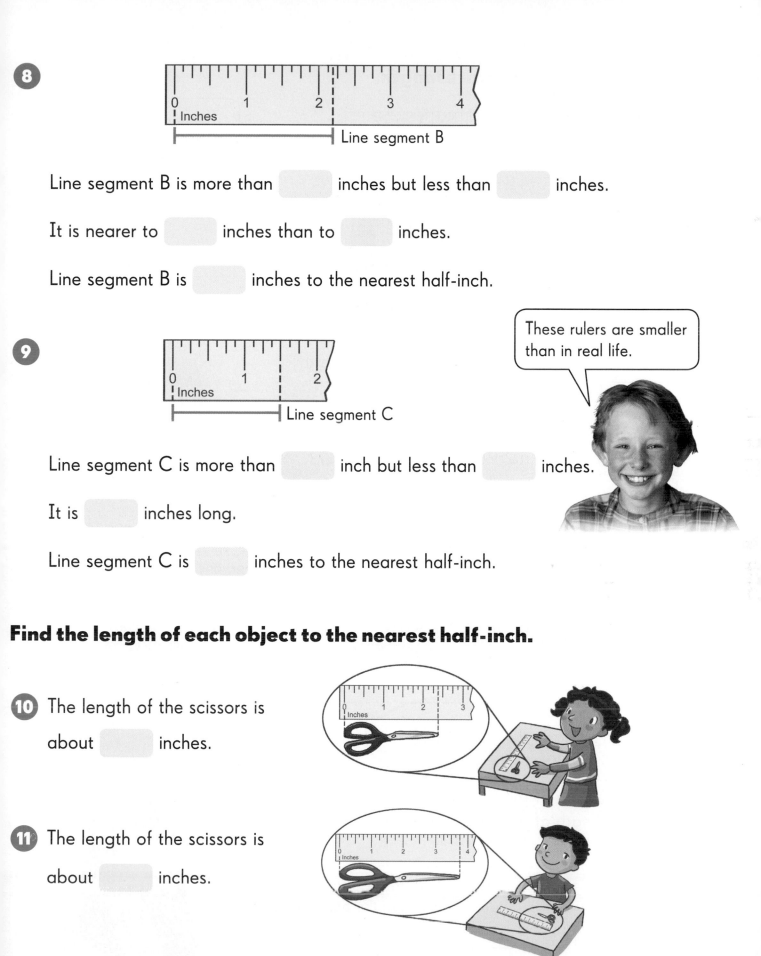

Line segment B is more than [ ] inches but less than [ ] inches.

It is nearer to [ ] inches than to [ ] inches.

Line segment B is [ ] inches to the nearest half-inch.

9

Line segment C is more than [ ] inch but less than [ ] inches.

It is [ ] inches long.

Line segment C is [ ] inches to the nearest half-inch.

These rulers are smaller than in real life.

Find the length of each object to the nearest half-inch.

10 The length of the scissors is about [ ] inches.

11 The length of the scissors is about [ ] inches.

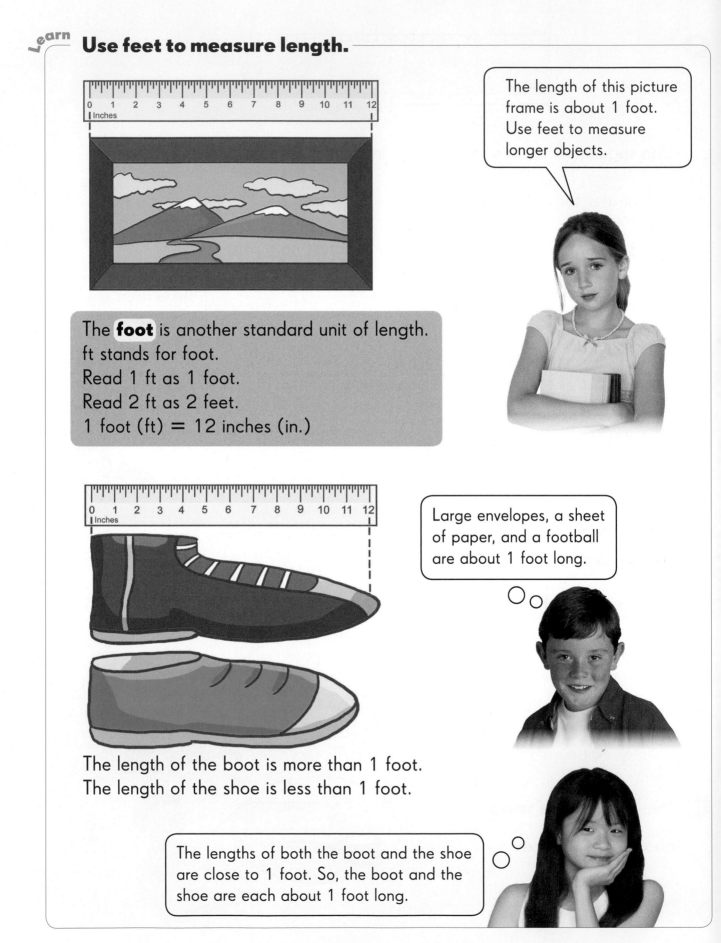

The length of this picture frame is about 1 foot. Use feet to measure longer objects.

The **foot** is another standard unit of length.
ft stands for foot.
Read 1 ft as 1 foot.
Read 2 ft as 2 feet.
1 foot (ft) = 12 inches (in.)

Large envelopes, a sheet of paper, and a football are about 1 foot long.

The length of the boot is more than 1 foot.
The length of the shoe is less than 1 foot.

The lengths of both the boot and the shoe are close to 1 foot. So, the boot and the shoe are each about 1 foot long.

Guided Practice

Complete.

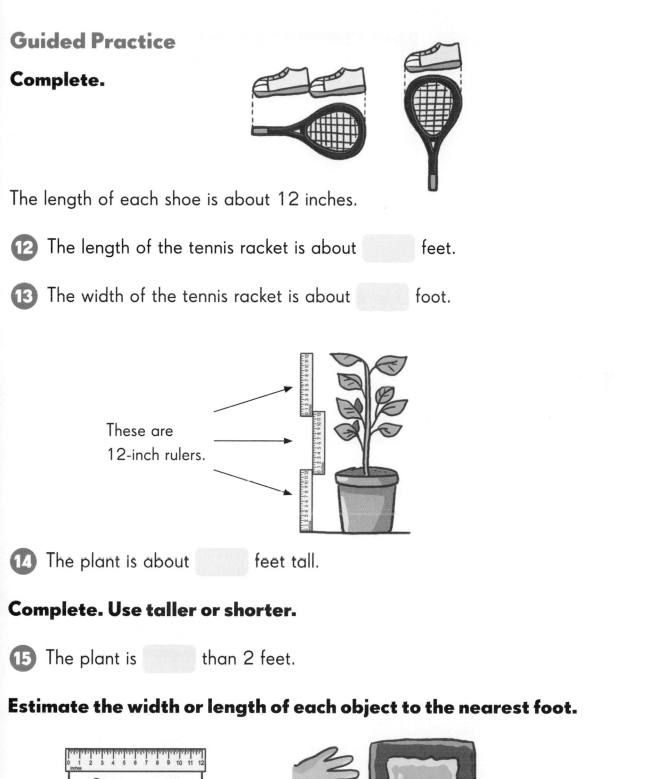

The length of each shoe is about 12 inches.

12 The length of the tennis racket is about ⬜ feet.

13 The width of the tennis racket is about ⬜ foot.

These are
12-inch rulers.

14 The plant is about ⬜ feet tall.

Complete. Use taller or shorter.

15 The plant is ⬜ than 2 feet.

Estimate the width or length of each object to the nearest foot.

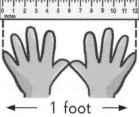

← 1 foot →

16 The place mat is about ⬜ foot long.

17 The height of the television set is about [ ] feet.

 **Hands-On Activity**

Materials:
• 12-inch rulers

First, estimate the length of each object in feet. Then, use rulers to measure the length.

Objects	Estimate	Measured Length
Length of a bulletin board		
Height of the teacher's desk		
Length of your desk		
Height of your chair		
Length of the white board		

Use yards to measure length.

1 yard

A yardstick is 3 times as long as a 12-inch ruler.

> The **yard** is another standard customary unit of length.
> It is used for measuring long lengths and short distances.
> yd stands for yard.
>   1 yard (yd) = 3 feet (ft)
>   1 yard (yd) = 36 inches (in.)

A baseball bat is about 1 yard long.
A doorway is about 1 yard wide.

1 ft = 12 in.
3 ft = 12 × 3
    = 36 in.

The height of a doorway is about 2 yards. The length of my garden is about 10 yards. The distance from my house to my neighbor's house is about 40 yards.

The boy is shorter than 1 yard.
The girl is taller than 1 yard.

This is a yardstick.

The heights of both the boy and the girl are close to 1 yard. So, they are about 1 yard tall.

Continued on next page

The length of the table is 1 yard.

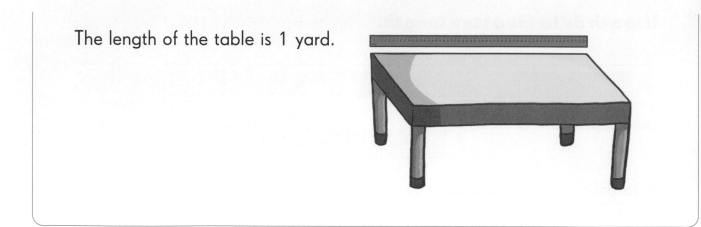

Guided Practice

Estimate the height of each object to the nearest yard.

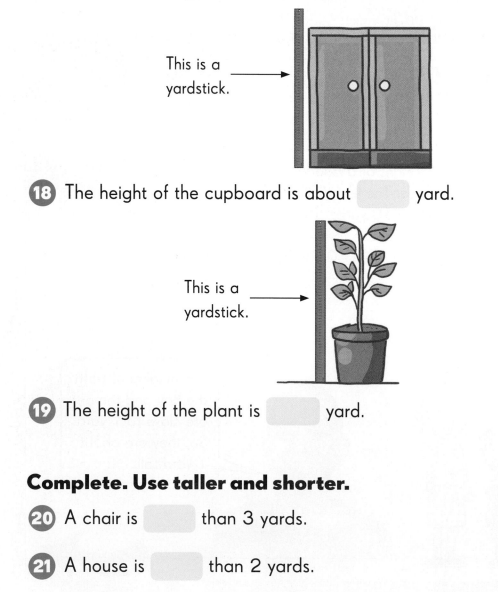

This is a
yardstick.

18 The height of the cupboard is about [ ] yard.

This is a
yardstick.

19 The height of the plant is [ ] yard.

Complete. Use taller and shorter.

20 A chair is [ ] than 3 yards.

21 A house is [ ] than 2 yards.

Estimate the length of each object to the nearest yard.

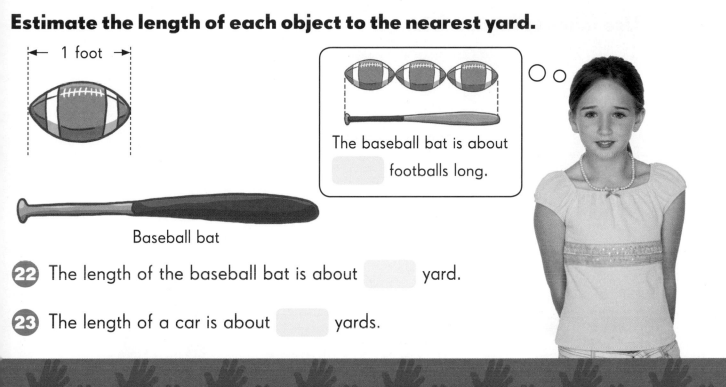

←— 1 foot —→

The baseball bat is about [   ] footballs long.

Baseball bat

22 The length of the baseball bat is about [   ] yard.

23 The length of a car is about [   ] yards.

 **Hands-On Activity**

Estimate the length of each object in yards. Then, use a 1-yard measuring tape to measure each object.

Materials:
• 1-yard measuring tape

Objects	Estimate	Measured Length
Length of your classroom		
Width of your classroom		
Height of a door		
Width of a door		
Length of a hallway		
Width of a hallway		

Use miles to measure length.

The standard customary unit for measuring distance is the **mile**. mi stands for mile.
The distance you can briskly walk in 20 minutes is about 1 mile. Jerome estimates that the distance between his home and school is 1 mile.

1 mile (mi) = 1,760 yards (yd)
1 mile (mi) = 5,280 feet (ft)

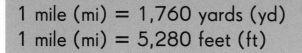

1 yd = 3 ft

There are 1,760 yards, or 1 mile, between my home and school.

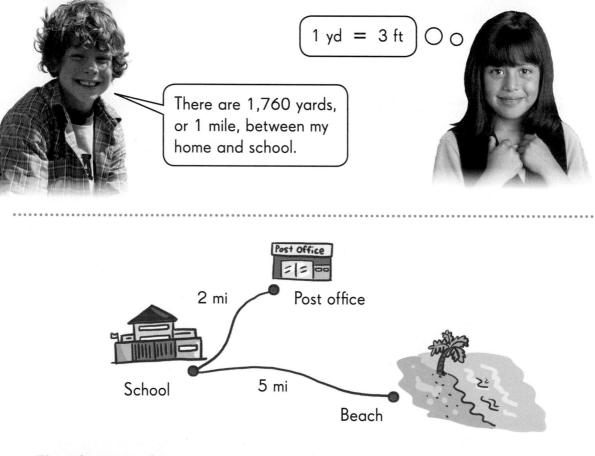

2 mi   Post office

School   5 mi   Beach

The distance between school and the post office is 2 miles.

Is the school about 3,500 yards from the post office?

Yes. The post office is also about 10,000 feet away from the school.

The distance between school and the beach is 5 miles.

Is the school about 5,000 yards from the beach?

No. It is further than 5,000 yards away. It is 5 miles. So, it is about 8,800 yards from the beach.

Guided Practice

Complete.

24 A helicopter is flying at a height of 5,257 feet.

It is about [ ] mile high. [1 mi = 5,280 ft] ○ ○

Rebecca estimated the distance between her home and school to be about 1 mile.

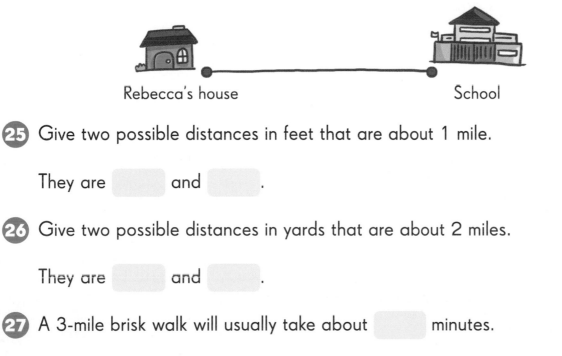

Rebecca's house   School

25 Give two possible distances in feet that are about 1 mile.

They are [ ] and [ ].

26 Give two possible distances in yards that are about 2 miles.

They are [ ] and [ ].

27 A 3-mile brisk walk will usually take about [ ] minutes.

Let's Practice

Measure the line segment to the nearest inch.

Line segment A

1 Line segment A is about [ ] inches.

Measure each line segment to the nearest half-inch.

Line segment B

These ruler are smaller than in real life.

2 Line segment B is about [ ] inches.

Line segment C

3 Line segment C is about [ ] inches.

**Choose the unit you would use to measure each.
Use inch, foot, yard, or mile.**

4 the length of a pair of glasses [ ]

5 the length of a football field [ ]

Choose the best estimate of the objects.

6 The length of a two football field is about 2 inches/feet/yards/miles .

7 The distance a person might travel to school is about
2 inches/feet/yards/miles .

Complete.

8 The width of 2 fingers is about 1 inch.
Which of these objects is about 1 inch long?

fork   bottle cap   exercise book

9 1 foot is equal to 12 inches. Which of these objects is about 1 foot long?

cushion

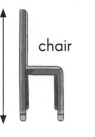

chair

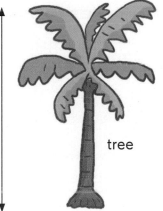

tree

10 Which of these objects is about 1 yard long?

house

bottle

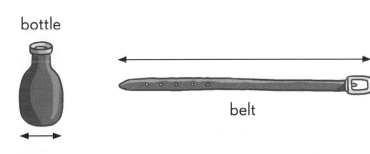

belt

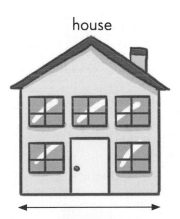

11 How long do you take to briskly walk 2 miles?

ON YOUR OWN

**Go to Workbook B:
Practice 1, pages 119–126**

Lesson 15.2 Measuring Weight

Lesson Objectives

- Use ounce, pound, and ton as units of measurement for weight.
- Read scales in ounces (oz) and pounds (lb).
- Estimate and find actual weights of objects by using different scales.
- Use referents to estimate weight.

Vocabulary
ounce (oz)
pound (lb)
ton (T)

Learn Use ounces to measure weight.

The **ounce** is a standard customary unit of weight.
It is used for measuring light objects.
oz stands for ounce.

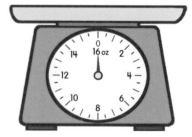

This is a scale that measures light objects in ounces.

The scale shows the weight of 1 slice of bread.
The weight of the slice of bread is about 1 ounce.

The balance shows the weight of some carrots.

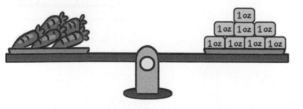

The weight of the carrots is about 8 ounces.

Guided Practice

Complete.

The scale shows the weight of 5 grapes.
The weight of the grapes is 1 ounce.

1 Make a guess. What is the weight of a bunch of grapes?

2 The weight of the bunch of grapes above is [   ] ounces.

Weigh objects to the nearest ounce.

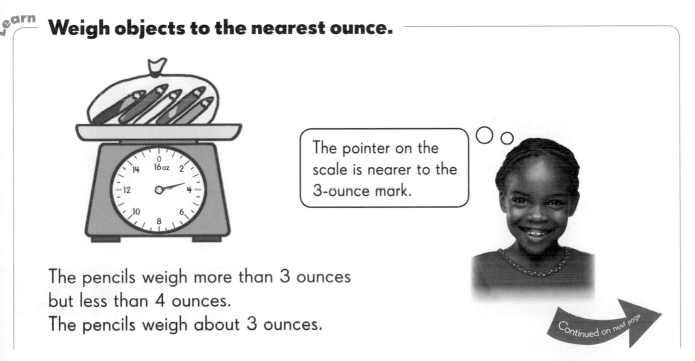

The pointer on the scale is nearer to the 3-ounce mark.

The pencils weigh more than 3 ounces
but less than 4 ounces.
The pencils weigh about 3 ounces.

Continued on next page

The cherries weigh more than 9 ounces
but less than 10 ounces.

The pointer on the
scale is nearer to the
10-ounce mark.

The cherries weigh about 10 ounces.

The bag of mushrooms weighs more than
8 ounces but less than 9 ounces.
The pointer is at the halfway mark between
8 ounces and 9 ounces.

The bag of mushrooms weighs about 9 ounces.

A slice of bread weighs about 1 ounce.
You can use the slice of bread to estimate
the weights of other light objects.

1 slice of bread weighs
about 1 ounce.
4 slices of bread weigh
about 4 ounces.

The apple is about 4 ounces.

Guided Practice

Complete.

3 What is the weight of the 3 apples? [ ] ounces

4 What is the weight of the tube of toothpaste? About [ ] ounces

5 What is the weight of 2 tennis balls? About [ ] ounces

A slice of cheese weighs about 1 ounce.

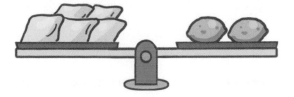

6 The 2 limes weigh about [ ] ounces.

Hands-On Activity

WORKING TOGETHER

Work with your friends and weigh these objects found in your classroom.

Make a copy of this table.
Guess the weight of each object in ounces.
Add three more objects to the table.

Then measure with a scale in ounces.
Record your answers in your copy of this table.

Objects	Estimate	Measured Weight
Your math book		
A marker		
A whiteboard duster		
Two files		

Use pounds to measure weight.

The **pound** is a another standard customary unit of weight.
It is used for measuring heavy objects.
lb stands for pound.

This is a scale that measures heavy
objects in pounds.

The scale shows the weight of 1 loaf
of bread.
The weight of the loaf of bread
is about 1 pound.

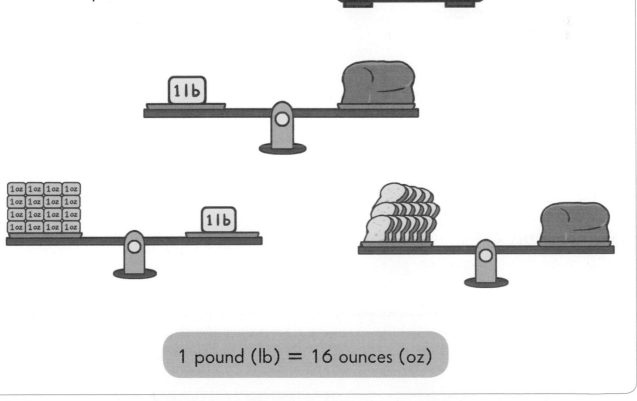

1 pound (lb) = 16 ounces (oz)

Guided Practice

Complete.

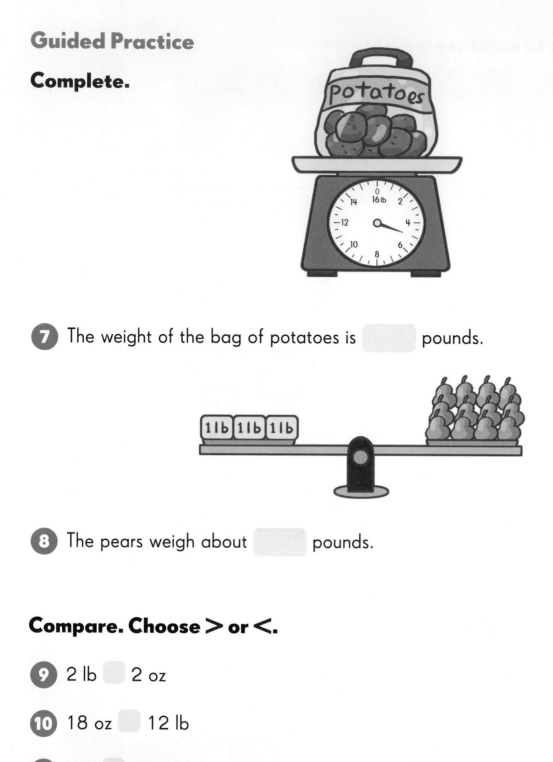

7 The weight of the bag of potatoes is [   ] pounds.

8 The pears weigh about [   ] pounds.

Compare. Choose > or <.

9 2 lb [   ] 2 oz

10 18 oz [   ] 12 lb

11 2 lb [   ] 20 oz

Weigh objects to the nearest pound.

The bananas weigh more than
2 pounds but less than 3 pounds.

The bananas weigh about 2 pounds.

> The pointer on the scale is closer to the 2-pound mark.

The pumpkin weighs more than
2 pounds but less than 3 pounds.

The pumpkin weighs about 3 pounds.

> The pointer on the scale is closer to the 3-pound mark.

Continued on next page

The fish and shrimp weigh more than 13 pounds and less than 14 pounds.
The pointer is at the halfway mark between 13 pounds and 14 pounds.

The fish and shrimp weigh about 14 pounds.

A loaf of bread weighs about 1 pound.
You can use the loaf of bread to estimate the weights of other heavy objects.

1 loaf of bread weighs about 1 pound.
2 loaves of bread weigh about 2 pounds.

The leg of lamb weighs about 2 pounds.

Guided Practice

Complete.

12 The bag of flour weighs [ ] pounds.

13 The watermelon weighs about [ ] pounds.

14 The bag of tomatoes weighs about [ ] pounds.

Estimate the weight in pounds.

1 loaf of bread is 1 pound.

15 The sticks of butter weigh about ____ pounds.

Choose the correct answer.

16 A basket of fruit weighs about 10 ounces/pounds .

17 A box of cereal weighs about 18 ounces/pounds .

18 15 pounds is heavier than/lighter than 12 ounces.

19 25 ounces is heavier than/lighter than 15 pounds.

20 20 ounces is heavier than/lighter than 20 pounds.

21 50 pounds is heavier than/lighter than 55 ounces.

Complete.

22 A slice of bread weighs about 1 ounce. Name another object around you that weighs about 1 ounce.

23 A loaf of bread weighs about 1 pound. Name another object around you that weighs about 1 pound.

Hands-On Activity

Materials:
• weighing scale

1

Guess the weight of each object in pounds.
Then measure with a scale in pounds.

Objects	Estimate	Measured Weight
Your school bag		
A stack of 2 books		
4 bottles of water		

2 Think about a supermarket.

Can you name 5 objects that are measured in

a ounces?

b pounds?

Examples

green beans, cheese, olives, potatoes, butter, and onions

The **ton** is another customary unit of weight.
It is used for measuring very heavy objects.
T stands for ton.

A car

1 ton = 2,000 pounds

A car weighs about 1 ton (T).

Which objects can be measured in tons?

An elephant, a whale, a helicopter, a polar bear....

A handful of mushrooms weighs about 8 ounces.
A bunch of grapes and a pineapple weigh about 4 pounds.
A large tractor weighs about 2 tons.

Guided Practice

Choose the best unit to measure each object.
Use ounce, pound, or ton.

24 a bunch of bananas

25 a slice of cheese

26 helicopter

27 a whale

Let's Practice

Find the weights of each object to the nearest ounce.

1

_____ ounces

2

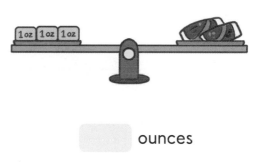

_____ ounces

Find the weights of each object to the nearest pound.

3

_____ pounds

4

_____ pounds

Estimate the weight of each object.

 5 The weight of the bag of apples is about [ ] pounds.

6 The weight of the 5 limes is about [ ] ounces.

7 The weight of the book is about [ ] pounds.

8 The weight of the pack of rice is about [ ] ounces.

Complete.

 9 A slice of bread is about 1 ounce.
Choose another object that weighs about 1 ounce.

slice of cheese   carton of mik   1 grape

10 A pound is equal to 16 ounces. Choose the object that weighs about 1 pound.

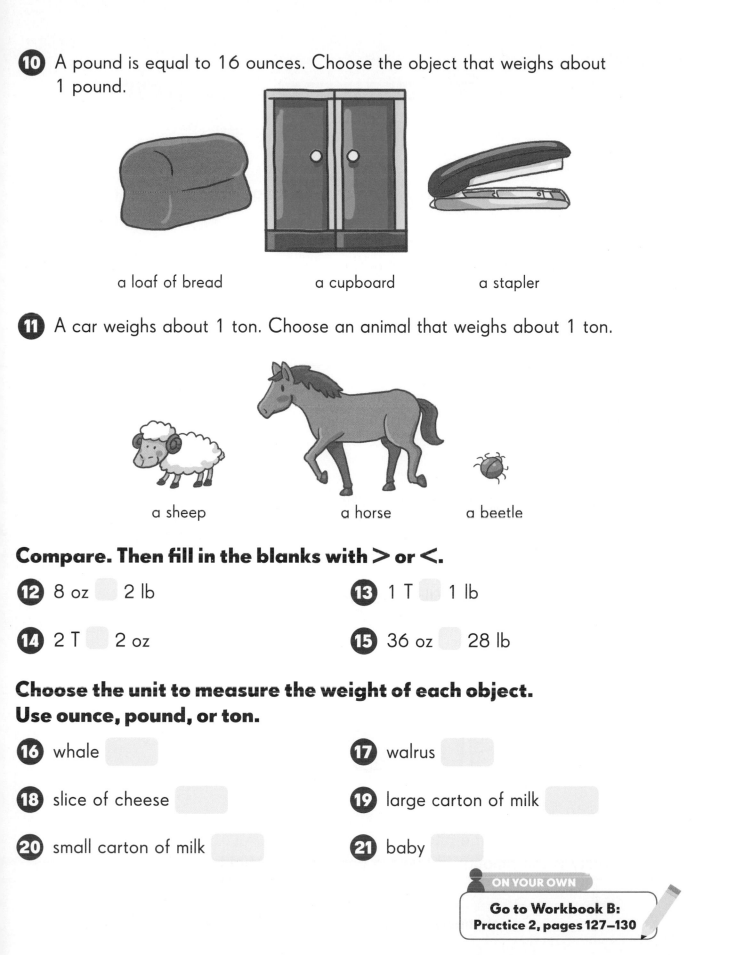

a loaf of bread   a cupboard   a stapler

11 A car weighs about 1 ton. Choose an animal that weighs about 1 ton.

a sheep   a horse   a beetle

Compare. Then fill in the blanks with > or <.

12 8 oz ___ 2 lb

13 1 T ___ 1 lb

14 2 T ___ 2 oz

15 36 oz ___ 28 lb

Choose the unit to measure the weight of each object. Use ounce, pound, or ton.

16 whale ___

17 walrus ___

18 slice of cheese ___

19 large carton of milk ___

20 small carton of milk ___

21 baby ___

ON YOUR OWN

**Go to Workbook B:
Practice 2, pages 127–130**

Lesson Objectives

- Measure capacity with cup (c), pint (pt), quart (qt), and gallon (gal).
- Estimate and find the actual capacity of a container.
- Relate units of capacity to one another.

 Use cups to measure capacity.

This is a cup.

The **cup** is a standard customary unit for measuring capacity.
c stands for cup.

The pitcher is completely filled with water.

The water in the pitcher fills 5 cups.
So, the capacity of the pitcher is 5 cups.
Capacity is the amount of liquid a container can hold.

Guided Practice

Complete.

1 The pitcher is completely filled with water.
The water is emptied into cups.

What is the capacity of the pitcher? ___ cups

2 9 cups of water are poured to completely fill a container.

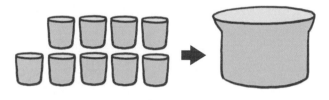

The capacity of the container is ___ cups.

ᴸᵉᵃʳⁿ Use pints to measure capacity.

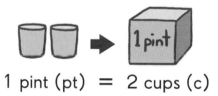

1 pint (pt) = 2 cups (c)

The 2 cups are completely filled with water.
The 2 cups of water completely fill the pint carton.

> The **pint** is a standard customary unit for measuring capacity.
> The capacity of the carton is 1 pint.
> pt stands for pint.

1 pint of water is the same as 2 cups of water.

Guided Practice

Complete.

Each carton contains 1 pint of milk.
The total amount of milk in the five cartons is [   ] cups.

4 Suppose cranberry juice is your favorite drink. Would you rather have

2 pints or 2 cups of cranberry juice? [   ]

5 Suppose you dislike yogurt. Would you rather have 3 cups or 1 pint of

yogurt? [   ]

Learn **Use quarts to measure capacity.**

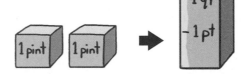

These 2 pints of milk can completely fill a bigger carton.

> The **quart** is a standard customary unit for measuring capacity.
> The capacity of the bigger carton is 1 quart.
> qt stands for quart.

1 quart (qt) = 2 pints (pt)

1 quart of milk is the same as 2 pints of milk.

How many cups are there in 1 quart?
Multiply to change pints to cups.

1 pt = 2 c
2 pt = 4 c

So, 1 quart (qt) = 2 pints (pt)
       1 quart (qt) = 4 cups (c)

1 pt = 2 c
1 qt = 2 pt
1 qt = ? c

Guided Practice

Complete.

6 Rodney spilled 2 cups of orange juice. Noel spilled 1 quart
of cranberry juice. Who spilled more juice?

7 Lillian has a pitcher that can hold 1 quart of water. She has a small
bottle with a capacity of 1 pint. How many times must she pour water
into the pitcher with her small bottle to fill the pitcher?

8 Tabitha bought 3 one-quart cans of blue paint and 4 one-pint cans
of yellow paint. Did she buy more blue or yellow paint?

Multiply to change quarts
to pints and pints to cups.

Use gallons to measure capacity.

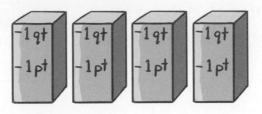

A carton can hold 1 quart of milk.
These 4 cartons hold 4 quarts of milk.
These 4 quarts of milk can completely fill the container.

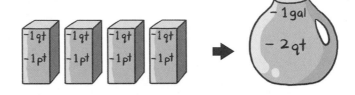

The **gallon** is a standard customary unit
for measuring capacity.
The capacity for the container is 1 gallon.
gal stands for gallon.

How many pints are there in 1 gallon?
Multiply to change gallon to pints.

1 qt = 2 pt
4 qt = 8 pt
So, 1 gallon (gal) = 4 quarts (qt)
    1 gallon (gal) = 8 pints (pt)

How many cups are there in 1 gallon?

1 gallon of water is the same as 4 quarts of water.

1 pt = 2 c
1 gal = 8 pt
1 gal = 8 × 2
      = 16 c

There are 16 cups in 1 gallon.

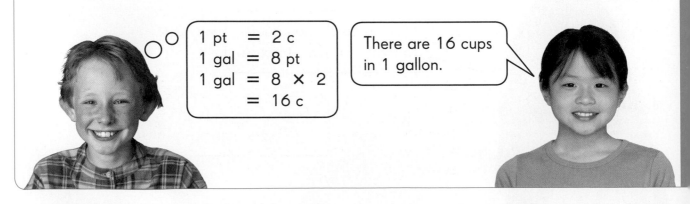

Capacity Measurements in the Customary System

You can relate the units of capacity to one another:

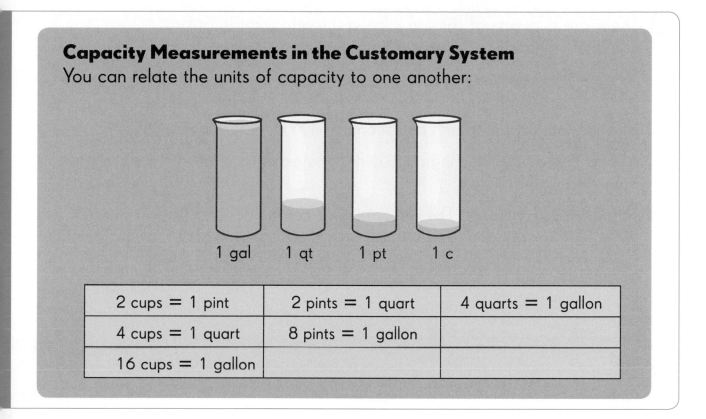

1 gal   1 qt   1 pt   1 c

2 cups = 1 pint	2 pints = 1 quart	4 quarts = 1 gallon
4 cups = 1 quart	8 pints = 1 gallon	
16 cups = 1 gallon		

Guided Practice

Choose the best unit for each measure. Use quart, cup, pint, or gallon.

9 milk for breakfast

10 a large can of paint

11 a small carton of orange juice

12 a medium-sized tomato juice container

Solve.

13 David and his 7 friends drink 1 gallon of milk each day.

How many cups is this?

1 gal = 4 qt
1 gal = 4 × 2
      = 8 pt
1 gal = 8 × 2
      = 16 c

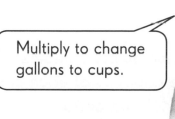

Multiply to change gallons to cups.

14 There are 6 quarts of tomato juice in the refrigerator. Suki needs 1 gallon of tomato juice for a recipe. Does she have enough? Answer yes or no. _____

15 A recipe calls for 2 quarts of coconut milk. How many times must a one-cup measuring cup be filled to equal 2 quarts? _____ times

16 John has 2 containers. The red container can hold 12 cups of water. The yellow container can hold 9 pints of water. What is the difference in the capacity of the two containers in pints? _____ pints

Hands-On Activity

WORK IN GROUPS

Materials:
- a pint container
- pitcher
- containers to measure
- 1-cup measuring cup

1 This carton has a standard capacity of 1 pint.

1 pint

Estimate the capacity of the pitcher given by your teacher.
Fill up the small cartons with water from the pitcher until the pitcher is empty.
What is the capacity of the pitcher in pints?
What is the capacity of the pitcher in quarts?

2 Bring some empty containers from your home.
Find the capacity of each container with some cups and 1-pint cartons.

Find the capacity of each container.

A container was completely filled with water. Gina poured out all the water from the container to fill up some one-pint cartons.

1 What is the capacity of the container in pints?   pints

2 What is the capacity of the container in cups?   cups

Complete.

3 The capacity of the container is about   cups.

Complete. Use greater or less.

4 The capacity of the container in Exercise **3** is   than 4 cups.

5 The capacity of the container in Exercise **3** is   than 2 cups.

Choose the best estimate.

6 15 pints of paint or 15 gallons of paint for painting the house

7 5 cups of milk or 5 quarts of milk for the baby each day

8 45 pints of water or 45 gallons of water in a wading pool

9 4 gallons of water or 20 gallons of water in a bathtub

Name two objects in a supermarket that use each measure:

10 cups [ ] , [ ]

11 pints [ ] , [ ]

12 quarts [ ] , [ ]

13 gallons [ ] , [ ]

The container is completely filled with water.
The water is emptied into cups.

Find the capacity of the container:

14 in cups [ ]

15 in pints [ ]

16 in quarts [ ]

ON YOUR OWN

Go to Workbook B:
Practice 3, pages 131–134

Math Journal

You are given an empty container and a cup.

Explain how you would find the capacity of the container.

CRITICAL THINKING SKILLS

Put On Your Thinking Cap!

PROBLEM SOLVING

1. Can containers of different shapes have the same capacity?
Explain why or why not.

A

B

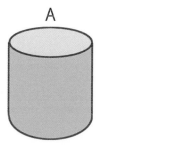
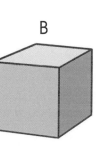

ON YOUR OWN

**Go to Workbook B:
Put on Your Thinking Cap!
pages 135–136**

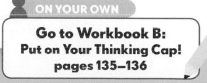

Chapter Wrap Up

Study Guide
You have learned...

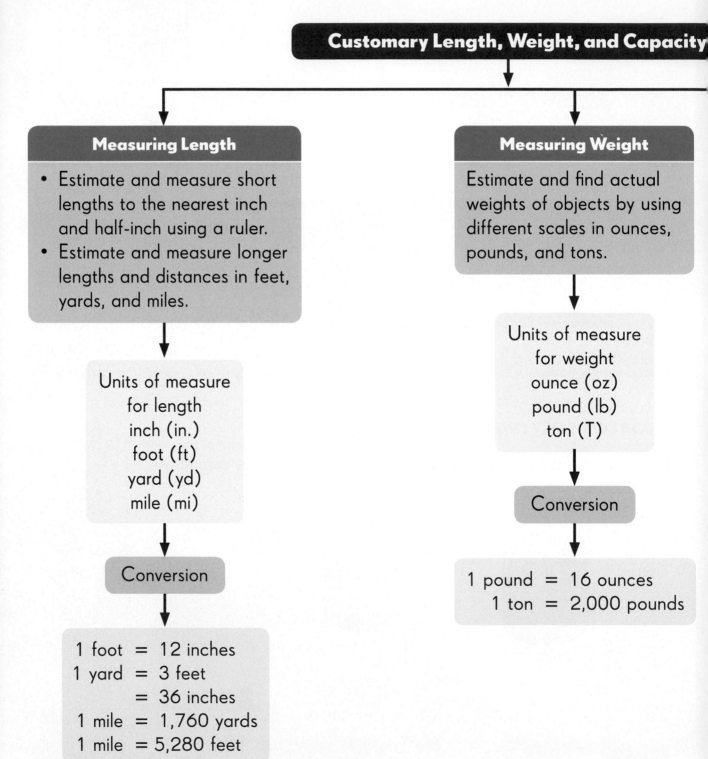

Customary Length, Weight, and Capacity

Measuring Length

- Estimate and measure short lengths to the nearest inch and half-inch using a ruler.
- Estimate and measure longer lengths and distances in feet, yards, and miles.

Units of measure
for length
inch (in.)
foot (ft)
yard (yd)
mile (mi)

Conversion

1 foot = 12 inches
1 yard = 3 feet
       = 36 inches
1 mile = 1,760 yards
1 mile = 5,280 feet

Measuring Weight

Estimate and find actual weights of objects by using different scales in ounces, pounds, and tons.

Units of measure
for weight
ounce (oz)
pound (lb)
ton (T)

Conversion

1 pound = 16 ounces
1 ton = 2,000 pounds

BIG IDEA

▶ Length, weight, and capacity can be measured using customary units.

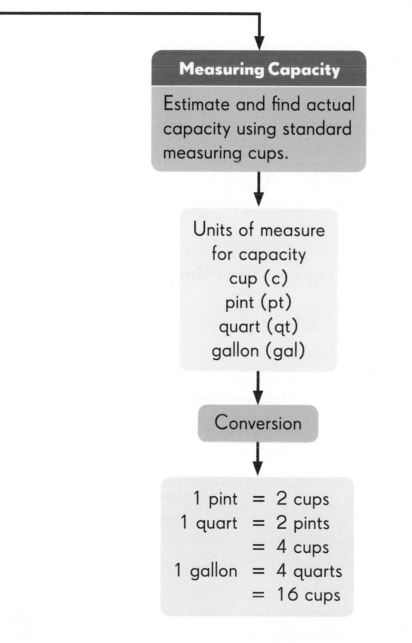

Measuring Capacity

Estimate and find actual capacity using standard measuring cups.

Units of measure
for capacity
cup (c)
pint (pt)
quart (qt)
gallon (gal)

Conversion

1 pint = 2 cups
1 quart = 2 pints
= 4 cups
1 gallon = 4 quarts
= 16 cups

Chapter Review/Test

Vocabulary

Fill in the blanks. Use the word in the box.

cups	feet	gallons	quarts	inches
ounces	pounds	tons	yards	pints

1 Rita uses _____ , _____ , and _____ to measure lengths.

2 Mary Anne uses _____ , _____ , and _____ to measure weights.

3 Sharon uses _____ , _____ , _____ , and _____ to measure capacity.

Concept and Skills

Study the picture carefully. Then answer the questions.

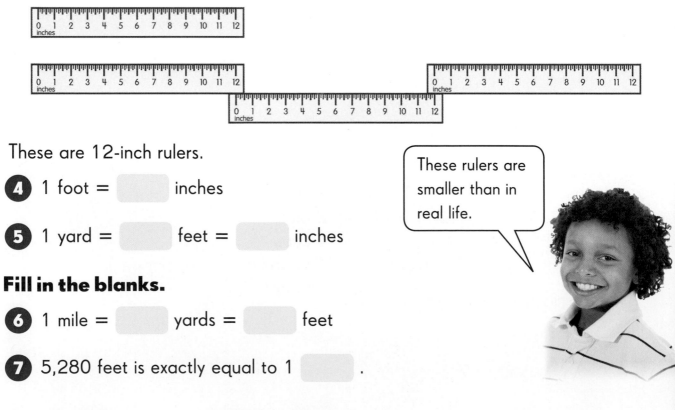

These are 12-inch rulers.

4 1 foot = _____ inches

5 1 yard = _____ feet = _____ inches

These rulers are smaller than in real life.

Fill in the blanks.

6 1 mile = _____ yards = _____ feet

7 5,280 feet is exactly equal to 1 _____ .

Use an inch ruler. Measure the length of each line segment to the nearest half-inch.

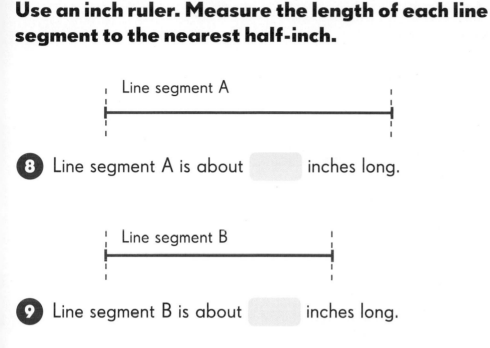

Line segment A

8 Line segment A is about _____ inches long.

Line segment B

9 Line segment B is about _____ inches long.

Old Mac Cartney goes on a farm trip. Help him to find the weight of each animal in pounds.

Complete the sentences.

10 A turkey weighs about _____ pounds.

11 A sheep weighs about _____ pounds.

12 A chick weighs about _____ pound.

Old Mac Cartney then finds out the amount of food some animals eat in pounds and ounces.

Help him to complete the sentences.

 The chicks eat [ ] ounces of grain.

 The sheep eats [ ] pounds of fresh green grass everyday.

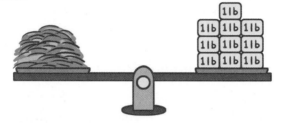

15 All the animals on the farm eat about [ ] tons of grain each year.

Old Mac Cartney finds out the amount of water and milk that Farmer Fred uses and sells.

Help him to complete the sentences.

16 Farmer Fred uses [ ] quarts and [ ] pints of water to water his small vegetable patch each day.

17 2 pints of water is equal to _____ cups.

18 Farmer Fred drinks 16 cups of water each day. It is equal to _____ gallon.

19 Farmer Fred sells _____ gallon of milk to the neighbors each day.

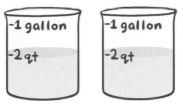

Farmer Fred cares for his farm animals. He measures the height of his cow, puppy, and sheep one day.

Help him to complete the sentences.

These are yardsticks.

20 The cow is about _____ yards tall.

These are 12-inch rulers.

21 The puppy is about _____ feet tall.

These are 12-inch rulers.

22 The sheep is about _____ inches tall.

Farmer Fred travels to his orchard barn each day. Help him to find the distance he travels each day.

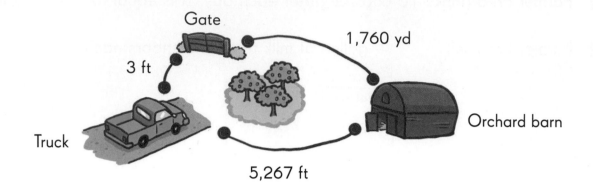

Gate

1,760 yd

3 ft

Truck

Orchard barn

5,267 ft

Complete the sentences.

23 Farmer Fred travels [ ] yard to the gate from his truck each day.

24 He travels [ ] mile from the gate to the orchard barn.

25 On his way back to the truck from the orchard barn, he travels about [ ] mile.

Problem Solving
Solve.

26 Farmer Fred has a container of orange juice that has a capacity of 4 quarts. He has 2 pints of orange juice in it now. How much more orange juice does he need to completely fill the container?

27 Farmer Fred makes 4 quarts of orange juice on Monday. He makes 2 quarts more orange juice on Tuesday than on Monday. He makes 2 more quarts on Wednesday than on Tuesday. He carries on making 2 more quarts of orange juice every day than the day before. In how many days will he make a total of 80 pints of orange juice?

Chapter 16

Time and Temperature

Lessons

BIG IDEA

▶ Time can be used to tell when activities start and end, or how long an activity will last.

▶ Temperature can be used to understand what the weather will be like.

219

Recall Prior Knowledge

Skip-counting by 5s to find minutes

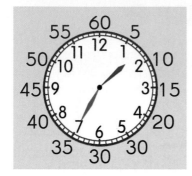

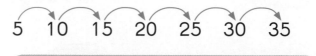

$7 \times 5 = 35$
The minute hand shows 35 minutes.

Knowing that 60 minutes is 1 hour

60 minutes = 1 hour

The minute hand moves one complete round in 60 minutes.
The hour hand moves from one number to the next number in 1 hour.

Telling time

Read 2:30 as two thirty.

A.M. shows the time after midnight but before noon.
P.M. shows the time after noon but before midnight.

Finding elapsed time

8:00 A.M. is 1 hour after 7:00 A.M.
7:00 A.M. is 1 hour before 8:00 A.M.

10:30 A.M. is 30 minutes or half an hour after 10 A.M.
10:30 A.M. is 30 minutes or half an hour before 11 A.M.

Reading numbers on a number line

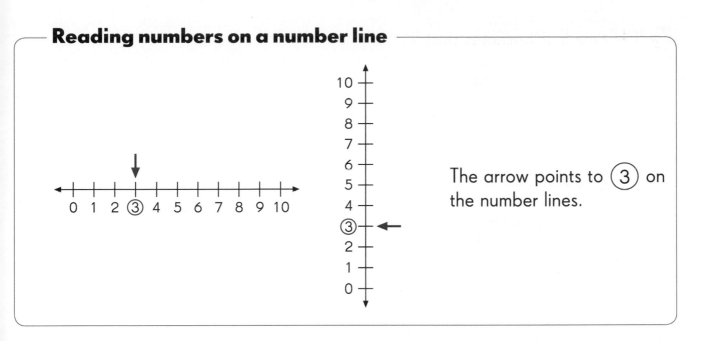

The arrow points to ③ on the number lines.

✔ Quick Check

Look at each clock. Then decide which number is missing.

1

The minute hand shows

[   ] minutes after the hour.

2

The minute hand shows

[   ] minutes after the hour.

Tell the time.

3

[   ]

4

[   ]

5 The time is 20 minutes past 7.

6 The time is 45 minutes before 10.

Complete the sentences with A.M. or P.M.

7

Robin eats breakfast at
7:50 [ ]

8

He eats dinner at 8:00 [ ]

Find the length of time.

9 3 P.M. is [ ] after 2 P.M.

10 4:30 A.M. is [ ] before 5 A.M.

11 Noon is [ ] after 11:30 A.M.

16.1 Telling Time

Lesson Objectives

- Tell time to the minute.
- Read time on a digital clock.

Learn **Tell time to the nearest minute.**

1 minute

Each small mark stands for 1 **minute**.

The minute hand shows 5 minutes.

Students are in the auditorium at 9:20 A.M. for an assembly.

It is 20 minutes after 9 o'clock.

You can also say the time is 20 minutes **past** 9.

The time is nine twenty.

9:20

Continued on next page

At 7:40 P.M., a group of people visit the Community Center for a charity dinner.

It is 20 minutes before 8 o'clock.

$60 - 40 = 20$

The time is seven forty.

You can also say the time is 20 minutes **to** 8.

Guided Practice

Find the missing numbers.

1

The time is six fifteen.

It is [ ] minutes after 6.

6:15 is [ ] minutes past 6.

2

The time is five forty-five.

It is [ ] minutes before 6.

5:45 is [ ] minutes to 6.

3

The time is three twenty-five.

It is [ ] minutes after 3.

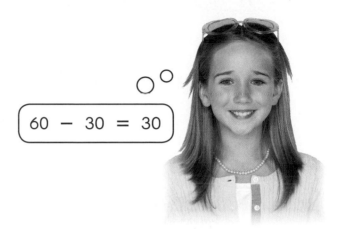

$60 - 30 = 30$

4

3:30

The time is half past three.

It is [ ] minutes before 4.

Complete using past or to.

5

8:07 is 7 minutes [ ] 8.

6

2:37 is 23 minutes [ ] 3.

7

5:05

5:05 is 5 minutes [ ] 5.

8

7:30

[ ] $- 30 =$ [ ]

7:30 is 30 minutes [ ] 8.

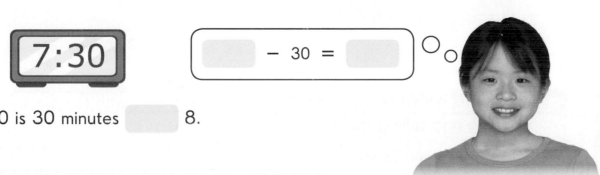

WORKING TOGETHER **Game**

Show and Tell Time!

Players: 2 groups of students

Materials:
• a clock with movable hands

STEP 1 A player from Group 1 shows a time by moving the hour hand and the minute hand.

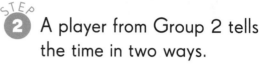

STEP 2 A player from Group 2 tells the time in two ways.

• two fifty
• 10 minutes to 3

STEP 3 Group 1 checks the answer. Group 2 gets 1 point for a correct answer.

STEP 4 Next, the player from Group 2 shows the time and the player from Group 1 tells the time.

• five seventeen
• 17 minutes past 5

STEP 5 Take turns within two groups in showing and telling the time.

The group with the most points wins!

Let's Practice

Tell the time in two ways.

1

2

3

4

Tell the time in a different way.

5 5 minutes past 11 is ⬚ .

6 5 minutes to 11 is ⬚ .

7 12 minutes past 6 is ⬚ .

8 15 minutes to 8 is ⬚ .

Fill in the blanks.

9 3:20 is ⬚ minutes past ⬚ .

10 12:35 is ⬚ minutes to ⬚ .

ON YOUR OWN

Go to Workbook B:
Practice 1, pages 147–150

Lesson 16.2 Converting Hours and Minutes

Lesson Objective

- Change minutes to hours or hours to minutes.

Vocabulary
hours (h)
minutes (min)

Learn — Convert hours (h) to minutes (min).

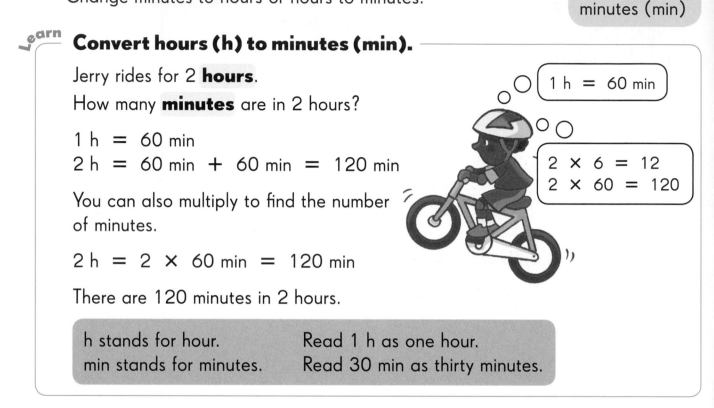

Jerry rides for 2 **hours**.
How many **minutes** are in 2 hours?

$1 \text{ h} = 60 \text{ min}$

$2 \text{ h} = 60 \text{ min} + 60 \text{ min} = 120 \text{ min}$

You can also multiply to find the number of minutes.

$2 \text{ h} = 2 \times 60 \text{ min} = 120 \text{ min}$

There are 120 minutes in 2 hours.

1 h = 60 min

$2 \times 6 = 12$
$2 \times 60 = 120$

> h stands for hour.   Read 1 h as one hour.
> min stands for minutes.   Read 30 min as thirty minutes.

Guided Practice

Express the time in minutes.

1. Jerry took 3 hours to do his homework.
   How many minutes are in 3 hours?

   $3 \text{ h} = $ ⬚ $\text{min} + $ ⬚ $\text{min} + $ ⬚ min

   $= $ ⬚ min

   You can also multiply.

   $3 \text{ h} = $ ⬚ $\times 60 \text{ min}$

   $= $ ⬚ min

   There are ⬚ minutes in 3 hours.

$3 \times 6 = $ ⬚
$3 \times 60 = $ ⬚

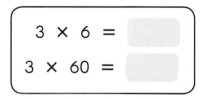

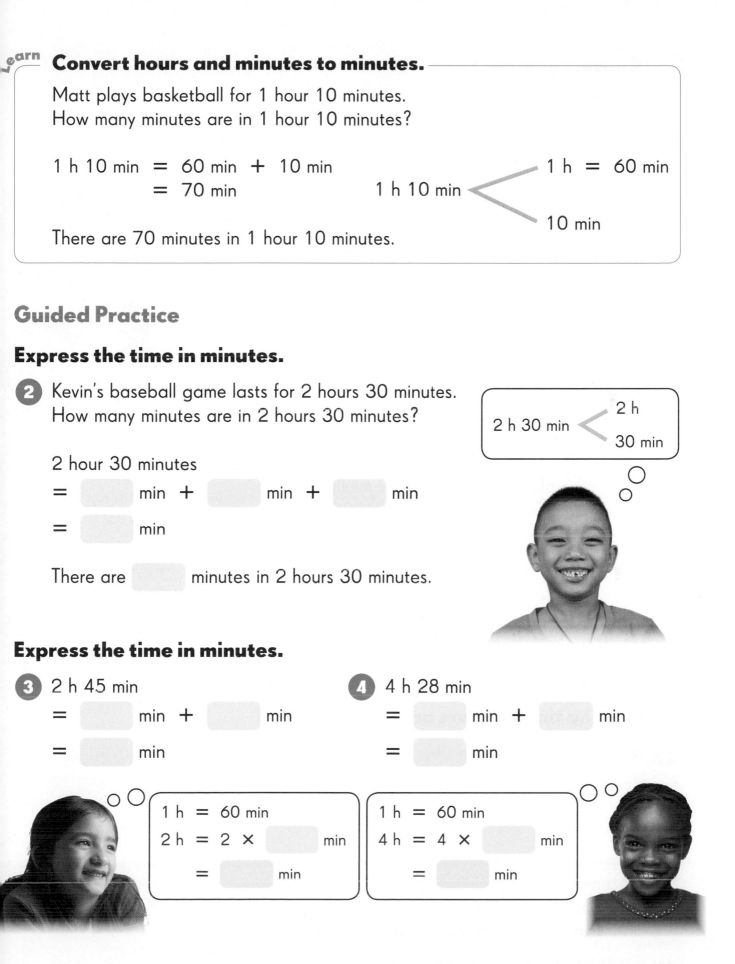

Convert hours and minutes to minutes.

Matt plays basketball for 1 hour 10 minutes.
How many minutes are in 1 hour 10 minutes?

1 h 10 min = 60 min + 10 min
= 70 min

1 h 10 min < 1 h = 60 min
10 min

There are 70 minutes in 1 hour 10 minutes.

Guided Practice

Express the time in minutes.

2 Kevin's baseball game lasts for 2 hours 30 minutes.
How many minutes are in 2 hours 30 minutes?

2 h 30 min < 2 h
30 min

2 hour 30 minutes

= ____ min + ____ min + ____ min

= ____ min

There are ____ minutes in 2 hours 30 minutes.

Express the time in minutes.

3 2 h 45 min

= ____ min + ____ min

= ____ min

1 h = 60 min
2 h = 2 × ____ min
= ____ min

4 4 h 28 min

= ____ min + ____ min

= ____ min

1 h = 60 min
4 h = 4 × ____ min
= ____ min

Learn Convert minutes to hours and minutes.

Marshall takes 135 minutes to mow the lawn.
How many hours and minutes are in 135 minutes?

135 min = 120 min + 15 min
        = 2 h 15 min

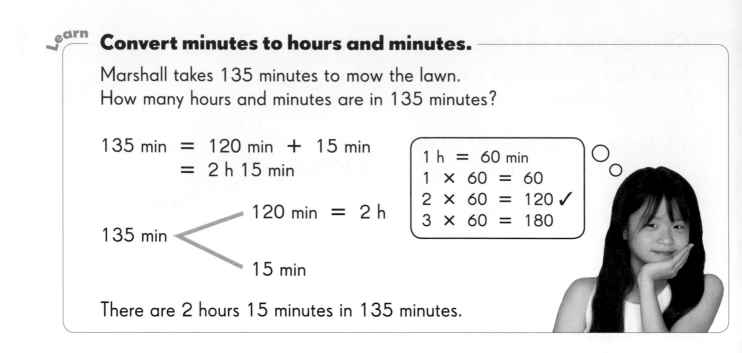

$$120 \text{ min} = 2 \text{ h}$$

135 min

15 min

1 h = 60 min
1 × 60 = 60
2 × 60 = 120 ✓
3 × 60 = 180

There are 2 hours 15 minutes in 135 minutes.

Guided Practice

Express the time in hours and minutes.

5 Samantha plays the piano for 82 minutes.
How many hours and minutes are in 82 minutes?

82 min = _____ min + _____ min

    = _____ h _____ min

There are _____ hour _____ minutes in 82 minutes.

Express the time in hours and minutes.

6 90 min = _____ min + _____ min

     = _____ h _____ min

7 130 min

8 145 min

9 192 min

WORKING TOGETHER **Game**

Let's Play Time Bingo!

STEP 1 Group 1 draws a card from the stack of Time Cards.
Examples of Time Cards:

1 h 25 min = ____ min

75 min = ____ h ____ min

STEP 2 Write the time in another form to complete the equation.

STEP 3 Groups take turns. Group 1 marks their answers on the Bingo Board with an X. Group 2 marks their answers with an O.

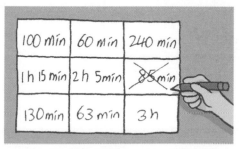

The first group to mark three correct answers in a straight line (↕, ↔ , ↘) on the Bingo Board wins!

Let's Practice

Complete each number bond.

1 1 h 45 min < ⬚ h / ⬚ min

2 3 h 40 min < ⬚ h / ⬚ min

Complete each number bond.

3 75 min < ⬚ h / ⬚ min

4 140 min < ⬚ h / ⬚ min

Express the time in hours.

5 60 min = ⬚ h

6 120 min = 60 min + ⬚ min

= ⬚ h

120 min
= ⬚ × 60 min

7 180 min = 60 min + 60 min + ⬚ min

= ⬚ h

180 min
= ⬚ × 60 min

Express the time in minutes.

8 4 h 33 min = ⬚

9 3 h 54 min = ⬚

ON YOUR OWN

Go to Workbook B:
Practice 2, pages 151–154

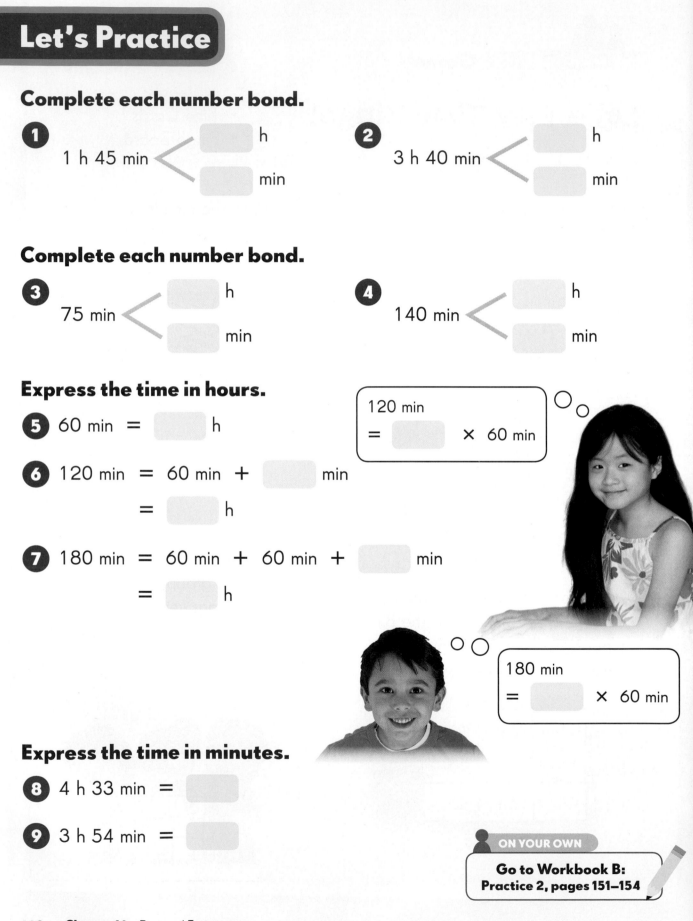

16.3 Adding Hours and Minutes

Lesson Objective

- Add time with and without regrouping.

Learn Add time without regrouping.

Today, Mr. Carlson works 2 hours 15 minutes in the morning.
He works 5 hours 10 minutes in the afternoon.
How long did he work today?

2 h 15 min + 5 h 10 min = ?

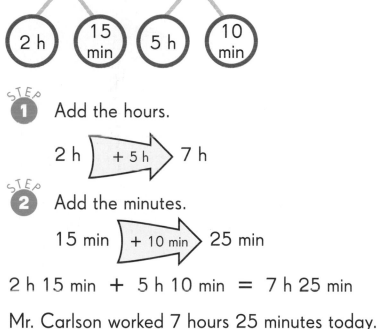

STEP 1 Add the hours.

2 h + 5 h → 7 h

STEP 2 Add the minutes.

15 min + 10 min → 25 min

2 h 15 min + 5 h 10 min = 7 h 25 min

Mr. Carlson worked 7 hours 25 minutes today.

Guided Practice

Complete.

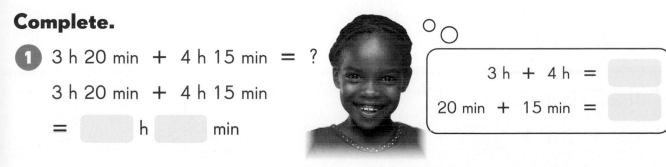

1) 3 h 20 min + 4 h 15 min = ?

3 h 20 min + 4 h 15 min

= ☐ h ☐ min

3 h + 4 h = ☐

20 min + 15 min = ☐

Add time with regrouping.

Emily takes a flight from Chicago to New York.
She waits 40 minutes to check her luggage.
Then she waits 1 hour 55 minutes before boarding the airplane.
How long does she wait in all?

40 min + 1 h 55 min = ?

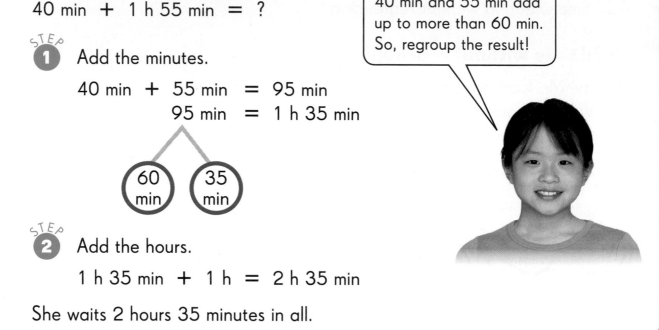

STEP
1 Add the minutes.

40 min + 55 min = 95 min
95 min = 1 h 35 min

60 min   35 min

> 40 min and 55 min add up to more than 60 min. So, regroup the result!

STEP
2 Add the hours.

1 h 35 min + 1 h = 2 h 35 min

She waits 2 hours 35 minutes in all.

Guided Practice

Complete.

2 2 h 45 min + 5 h 35 min = ?

First, add the minutes.

45 min + 35 min = ☐ min

☐ min = ☐ h ☐ min

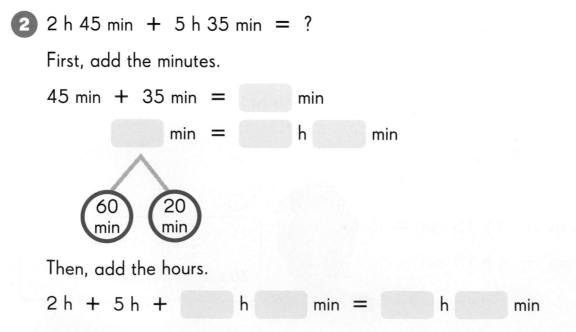

60 min   20 min

Then, add the hours.

2 h + 5 h + ☐ h ☐ min = ☐ h ☐ min

Let's Play Time Shuffle!

Players: 2
Materials:
• a counter
• game board

1 Player 1 tosses a counter until it lands on a clock on the game board.

STEP
2 The player writes a time that is shown on the clock picture.
For example, the player gets 50 minutes if the counter lands on the clock showing 50 minutes.

STEP
3 Player 1 tosses the counter again and writes another time.
For example, the player gets 2 hours.
The player then adds the two times.
50 min + 2 h = 2 h 50 min

STEP
4 Player 2 checks the answer.
Player 1 gets 1 point for a correct answer.

STEP
5 Take turns.
Play five rounds each.

The player with the most points wins!

Let's Practice

Add. Use number bonds to help you.

1 4 h 15 min + 5 h 30 min

2 7 h 10 min + 2 h 45 min

3 2 h 35 min + 2 h 20 min

4 4 h 25 min + 1 h 15 min

5 1 h 40 min + 2 h 10 min

6 6 h 5 min + 1 h 35 min

Add. Use number bonds to help you.

7 3 h 40 min + 5 h 25 min

8 4 h 55 min + 6 h 15 min

9 2 h 57 min + 2 h 8 min

10 3 h 45 min + 1 h 40 min

57 min + 8 min = _____ min

= _____ h _____ min

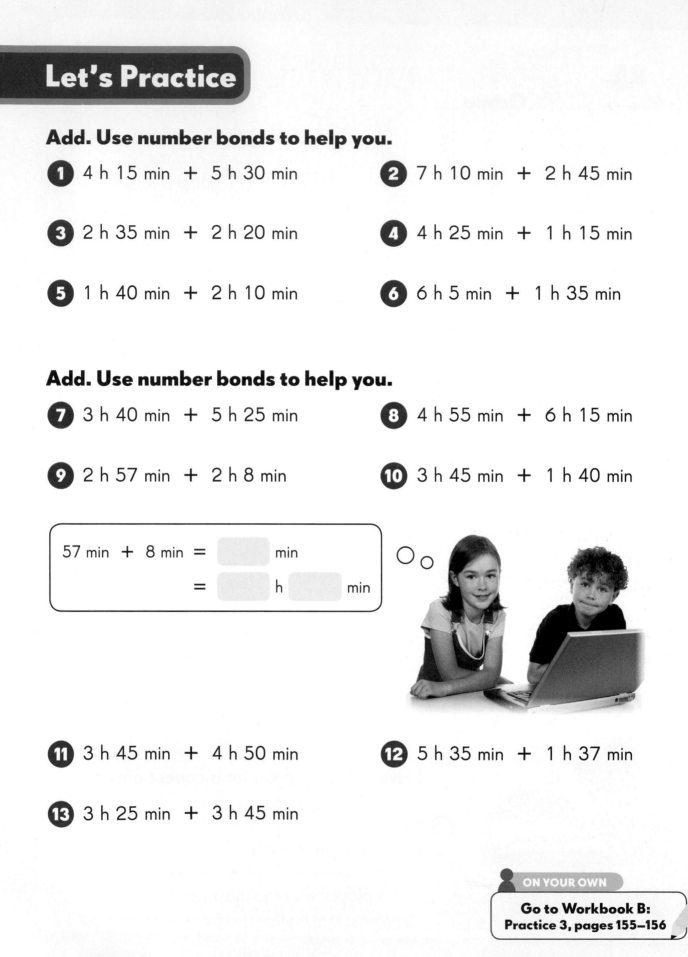

11 3 h 45 min + 4 h 50 min

12 5 h 35 min + 1 h 37 min

13 3 h 25 min + 3 h 45 min

ON YOUR OWN

Go to Workbook B:
Practice 3, pages 155–156

Lesson 16.4 Subtracting Hours and Minutes

Lesson Objective

- Subtract time with and without regrouping.

Learn **Subtract time without regrouping.**

Mr. Jackson takes 2 hours 15 minutes to paint his bedroom.
He takes 1 hour 5 minutes to paint his dining room.
How much longer does he take to paint the bedroom than dining room?

2 h 15 min — 1 h 5 min = ?

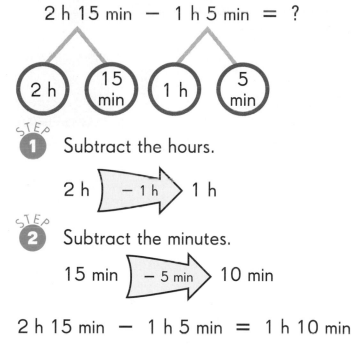

STEP 1 Subtract the hours.

2 h $\boxed{- 1 h}$ 1 h

STEP 2 Subtract the minutes.

15 min $\boxed{- 5 min}$ 10 min

2 h 15 min — 1 h 5 min = 1 h 10 min

He takes 1 hour 10 minutes longer to paint the bedroom than the dining room.

Guided Practice

Complete.

$$8 h - 3 h = \boxed{} h$$
$$45 min - 20 min = \boxed{} min$$

1 8 h 45 min — 3 h 20 min = ?

8 h 45 min — 3 h 20 min

= $\boxed{}$ h $\boxed{}$ min

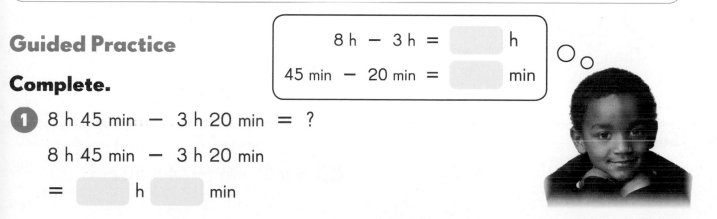

Subtract time with regrouping.

Kyle bikes for 4 hours 30 minutes.
Joey bikes for 2 hours 50 minutes.
How much longer does Kyle bike than Joey?

4 h 30 min — 2 h 50 min = ?

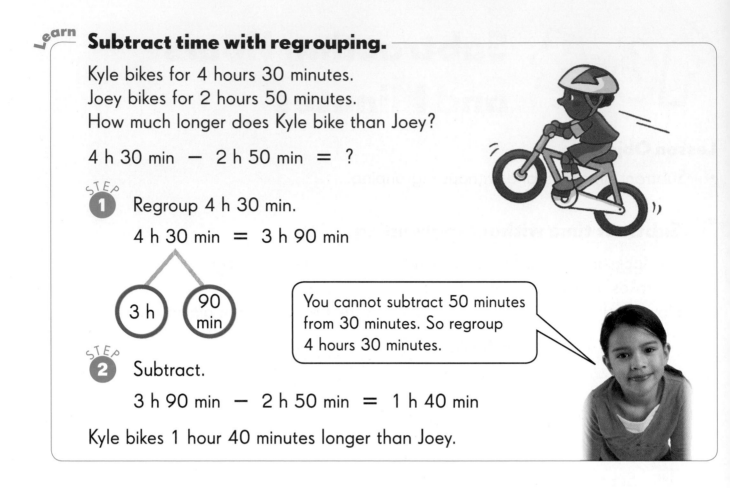

STEP
1 Regroup 4 h 30 min.

4 h 30 min = 3 h 90 min

3 h   90 min

You cannot subtract 50 minutes from 30 minutes. So regroup 4 hours 30 minutes.

STEP
2 Subtract.

3 h 90 min — 2 h 50 min = 1 h 40 min

Kyle bikes 1 hour 40 minutes longer than Joey.

Guided Practice

Complete.

2 7 h 20 min — 4 h 45 min = ?

First, regroup 7 h 20 min.

7 h 20 min = 6 h [ ] min

6 h

Then, subtract.

6 h [ ] min — 4 h [ ] min = [ ] h [ ] min

Subtract.

3 4 h 30 min – 2 h 45 min

4 8 h 35 min — 4 h 50 min

WORKING TOGETHER **Game**

Let's Subtract!

Players: 4
Materials:
- paper strips
- a bag

STEP **1** Each player writes four time subtraction problems on separate strips of paper.

Example

2 h 15 min — 1 h 20 min =

STEP **2** Players put their problems in a bag.

STEP **3** Player 1 picks a problem from the bag and solves it.

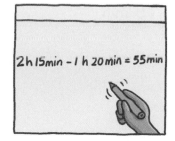

2h 15min – 1 h 20min = 55min

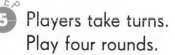

I got it correct!

STEP **4** The other players check the answer. Player 1 gets 1 point for a correct answer.
The player with the greatest difference in time in each round also gets an extra point.

STEP **5** Players take turns. Play four rounds.

The player with the most points wins!

Let's Practice

Subtract.

1 12 h 35 min − 7 h 10 min = [   ] h [   ] min

2 15 h 40 min − 9 h 25 min = [   ] h [   ] min

3 3 h 20 min − 2 h 10 min = [   ] h [   ] min

4 5 h 15 min − 1 h 5 min = [   ] h [   ] min

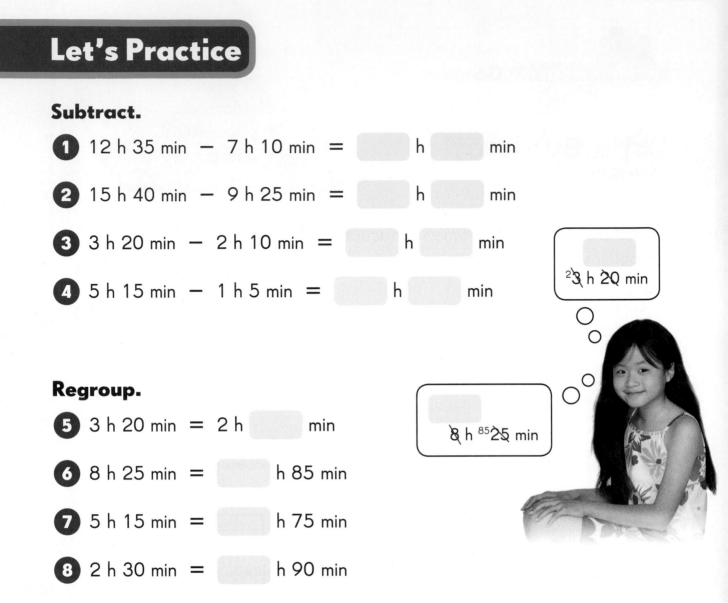

[   ]
²3̷ h 2̷0̸ min

[   ]
8̷ h ⁸⁵2̷5̸ min

Regroup.

5 3 h 20 min = 2 h [   ] min

6 8 h 25 min = [   ] h 85 min

7 5 h 15 min = [   ] h 75 min

8 2 h 30 min = [   ] h 90 min

Subtract.

9 5 h 38 min − 1 h 55 min

10 3 h 20 min − 1 h 45 min

11 9 h 15 min − 8 h 35 min

12 8 h 20 min − 6 h 24 min

13 3 h − 1 h 30 min

14 5 h 46 min − 55 min

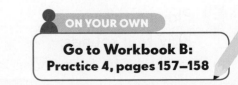

ON YOUR OWN

Go to Workbook B:
Practice 4, pages 157–158

Elapsed Time

Lesson Objective

- Find elapsed time.

Vocabulary
elapsed time
time line

Learn

Introduction to finding elapsed time.

Tom's soccer practice started at 3:00 P.M.
It ended at 5:00 P.M.
How long was his soccer practice?

Start:

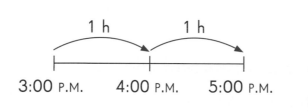

End:

The soccer practice lasted 2 hours.

Elapsed time is the amount of time that has passed between the start and the end of an activity.

Anita started her dinner at 6:45 P.M.
She finished at 7:20 P.M.
How long did her dinner last?

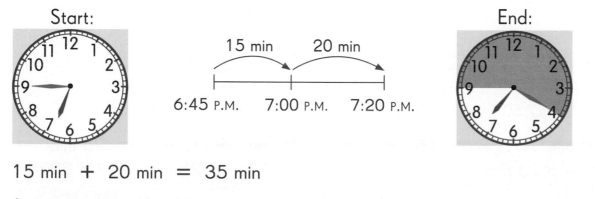

15 min + 20 min = 35 min

Anita ate dinner for 35 minutes.

Guided Practice

Answer each question.

1 What time is 3 hours after 7:00 P.M.?

2 What time is 2 hours after 7:15 P.M.?

3 How many hours are there from 9:00 to noon?

4 How many hours are there from 2:30 P.M. to 4:30 P.M.?

5 What time is 15 minutes after 11:00 A.M.?

6 What time is 45 minutes after 11:30 A.M.?

7 How many minutes are there from 11:50 A.M. to 12:25 P.M.?

Learn Find elapsed time in hours and minutes.

Rachel and Shannon went to a fair.
They arrived at 7:50 P.M. and left at 9:15 P.M.
How long were they at the fair?

BOOK FAIR

 Arrived:
7:50 P.M. or
10 minutes to 8.

 Left:
9:15 P.M. or
15 minutes past 9.

You can use a **timeline** to find elapsed time.

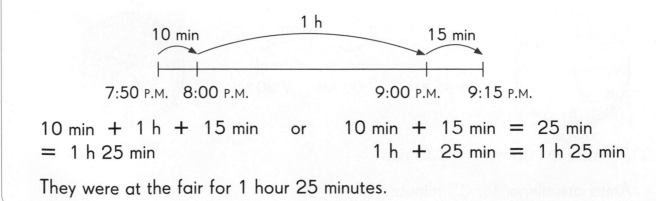

10 min + 1 h + 15 min   or   10 min + 15 min = 25 min
= 1 h 25 min   1 h + 25 min = 1 h 25 min

They were at the fair for 1 hour 25 minutes.

Guided Practice

8 Kevin had a birthday party.
What time did the guests arrive?
What time did the guests leave?
Look at the clocks. Complete the times.
Use past or to.

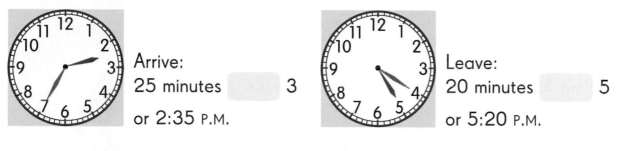

Arrive:
25 minutes ☐ 3
or 2:35 P.M.

Leave:
20 minutes ☐ 5
or 5:20 P.M.

How long did the party last?

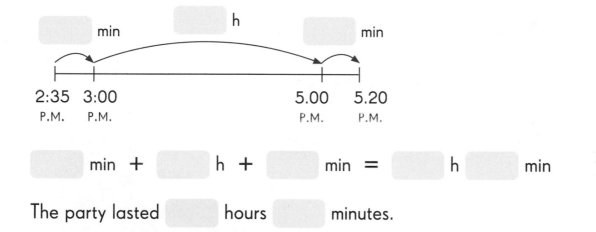

☐ min   ☐ h   ☐ min

2:35   3:00   5.00   5.20
P.M.   P.M.   P.M.   P.M.

☐ min + ☐ h + ☐ min = ☐ h ☐ min

The party lasted ☐ hours ☐ minutes.

Find the end time given the start time and elapsed time.

After a party, Emily cleans her house.
She starts cleaning at 10:30 P.M. and finishes in 1 hour 45 minutes.
What time did she finish cleaning the house?

Emily works past midnight. So, P.M. time becomes A.M. time.

Count on the hours and minutes from 12 A.M.

Continued on next page

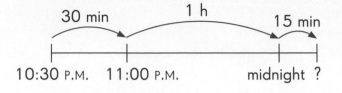

10:30 P.M. 11:00 P.M. midnight ?

30 minutes after 10:30 P.M. is 11:00 P.M.
1 hour after 11:00 P.M. is midnight.
So, midnight is 12 A.M.
15 minutes after midnight is 12:15 A.M.

Emily finished cleaning the house at 12:15 A.M.

Guided Practice

Complete. Use the time line to help you.

9 Taylor makes posters for his family.
He takes 2 hours and 35 minutes to make
the posters.
He started making them at 10:10 A.M.
When did he finish making them?

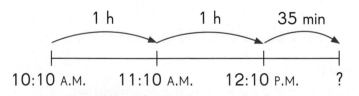

10:10 A.M.   11:10 A.M.   12:10 P.M.   ?

2 hours after 10:10 A.M. is 12:10 P.M.

35 minutes after 12:10 P.M. is ⬚.

He finished making them at ⬚.

Taylor works past noon.
So, A.M. time becomes
P.M. time.

Find the start time given the elapsed time and end time.

Brooke was painting a sign. She finished painting it at 3 P.M.
She took 1 hour 50 minutes to paint it. When did she begin?

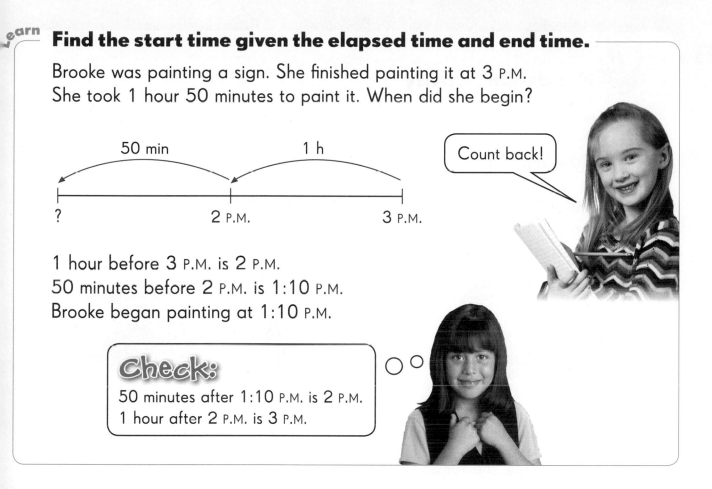

Count back!

1 hour before 3 P.M. is 2 P.M.
50 minutes before 2 P.M. is 1:10 P.M.
Brooke began painting at 1:10 P.M.

Check:
50 minutes after 1:10 P.M. is 2 P.M.
1 hour after 2 P.M. is 3 P.M.

Guided Practice

Complete using the timeline.

10 Jamal spent 45 minutes opening his birthday gifts.
He finished opening his gifts at 12:05 A.M.
What time did he start?

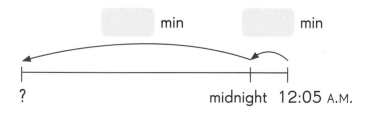

[____] min   [____] min

?   midnight   12:05 A.M.

Jamal started opening his gifts at [____] .

Hands-On Activity

WORKING TOGETHER

1 In groups of four, take turns telling one another the last time you did each activity. Include the time you think you started and ended each one.

Reading a story

Playing a game

Having lunch

2 Write down your start time and end time for each activity.

3 Draw a time line for each activity. Then find the elapsed time.

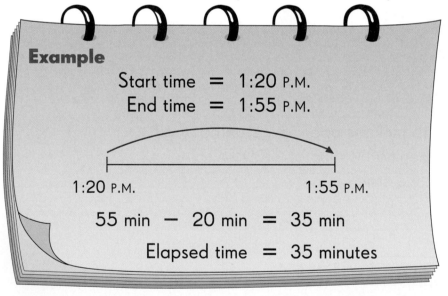

Example

Start time = 1:20 P.M.
End time = 1:55 P.M.

1:20 P.M.   1:55 P.M.

55 min — 20 min = 35 min

Elapsed time = 35 minutes

4 Solve.

a Who takes the longest time to read a story?

b Who takes the shortest time to have lunch?

c Who takes the shortest time to play a game?

Let's Practice

Tell what time it will be.

1 2 hours after 7:00 P.M.

2 3 hours after 2:45 A.M.

3 35 minutes after 9:00 P.M.

4 25 minutes after 8:50 A.M.

Find how much time has passed. Draw a timeline to help you.

5 5:45 P.M. to 6:20 P.M.

6 3:25 A.M. to 4:10 A.M.

7 noon to 4:55 P.M.

8 11:20 A.M. to 2:35 P.M.

Solve.

9 A train leaves Town P at 7:30 A.M.
It arrives at Town Q at 11:45 A.M.
How long is the trip?

10 A movie starts at 7:15 P.M.
It lasts 2 hours 15 minutes.
What time does it end?

11 A chef starts work at 8:45 A.M.
He usually works for 8 hours.
Today, he leaves a half hour early.
What time does he leave the restaurant?

12 Mr. Williams takes 2 hours 40 minutes to drive from Town A to Town B.
He arrives at Town B at 2:25 P.M.
What time did he start from Town A?

13 Sally finished her hike at 4:35 P.M.
She hiked for 2 hours 20 minutes.
She took a 15-minute rest during her hike.
What time did she begin hiking?

14 A hospital nurse gave a patient medicine every 4 hours, 4 times a day.
The patient took his first tablet for the day at 9:30 A.M.
At what time should he take the last tablet for the day?

ON YOUR OWN

**Go to Workbook B:
Practice 5, pages 159–162**

Lesson 16.6 Measuring Temperature

Lesson Objectives

- Read a Fahrenheit thermometer.
- Choose the appropriate tool and unit to measure temperature.
- Use a referent to estimate temperature.

Learn Introduction to measuring temperature.

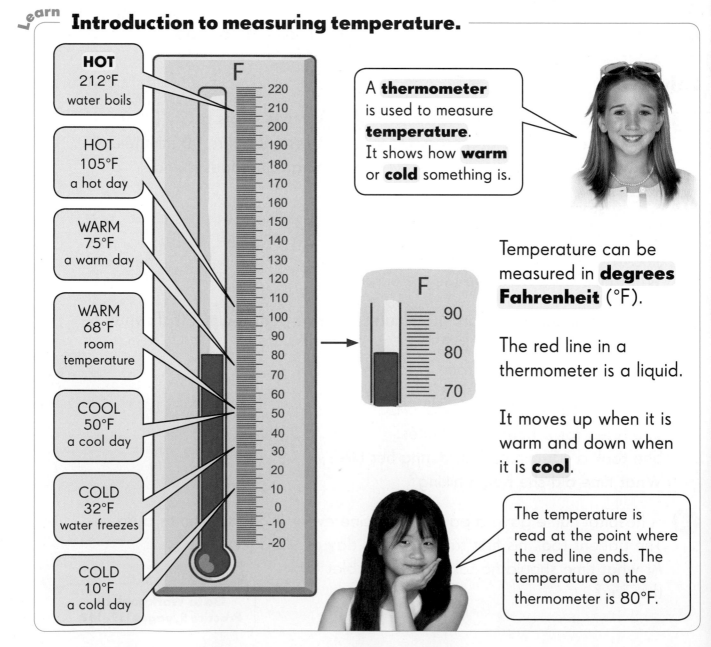

A **thermometer** is used to measure **temperature**. It shows how **warm** or **cold** something is.

Temperature can be measured in **degrees Fahrenheit** (°F).

The red line in a thermometer is a liquid.

It moves up when it is warm and down when it is **cool**.

The temperature is read at the point where the red line ends. The temperature on the thermometer is 80°F.

Guided Practice

Find each temperature, including its unit. Then describe the temperature as hot, warm, cool, or cold.

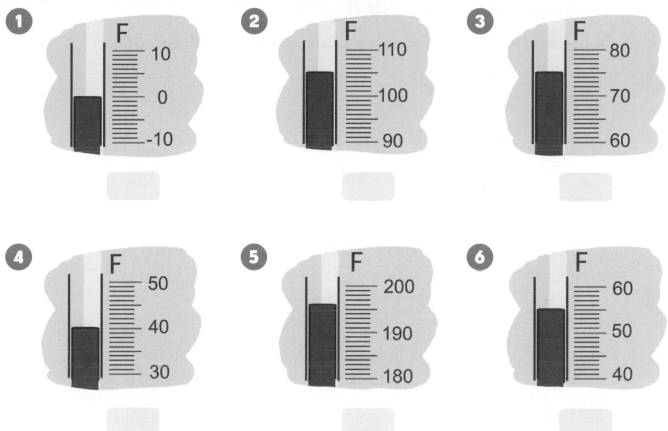

① F
10
0
-10

② F
110
100
90

③ F
80
70
60

④ F
50
40
30

⑤ F
200
190
180

⑥ F
60
50
40

Decide which temperature matches the activity.

⑦ A 72°F B 38°F

⑧ A 60°F B 10°F

⑨ A 50°F B 212°F

Let's Practice

Find each temperature. Include its unit.

Then describe the temperature as hot, warm, cool, or cold.

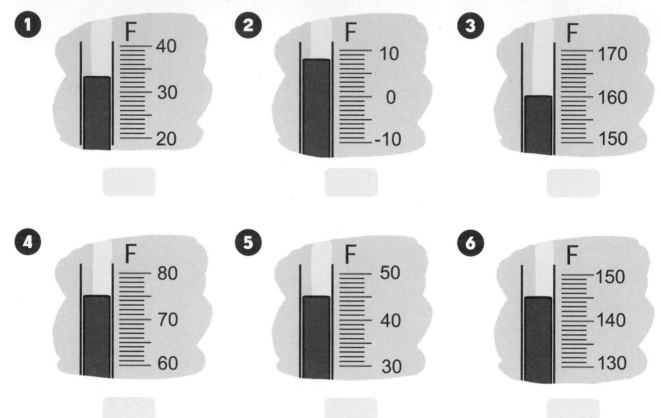

1 F — 40 — 30 — 20

2 F — 10 — 0 — -10

3 F — 170 — 160 — 150

4 F — 80 — 70 — 60

5 F — 50 — 40 — 30

6 F — 150 — 140 — 130

Decide which temperature matches the activity.

7

60°F   20°F

ON YOUR OWN

Go to Workbook B:
Practice 6, pages 163–166

16.7 Real-World Problems: Time and Temperature

Lesson Objectives

- Solve up to two-step word problems on time.
- Solve word problems involving temperature.

Learn Solve one- or two-step real-world word problems involving time.

Rafael is a city tour guide.
He gives 45-minute tours.
He is paid $30 an hour.
On Saturday, he gave 8 tours.

a How many hours did Rafael spend giving the 8 tours on Saturday?

b How much did Rafael earn by giving 8 tours?

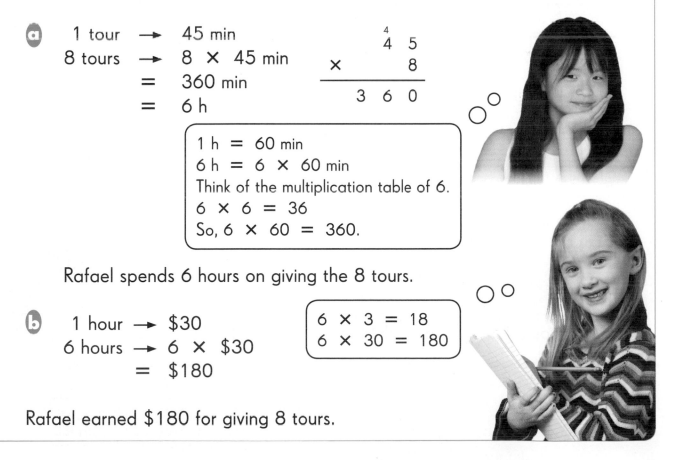

a

1 tour → 45 min

8 tours → 8 × 45 min

= 360 min

= 6 h

$$\begin{array}{r} \overset{4}{4}\ 5 \\ \times\qquad 8 \\ \hline 3\ 6\ 0 \end{array}$$

> 1 h = 60 min
> 6 h = 6 × 60 min
> Think of the multiplication table of 6.
> 6 × 6 = 36
> So, 6 × 60 = 360.

Rafael spends 6 hours on giving the 8 tours.

b

1 hour → $30

6 hours → 6 × $30

= $180

> 6 × 3 = 18
> 6 × 30 = 180

Rafael earned $180 for giving 8 tours.

Guided Practice

Solve.

1 A scenic train makes several 45-minute tours three times a week. Each tour costs $13 for each child.

45-minute Scenic Train Tour

Day	Mon	Wed	Fri
Number of Tours	6	6	6
Length of each Tour	45 min		

(a) How many hours and minutes does the train go on Wednesday?

(b) How much does it cost for 1 child to go on tours for 90 minutes?

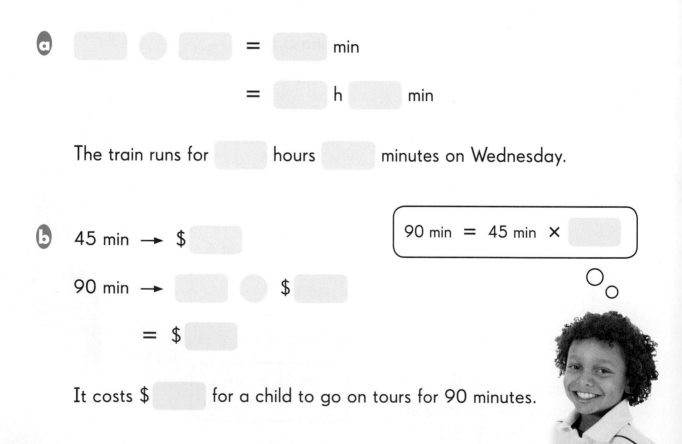

(a) ☐ ● ☐ = ☐ min

= ☐ h ☐ min

The train runs for ☐ hours ☐ minutes on Wednesday.

(b) 45 min → $ ☐

90 min → ☐ ● $ ☐

= $ ☐

90 min = 45 min × ☐

It costs $ ☐ for a child to go on tours for 90 minutes.

2 Raul spends 1 hour 40 minutes doing his homework.
Then he spends another 45 minutes on his piano practice.
He finishes his homework and piano practice at 5:30 P.M.
What time did he begin doing his homework?

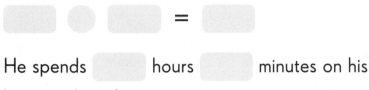

He spends [   ] hours [   ] minutes on his
homework and piano practice.

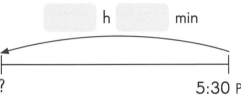

[   ] h [   ] min

?   5:30 P.M.

First, find the total time
spent on his homework
and piano lesson.

Raul began doing his homework at [   ] P.M.

3 Melissa arrives at a train station.
Her watch shows the time as 6:45 A.M.
Her watch is 20 minutes slow.

a What is the actual time shown on the train station's clock?

b The train arrives 10 minutes later.
What time does the train arrive according to the train station's clock?

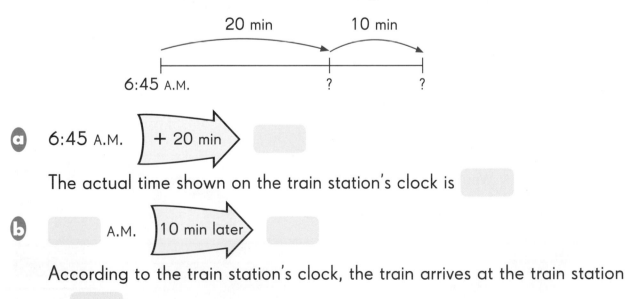

20 min   10 min

6:45 A.M.   ?   ?

a 6:45 A.M. ⟩ + 20 min ⟩ [   ]

The actual time shown on the train station's clock is [   ]

b [   ] A.M. ⟩ 10 min later ⟩ [   ]

According to the train station's clock, the train arrives at the train station
at [   ]

Solve real-world word problems involving temperature.

The temperature in the mountains today is 65°F.
The temperature in the desert today is 130°F.

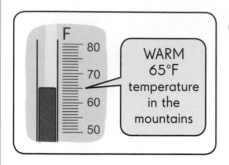

WARM
65°F
temperature
in the
mountains

HOT
130°F
temperature
in the
desert

Find the difference between the temperatures.

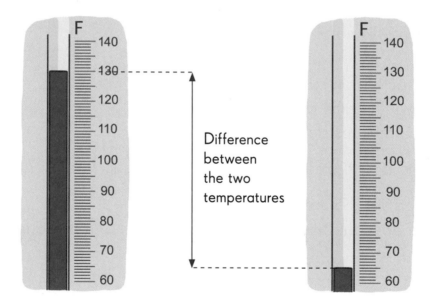

Difference
between
the two
temperatures

Count on.
The difference is 65°F.

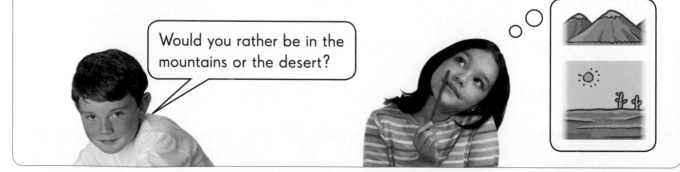

Would you rather be in the
mountains or the desert?

Guided Practice

Complete the story.
Use the numbers shown.

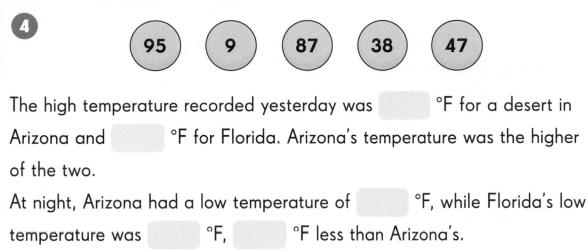

4

(95) (9) (87) (38) (47)

The high temperature recorded yesterday was [   ] °F for a desert in
Arizona and [   ] °F for Florida. Arizona's temperature was the higher
of the two.

At night, Arizona had a low temperature of [   ] °F, while Florida's low
temperature was [   ] °F, [   ] °F less than Arizona's.

Let's Practice

Solve.

1 Ken takes 45 minutes to paint a chair.
How long would he take to paint 7 similar chairs?

2 A clock shows 11:40 A.M.
It is 35 minutes slow.
What is the actual time?

3 A clock shows 3:10 P.M.
It is 25 minutes fast.
What is the actual time?

4 Chris leaves his grandmother's house at 7:15 P.M.
He takes 1 hour 40 minutes to travel home.
What time does he reach home?

5 Florence takes 4 hours 55 minutes to drive from Town A to Town B.
She reaches Town B at 4:45 P.M.
What time does she leave Town A?

6 Ms. Ramirez prepares meals for senior citizens.
It takes her 15 minutes to prepare each meal.
She prepares 8 meals.

a How many hours does she spend preparing the 8 meals?

b How many meals could she prepare in 3 hours?

7 Darryl drove 1 hour 35 minutes from Town A to Town B.
After that, he drove 2 hours 45 minutes from Town B to Town C.
He reached Town C at 7:15 P.M.
What time did he leave Town A?

8 Tonya went to school for a band concert.
She arrived at school at 7:15 P.M. according to her watch.
Her watch was 30 minutes fast.

a What was the actual time?

b She arrived just in time for the concert.
The concert ended at 9:00 P.M.
How long did the concert last?

9 When Max went to camp in the morning, the temperature was 67°F.
When he got home after dinner, it was 48°F.
Is the temperature shown on each thermometer correct?

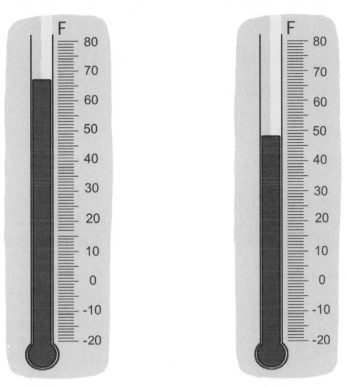

Mid-morning   Night

Was it cooler in the morning or at night?
Explain your answer.

10 Rachel is going on a trip.
It is 72°F where she is going.
Describe what kind of clothes she should pack.
Explain your thinking.

ON YOUR OWN

Go to Workbook B:
Practice 7, pages 167–174

Math Journal

1 The steps for finding the elapsed time from 10:20 A.M. to 1:30 P.M. are not in order. Put them in the correct order.

a Find the elapsed time from 10:20 A.M. to 11:00 A.M.

b Mark the hours between the two end points.

c Add the elapsed times.

d Find the elapsed time from 11:00 A.M. to 1:00 P.M.

e Find the elapsed time from 1:00 P.M. to 1:30 P.M.

f Mark the beginning time and end time on the time line.

g Draw the time line.

2 Find the elapsed time from 1:15 P.M. to 11:20 P.M. Determine whether the steps are the same as **1** and rewrite the steps that are different.

PROBLEM SOLVING

1 Andrew takes a plane from Dallas to Chicago at 8:15 A.M.
The flight takes 3 hours 40 minutes.
There are flights from Chicago to Dallas every 3 hours from 8:15 A.M.
Andrew wants to return to Dallas on the same day.
What is the latest flight that he can take?

2 Complete the story. Use the numbers shown.

86   43   32   8

11   5   78

The high temperature yesterday was [   ] degrees Fahrenheit. It is the highest it has been for the past [   ] days. The low temperature was [   ] degrees Fahrenheit, which was about half the high. It is only [   ] degrees above freezing (which is [   ] degrees Fahrenheit).

Tomorrow's temperature is predicted to be [   ] degrees Fahrenheit, which is [   ] degrees lower than yesterday's high.

ON YOUR OWN

**Go to Workbook B:
Put on Your Thinking Cap!
pages 175–176**

Chapter Wrap Up

Study Guide
You have learned...

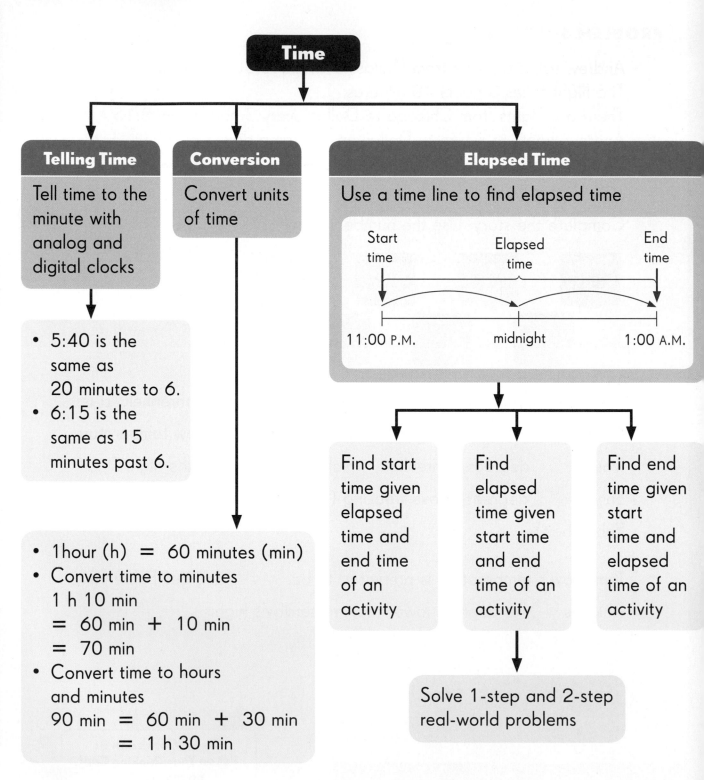

Time

Telling Time

Tell time to the minute with analog and digital clocks

- 5:40 is the same as 20 minutes to 6.
- 6:15 is the same as 15 minutes past 6.

Conversion

Convert units of time

- 1 hour (h) = 60 minutes (min)
- Convert time to minutes
  1 h 10 min
  = 60 min + 10 min
  = 70 min
- Convert time to hours and minutes
  90 min = 60 min + 30 min
  = 1 h 30 min

Elapsed Time

Use a time line to find elapsed time

Start time   Elapsed time   End time

11:00 P.M.   midnight   1:00 A.M.

Find start time given elapsed time and end time of an activity

Find elapsed time given start time and end time of an activity

Find end time given start time and elapsed time of an activity

Solve 1-step and 2-step real-world problems

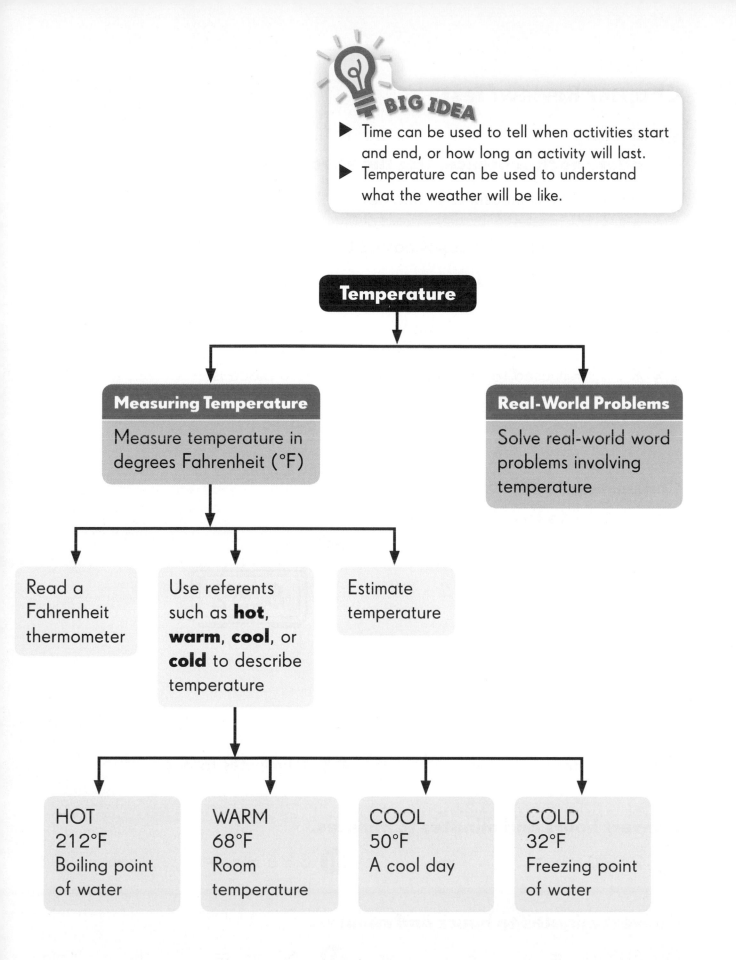

BIG IDEA

▶ Time can be used to tell when activities start and end, or how long an activity will last.
▶ Temperature can be used to understand what the weather will be like.

Temperature

Measuring Temperature

Measure temperature in degrees Fahrenheit (°F)

Real-World Problems

Solve real-world word problems involving temperature

Read a Fahrenheit thermometer

Use referents such as **hot**, **warm**, **cool**, or **cold** to describe temperature

Estimate temperature

HOT
212°F
Boiling point of water

WARM
68°F
Room temperature

COOL
50°F
A cool day

COLD
32°F
Freezing point of water

Chapter Review/Test

Vocabulary
Complete each sentence. Use the words shown.

 1 Temperature is measured in degrees [   ].

> elapsed time
> Fahrenheit
> hours
> minutes
> thermometer

2 The amount of time that has passed between one time and another is called [   ].

3 There are 24 [   ] in a day.

4 A [   ] is used to find out how hot or cold a place is.

5 There are 45 [   ] between 7:30 P.M. to 8:15 P.M.

Concept and Skills
Use past or to to tell the time.

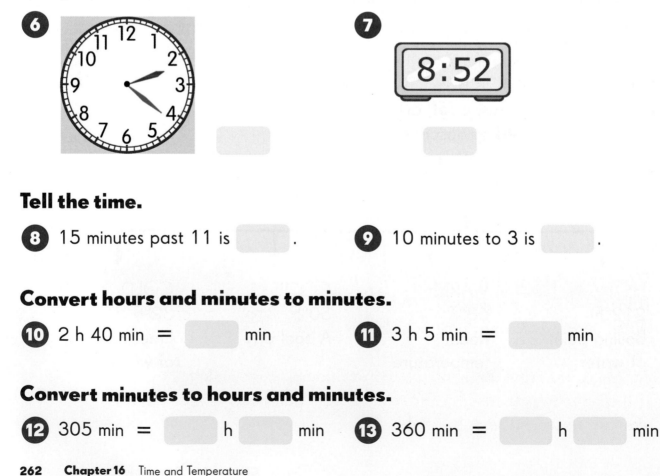

6 [   ]

7 8:52 [   ]

Tell the time.

8 15 minutes past 11 is [   ].

9 10 minutes to 3 is [   ].

Convert hours and minutes to minutes.

10 2 h 40 min = [   ] min

11 3 h 5 min = [   ] min

Convert minutes to hours and minutes.

12 305 min = [   ] h [   ] min

13 360 min = [   ] h [   ] min

Add or subtract.

14 4 h 50 min + 3 h 25 min

15 5 h 35 min − 3 h 55 min

Tell the time.

16 What time is 2 hours 15 minutes after 7:15 P.M.?

17 What time is 3 hours 40 minutes before 10:05 A.M.?

Find each temperature. Then describe hot, warm, cool, or cold.

18

F
— 30
— 20
— 10

_____ °F. It is _____ .

19

F
— 100
— 90
— 80

_____ °F. It is _____ .

Problem Solving

20 Robert jogs from 7:10 A.M. to 9:00 A.M. on Saturday mornings. How long does he jog?

21 Peter studies for 2 hours 10 minutes.
He started at 6:15 P.M.
What time did he stop?

22 A movie ended at 1 P.M.
It lasted 1 hour 50 minutes.
What time did the movie start?

23 At 9 A.M. one day, the temperature at Snowland was 35°F.
If the temperature rose by 2 degrees every half hour, what was the temperature at 11 A.M.?

Angles and Lines

Lessons

17.1 Understanding and Identifying Angles

17.2 Right Angles

17.3 Perpendicular Lines

17.4 Parallel Lines

BIG IDEA

▶ Angles and lines can be found all around us. These can be described with special names.

Recall Prior Knowledge

Identifying parts of lines and curves

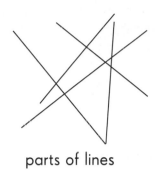

parts of lines

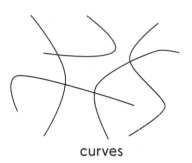

curves

✔ Quick Check

Which are parts of lines? Which are curves?

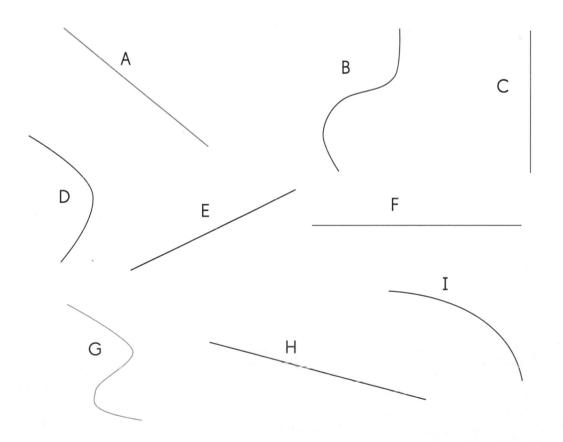

Lesson 17.1 Understanding and Identifying Angles

Lesson Objectives

- Finding angles in plane shapes and real-world objects.
- Compare the number of sides and angles of plane shapes.

Vocabulary

point	angle
line	endpoint
line segment	

Learn **Identify and name a point, line, and line segment**

A **point** is an exact location in space.

·
A

This is point A. Write point A as A.

A **line** is a straight path. It goes on without end in both directions as shown by the arrowheads.

This line passes through points A and B.
Name it line AB or line BA.

A **line segment** is part of a line. It has two **endpoints.**

This line segment has two endpoints, C and D.

Name it line segment CD or line segment DC.

Guided Practice

Identify each figure as a point, line, or line segment. Then name each figure.

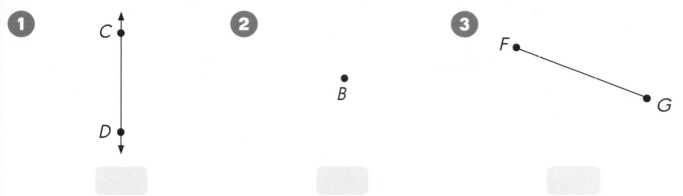

1 C, D

2 B

3 F, G

Find the number of line segments in each plane shape.

4

5

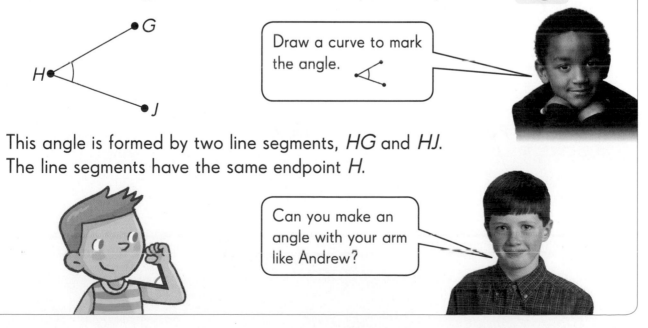

Learn Identify an angle.

When two line segments share the same endpoint, they form an **angle**.

Draw a curve to mark the angle.

This angle is formed by two line segments, *HG* and *HJ*. The line segments have the same endpoint *H*.

Can you make an angle with your arm like Andrew?

Guided Practice

Look at the pairs of craft sticks.

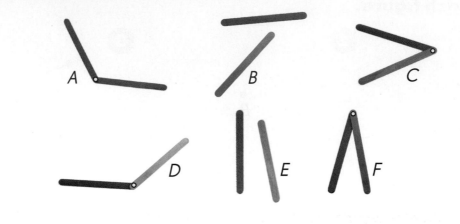

6 Which pairs form an angle?

7 Which pairs do not form an angle?

Which pairs form an angle?

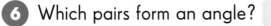

8

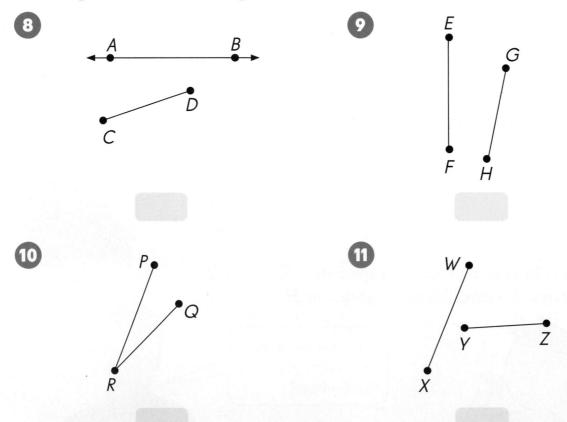

9

10

11

Find angles in plane shapes and real-world objects.

Look at the square and triangle.

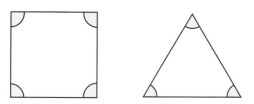

> In a plane shape, two sides meet at a corner to form an angle.

The square has four angles.
The triangle has three angles.

Here are some examples of angles found on objects.

> In an object, two sides meet at a corner to form an angle.

Can you find angles around you?

Guided Practice

Find the number of angles in each plane shape.

12

13

Find the number of angles on each object.

14

15

Compare the number of sides and angles of a plane shape.

The triangle has three sides and three angles.

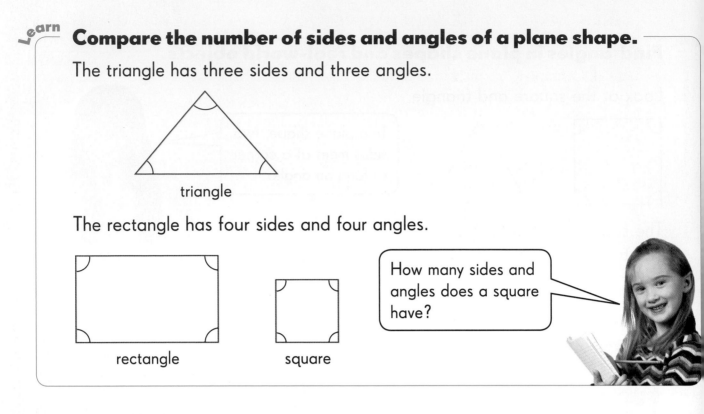

triangle

The rectangle has four sides and four angles.

rectangle   square

How many sides and angles does a square have?

Guided Practice

Complete.

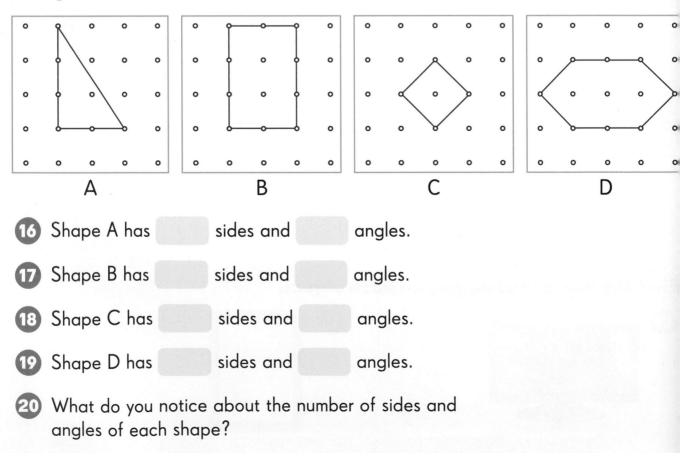

A   B   C   D

16 Shape A has ⬚ sides and ⬚ angles.

17 Shape B has ⬚ sides and ⬚ angles.

18 Shape C has ⬚ sides and ⬚ angles.

19 Shape D has ⬚ sides and ⬚ angles.

20 What do you notice about the number of sides and angles of each shape?

Hands-On Activity

STEP 1 Draw
- a 3-sided shape
- a 4-sided shape
- a 5-sided shape
- a 6-sided shape

STEP 2 Mark and color the angles in each shape.

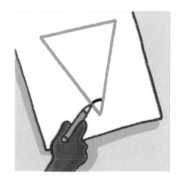

STEP 3 Copy and complete the table to show the number of angles in each shape.

Worksheet	
Type of Shape	Number of Angles
3-sided	
4-sided	
5-sided	
6-sided	

You can also do this activity using the computer drawing tool to draw the shapes.

Then print the shapes and do **STEP 2** and **STEP 3**.

Let's Explore!

Make triangles using the geoboard.

Example

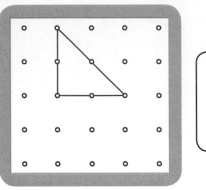

The triangles must look different from one another.

1 Make five different triangles. In what ways are they different?

2 How many sides and angles does each triangle have?

3 What can you say about the number of sides and angles in a triangle?

Make rectangles using the geoboard.

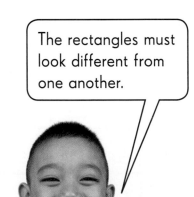

The rectangles must look different from one another.

4 Make five different rectangles. In what ways are they different?

5 How many sides does each rectangle have?

6 What can you say about the number of sides and angles in a rectangle?

Let's Practice

Name each figure as a point, line, or line segment.

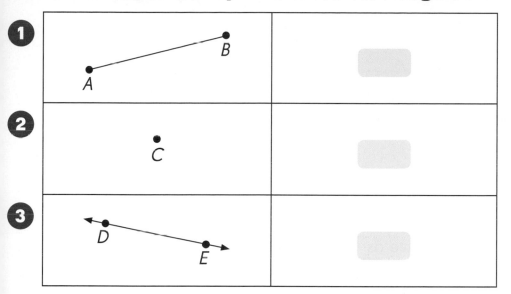

1 A —— B	
2 • C	
3 D ←——→ E	

Decide whether each pair of craft sticks forms an angle.

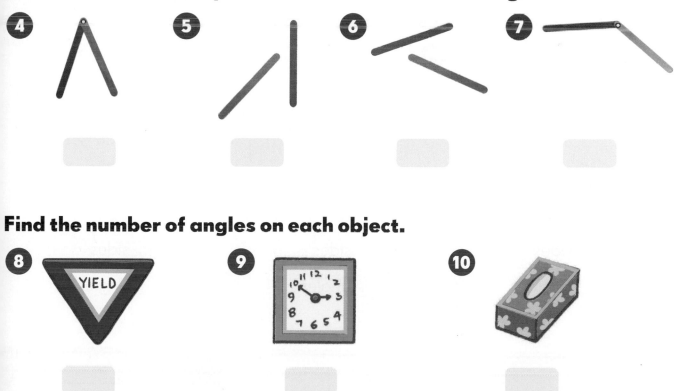

4   **5**   **6**   **7**

Find the number of angles on each object.

8   YIELD   **9**   **10**

Fill in the blanks with fan, box, or scissors.

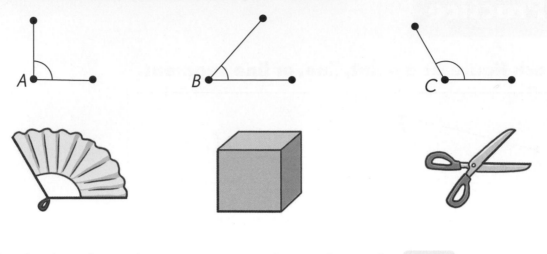

11 Angle *A* is about the same size as the angle on the ⬚ .

12 Angle *B* is about the same size as the angle on the ⬚ .

13 Angle *C* is about the same size as the angle on the ⬚ .

Count the number of sides and angles of each shape.

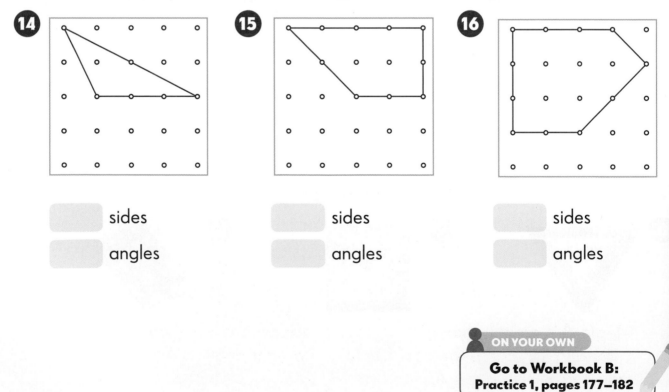

⬚ sides
⬚ angles

⬚ sides
⬚ angles

⬚ sides
⬚ angles

ON YOUR OWN

Go to Workbook B:
Practice 1, pages 177–182

 # Right Angles

Lesson Objectives

- Make a right angle.
- Compare angles to a right angle.
- Identify right angles in plane shapes.

Vocabulary

right angle (⌐)

greater than

less than

Learn **Make a right angle and compare other angles to it.**

Mia folded a sheet of paper twice to make an angle like this:

The corner of the folded paper is a **right angle**.

You can check for a right angle and mark it as shown.

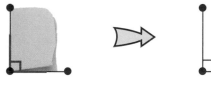

The symbol for right angle is ⌐ .

You can also use 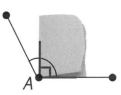 to check if other angles are

greater than or less than a right angle.

Angle *A* is greater than a right angle because the right angle fits within angle *A*.

Angle *B* is less than a right angle.

Guided Practice

Compare the angles. Use 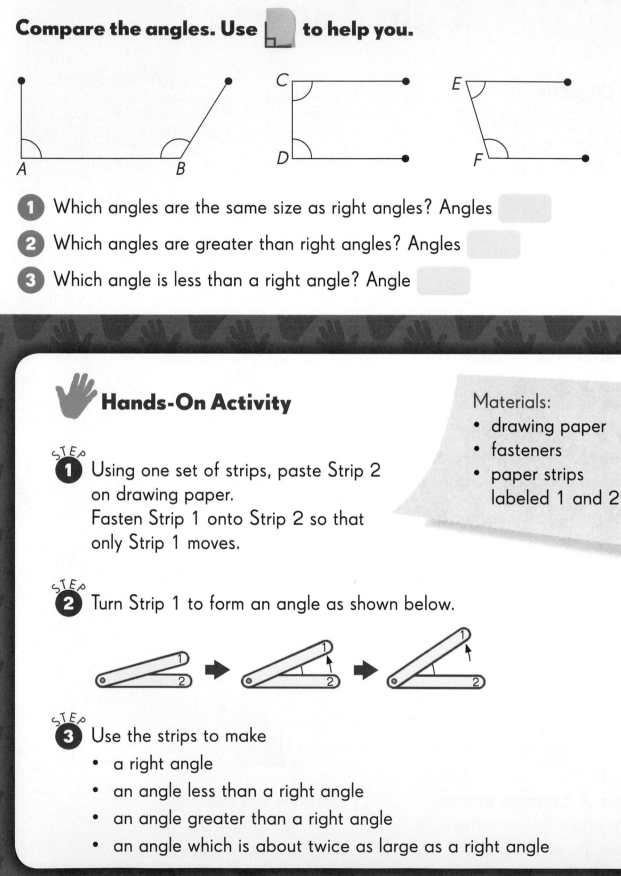 to help you.

1. Which angles are the same size as right angles? Angles ☐

2. Which angles are greater than right angles? Angles ☐

3. Which angle is less than a right angle? Angle ☐

Hands-On Activity

Materials:
- drawing paper
- fasteners
- paper strips labeled 1 and 2

STEP 1 Using one set of strips, paste Strip 2 on drawing paper.
Fasten Strip 1 onto Strip 2 so that only Strip 1 moves.

STEP 2 Turn Strip 1 to form an angle as shown below.

STEP 3 Use the strips to make
- a right angle
- an angle less than a right angle
- an angle greater than a right angle
- an angle which is about twice as large as a right angle

Find right angles in plane shapes.

This is a square. The sides of a square meet to form right angles.

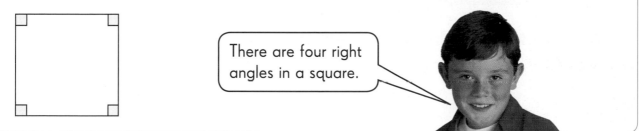

There are four right angles in a square.

Guided Practice

Find the number of right angles in each shape. Use [⌐] to help you.

4
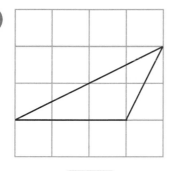

5
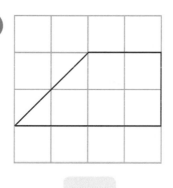

6
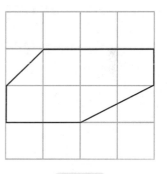

✋ Hands-On Activity

Make shapes using the geoboard. Then draw the shapes on grid paper.

Materials:
• a geoboard
• rubber bands
• grid paper

1 Make your own shape with seven sides and at least one right angle.
How many angles are greater than a right angle?
How many angles are less than a right angle?
How many angles are the same size as right angles?

2 Make a shape that has a right angle, two angles less than a right angle, and one angle greater than a right angle.

3 Make a shape that has a right angle, two angles greater than a right angle, and one angle less than a right angle.

Let's Practice

Decide whether each angle is greater than, same as, or less than a right angle.

1

2

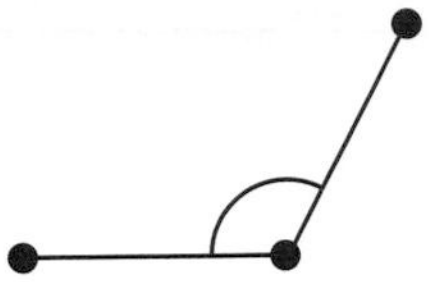

3

Find the number of right angles in each plane shape.

Use 🔲 to help you.

4

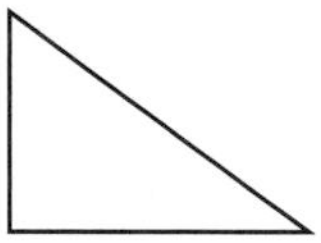

5

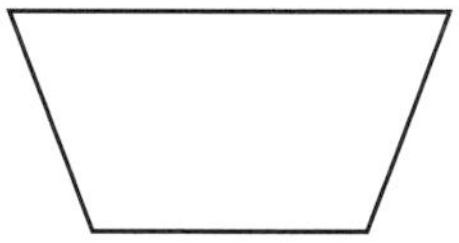

6

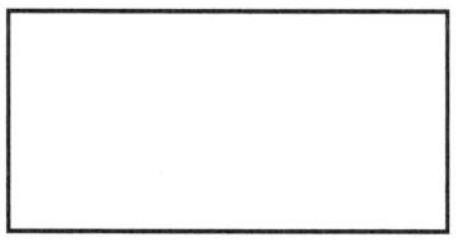

Find the number of angles less than a right angle.

Use 🔲 to help you.

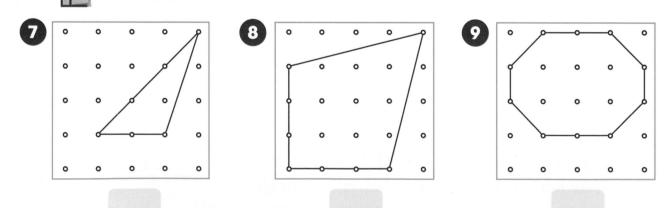

7

8

9

Draw the shape on grid paper.

10 Draw a four-sided shape with one angle greater than a right angle and one angle less than a right angle.

ON YOUR OWN

Go to Workbook B:
Practice 2, pages 183–184

Lesson 17.3 Perpendicular Lines

Lesson Objective
- Define and identify perpendicular lines.

Vocabulary
perpendicular lines
is perpendicular to

Learn — Identify perpendicular lines.

The lines shown are perpendicular line segments.

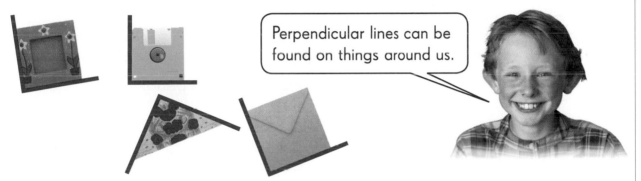

Perpendicular lines can be found on things around us.

What are perpendicular lines?

Perpendicular lines are two lines that meet at right angles.

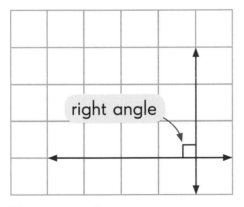

right angle

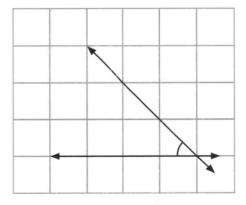

These two lines are perpendicular lines. They meet at right angles.

These two lines are not perpendicular lines. They do not meet at right angles.

Continued on next page

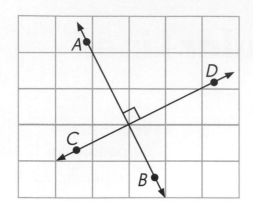

Line *AB* and line *CD* meet at right angles.
Line *AB* **is perpendicular to** line *CD*.

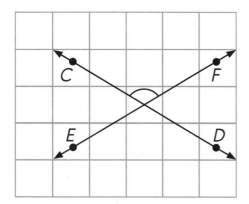

Is line *CD* perpendicular to line *EF*?

No.
The lines do not meet at right angles.
Line *CD* is not perpendicular to line *EF*.

How can you check whether the lines are perpendicular?

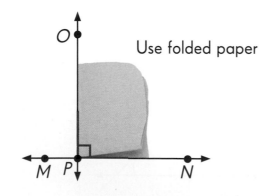

Use folded paper

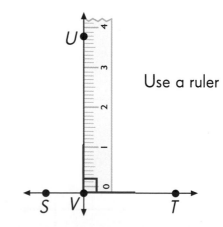

Use a ruler

Put the folded paper against
the two lines as shown.
The lines meet at a right angle.
So, line *OP* is perpendicular to
line *MN*.

Put a ruler against the two lines
as shown.
The lines meet at a right angle.
So, line *UV* is perpendicular to
line *ST*.

Guided Practice

Tell whether the lines are perpendicular.

1

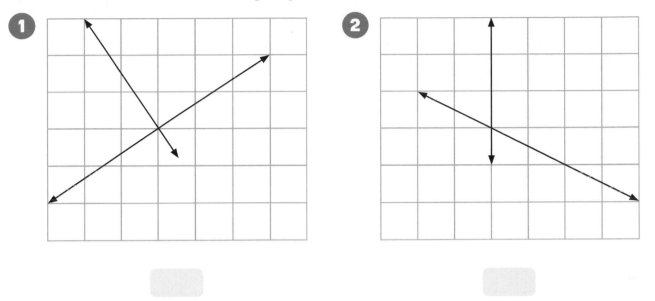

2

Find perpendicular lines.

3 Which line is perpendicular to line *AB*?

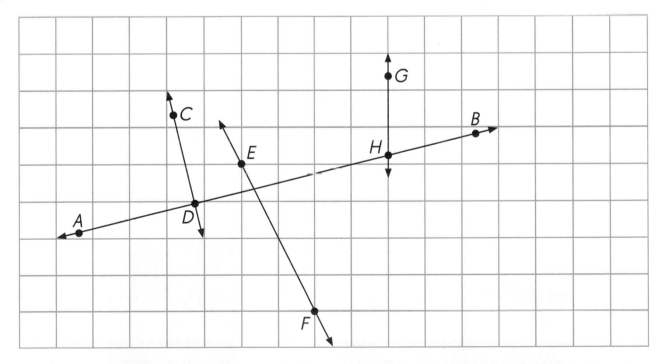

 is perpendicular to line *AB*.

4 Look at the pairs of perpendicular line segments on this box.

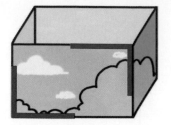

How many more pairs of perpendicular line segments can you find? [ ]

Copy the perpendicular lines onto grid paper.

5

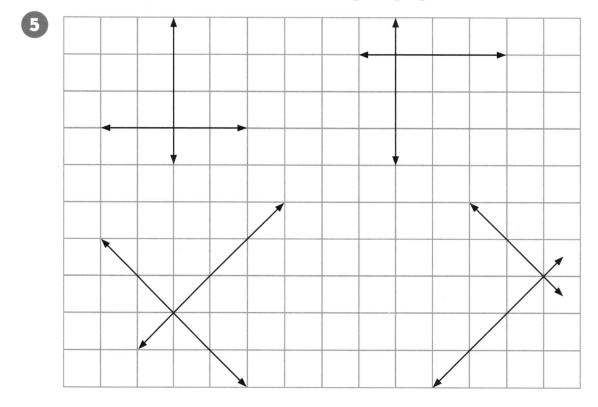

6 Find pairs of perpendicular line segments on each object.

Hands-On Activity

WORKING TOGETHER

 STEP 1 Look around your classroom and school.

 STEP 2 Find items with perpendicular line segments and items with no perpendicular line segments.

 STEP 3 Check the line segments with your folded paper or a ruler.

 STEP 4 Record the items and places in charts.

With Perpendicular Line Segments	Places Where I Found the Items
benches	hallways

With No Perpendicular Line Segments	Places Where I Found the Items
branches of plants	schoolyard

STEP 5 Compare your items with those found by other groups.

Tell whether the lines are perpendicular.

1

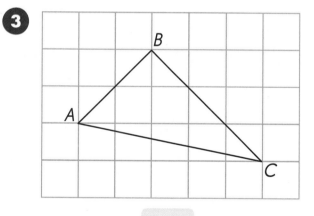

2

Identify the perpendicular line segments in each figure.

3

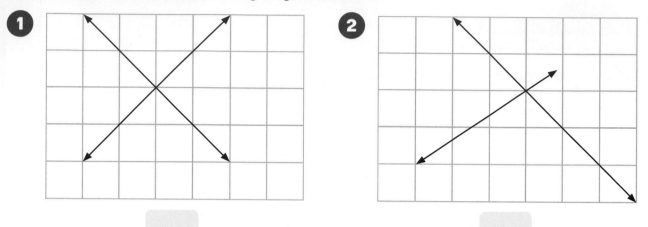

4

Find two pairs of perpendicular line segments on each object.

5

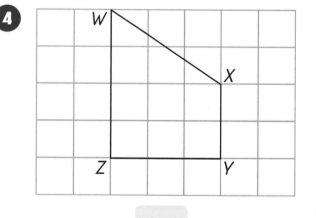

6

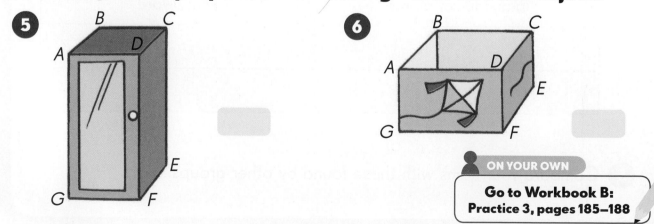

ON YOUR OWN

Go to Workbook B:
Practice 3, pages 185–188

Parallel Lines

Lesson Objective

• Define and identify parallel lines.

Vocabulary
parallel lines
is parallel to

Learn Identify parallel lines.

Parallel line segments can be found on objects around you.

Parallel lines are two lines that will not meet no matter how long you draw them.
The distance between them is always the same.

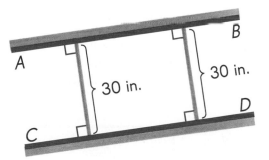

AB and *CD* are a pair of parallel line segments.

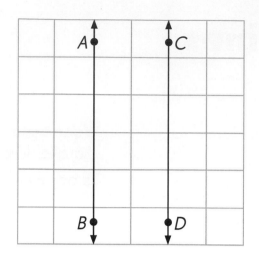

Line *AB* and line *CD* are parallel.
Line *AB* **is parallel to** line *CD*.

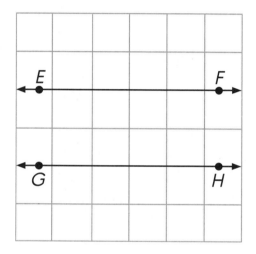

Line *EF* and line *GH* are parallel.
Line *EF* is parallel to line *GH*.

Look at the lines drawn on the grid.

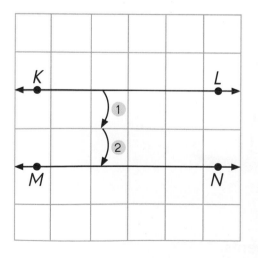

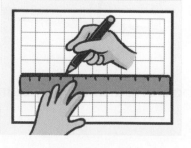

Line *KL* and line *MN* are parallel. You can use a ruler and draw them like this from left to right.

What is the distance between the lines?

Count the number of square units between the lines.

Line *KL* is always 2 square units from line *MN*.
So, line *KL* is parallel to line *MN*.

Line *OP* is always 2 square units from line *QR*.
So, line *OP* is parallel to line *QR*.

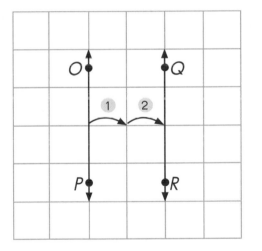

Line *OP* and line *QR* are parallel. You can use a ruler and draw them straight down like this.

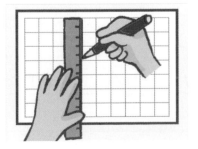

Continued on next page

Are line *ST* and line *UV* always the same distance apart?

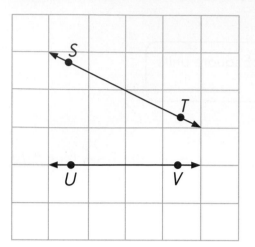

No.

Point *S* is 3 square units away from point *U*.

Point *T* is 1 square unit away from point *V*.

The distance between the lines is not the same.

Line *ST* and line *UV* are not parallel to each other.

Are line *PQ* and line *MN* parallel?

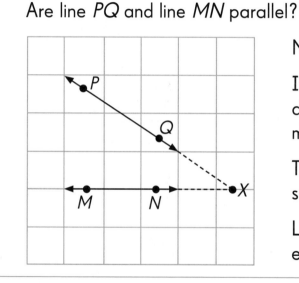

No.

If you make line *PQ* and line *MN* longer by drawing the dotted lines as shown, they will meet at point *X*.

The distance between the lines is not the same.

Line *PQ* and line *MN* are not parallel to each other.

Guided Practice

Find parallel lines.

Which pairs of lines are parallel?

1

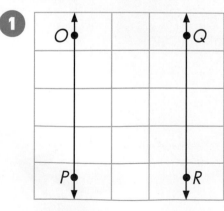

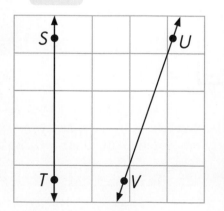

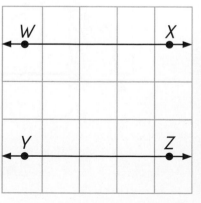

2 Name the pairs of parallel line segments in each figure.

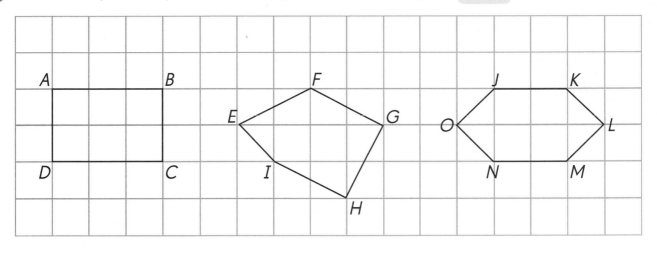

3 Find pairs of parallel line segments on each object.

Copy the parallel lines onto grid paper.

4

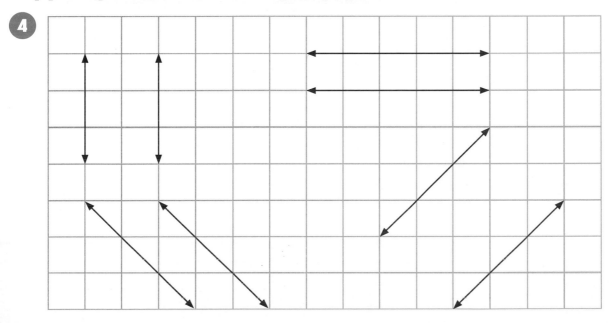

Hands-On Activity

STEP 1 Look around your classroom and school.

STEP 2 Find items with parallel line segments and items with no parallel line segments.

STEP 3 Record the items and places in charts.

With Parallel Line Segments	Places Where I Found the Items
benches	hallways

With No Parallel Line Segments	Places Where I Found the Items
branches of plants	schoolyard

STEP 4 Compare your items with those found by other groups.

Let's Practice

Tell whether the lines are parallel.

1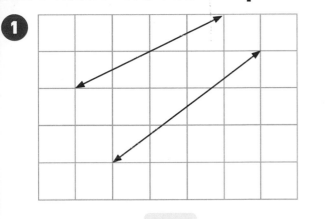

2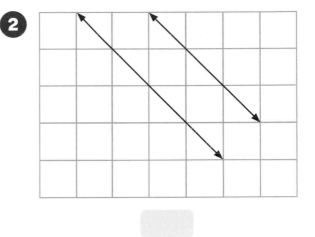

Identify the parallel line segments in each figure.

3

A   B

C   D

4

P

T   Q

S   R

Find two pairs of parallel line segments on each object.

5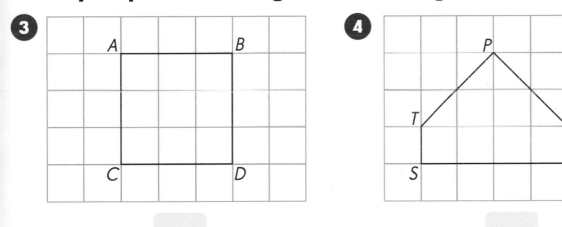

B
A   C
          D

          E
G   F

6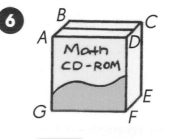

B   C
A   D
Math
CD-ROM

G   E
          F

ON YOUR OWN

Go to Workbook B:
Practice 4, pages 189–194

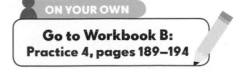

PROBLEM SOLVING

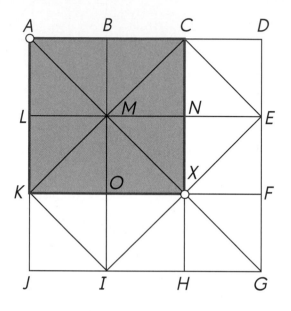

1 Name three pairs of perpendicular line segments in the diagram.

2 You are standing at *X*. You want to go to *A*. What is the shortest path to *A*?

3 Are there any line segments perpendicular to the shortest path? Name two.

4 Find three paths from *X* to *A* that are within the shaded area. Each path must be made up of one or more pairs of perpendicular line segments.

Use five craft sticks to make a figure that has four pairs of parallel line segments and four pairs of perpendicular line segments.

5 What shape do you get?

PROBLEM SOLVING

Cut out the seven pieces of a tangram.

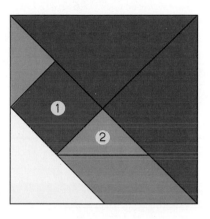

A tangram is a Chinese puzzle of seven pieces which can be pieced into a square.

6 The shape below is made up of two tangram pieces. It has two right angles, one angle smaller than a right angle, and one angle greater than a right angle.

Now, form two more shapes which have two right angles, one angle smaller than a right angle, and one angle greater than a right angle each, using

a three tangram pieces

b four tangram pieces

7 Arrange six pieces of the tangram to form a shape which has three right angles and two angles greater than a right angle.

ON YOUR OWN

Go to Workbook B:
Put on Your Thinking Cap!, pages 195–198

Chapter Wrap Up

Study Guide
You have learned...

Angles and Lines

Point, Line, Line Segment

A point is an exact location in space.
Point *A* (*A*)

•
A

A line is a straight path that goes on without ends in both directions.
Line *AB* or line *BA*

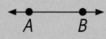

A line segment is part of a line. It has two endpoints.
Line segment *AB* or line segment *BA*

Angles

An angle is formed by two line segments with the same endpoint.

A folded piece of paper can be used to check for right angles.

It can also be used to check if other angles are greater than or less than a right angle.

less than   greater than
right angle   right angle

BIG IDEA

▶ Angles and lines can be found all around us. These can be described with special names.

Perpendicular Lines and Segments

Perpendicular lines and line segments meet at right angles.

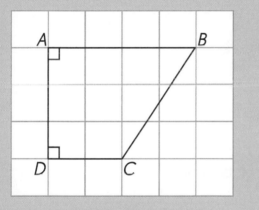

Perpendicular line segments:
Line segments *AB* and *AD*
Line segments *AD* and *DC*

Parallel Lines and Segments

Parallel lines and line segments will not meet no matter how long you draw them. The distance between them is always the same.

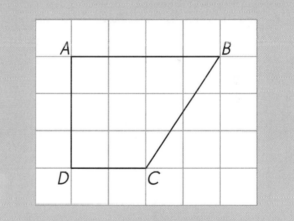

Parallel line segments:
Line segments *AB* and *DC*

Chapter Review/Test

Vocabulary
Choose the correct word.

line
line segment
right angle
perpendicular lines
parallel lines

1 A _____ has no endpoints.

2 _____ do not meet no matter how long you draw them.

3 A _____ is formed when two line segments meet at a point and are perpendicular to each other.

4 Two lines that meet at a right angle are called _____ .

Concepts and Skills

5 Which of these form an angle? _____

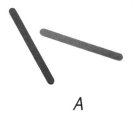

A

B

Find the number of angles in each object or shape.

6

_____

7

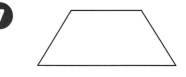

_____

8 Which angles are the same size as right angles? Angles _____

A

B

C

D

9 Find the number of sides and angles of the shape.

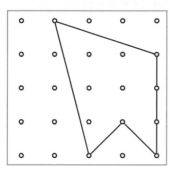

[____] sides [____] angles

10 Identify the perpendicular line segments. [____]

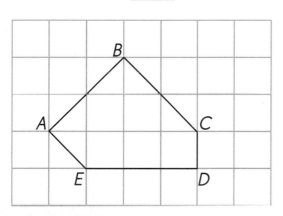

11 Identify the parallel line segments. [____]

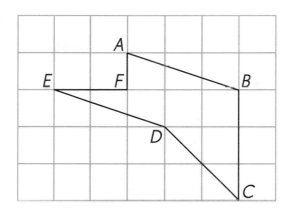

Problem Solving

12 You are walking parallel to Argos Road. On which road are you walking? [____]

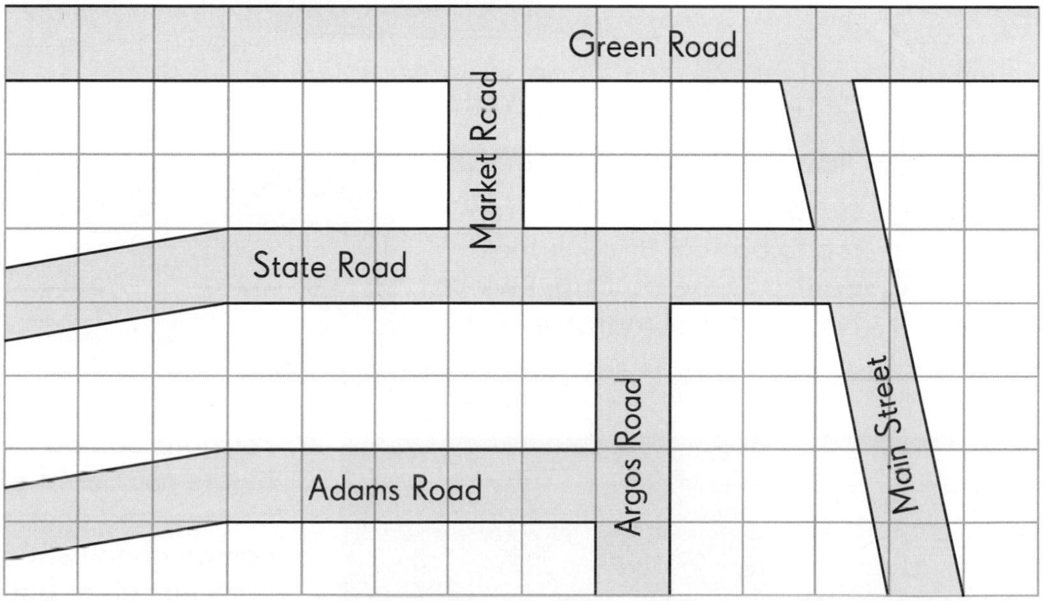

Green Road

Market Road

State Road

Argos Road

Main Street

Adams Road

18

Two-Dimensional Shapes

This is the White House. There are many plane shapes in this building.

Yes, I can see rectangles and triangles.

If I draw a straight line from top to bottom through the center of the building, I will get two parts that match exactly.

Lessons

BIG IDEA

▶ Polygons can be classified by the number of sides, corners, and angles. Figures can be congruent or symmetrical, or both.

Recall Prior Knowledge

Counting the number of sides, corners, and angles of plane shapes

Plane Shape	Number of Sides	Number of Corners	Number of Angles
circle	0	0	0
triangle	3	3	3
square	4	4	4
rectangle	4	4	4
trapezoid	4	4	4
hexagon	6	6	6

Combining plane shapes to form other plane shapes

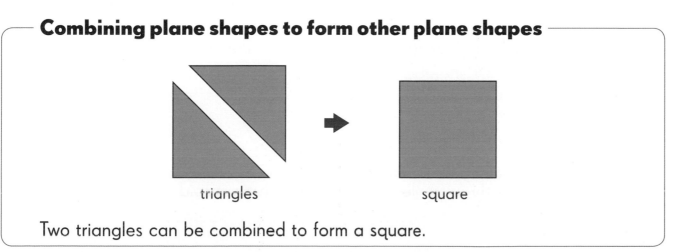

triangles → square

Two triangles can be combined to form a square.

Separating plane shapes into smaller plane shapes

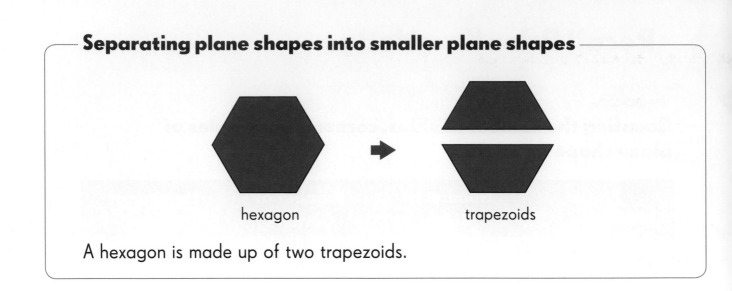

hexagon   trapezoids

A hexagon is made up of two trapezoids.

Drawing shapes on dot paper and grid paper

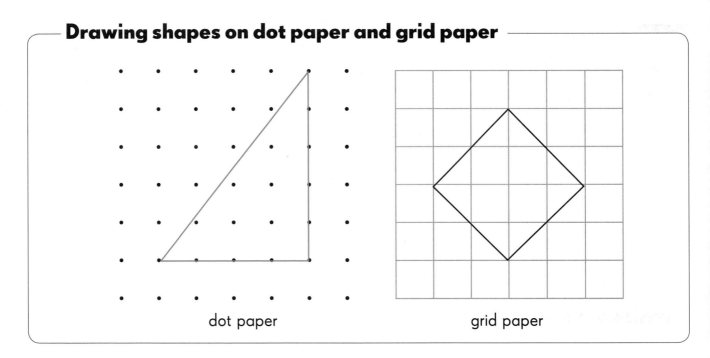

dot paper   grid paper

Identifying angles in shapes

In a shape, each angle is formed by two sides meeting at a point.

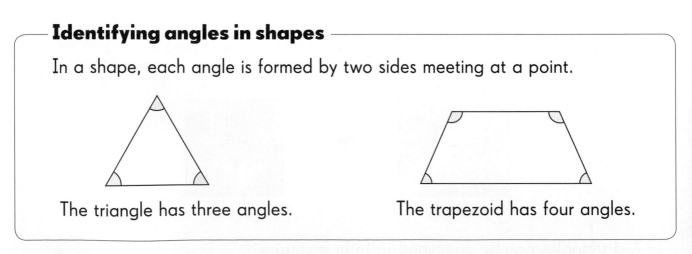

The triangle has three angles.   The trapezoid has four angles.

✔ Quick Check

What shape am I?

1. I have 3 sides and 3 corners. ______
2. I have 4 sides and 4 corners. ______

Which shape do you get when you combine two **?**

3.

A B C

Which sets of shapes make up **?**

4. 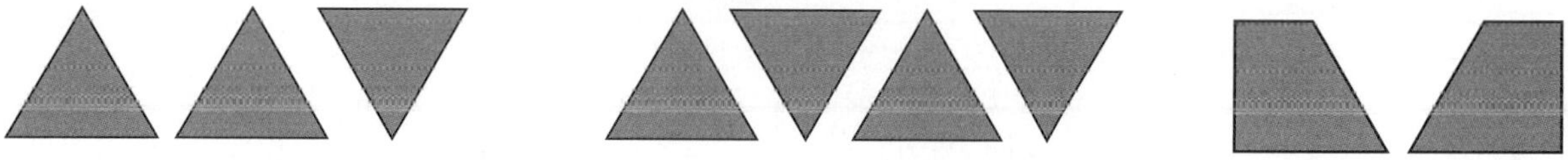

A B C

Combine the small triangles to make two different plane shapes.
Name the shapes.
State the number of triangles used.

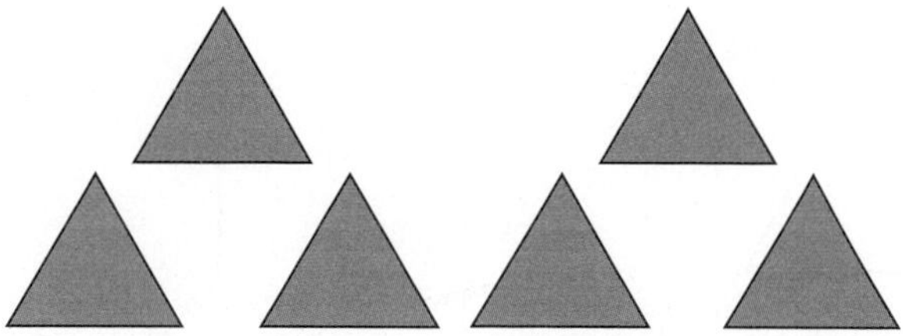

triangles

5. Name: ______

   Number: ______

6. Name: ______

   Number: ______

Separate the rectangle into smaller plane shapes in two different ways. Name the shapes. State the number of each shape formed.

Rectangle

7 Name:

Number:

8 Name:

Number:

Copy each shape onto dot paper or grid paper. Give the name of each shape drawn.

9

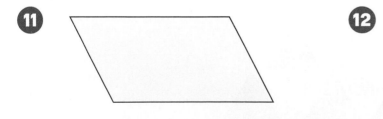

10

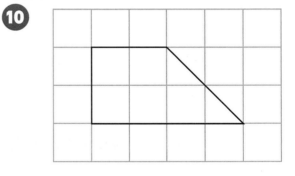

Identify all the angles in each shape.

11

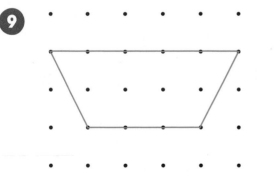

12

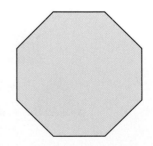

Lesson 18.1 Classifying Polygons

Lesson Objectives

- Identify open and closed figures.
- Identify special polygons and quadrilaterals.
- Classify polygons by the number of sides, vertices, and angles.
- Classify quadrilaterals by parallel sides, length of sides, and angles.
- Combine and separate polygons to make other polygons.

Vocabulary

plane figure	vertex	parallelogram
open figure	quadrilateral	pentagon
closed figure	parallel	octagon
polygon	rhombus	tangram

Learn **Identify open and closed plane figures.**

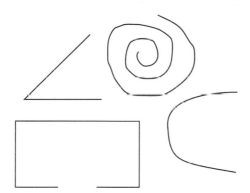

Group A

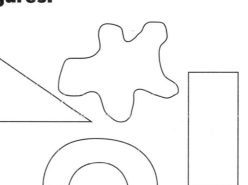

Group B

Compare groups A and B. How are they different?
The figures in Group A do not start and end at the same point.
They are **open plane figures**.

The figures in Group B start and end at the same point.
They are **closed plane figures**.

Plane figures are flat figures. They have length and width.
They may be open or closed figures.

Guided Practice

Tell whether each plane figure is closed or open.

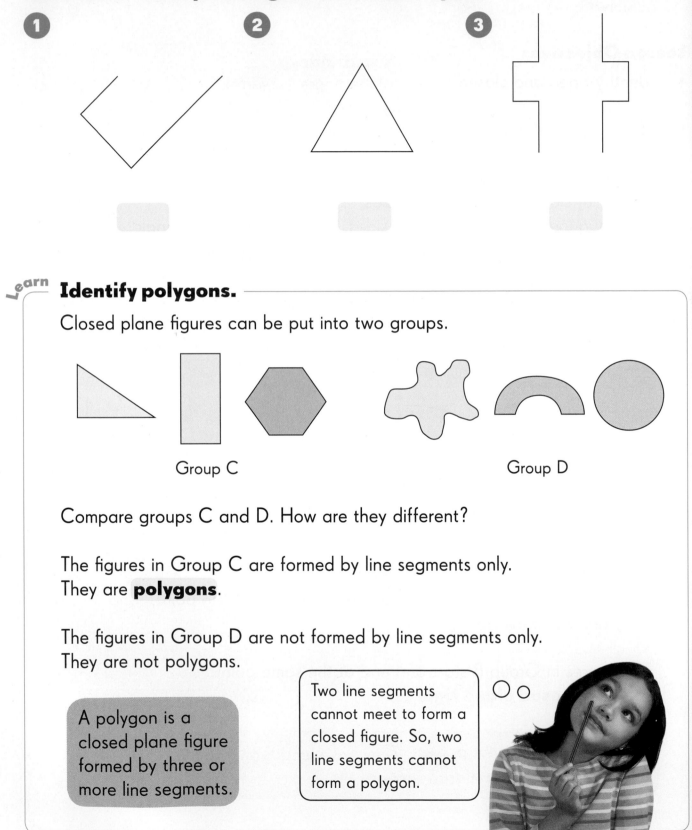

1

2

3

Learn Identify polygons.

Closed plane figures can be put into two groups.

Group C

Group D

Compare groups C and D. How are they different?

The figures in Group C are formed by line segments only.
They are **polygons**.

The figures in Group D are not formed by line segments only.
They are not polygons.

Two line segments
cannot meet to form a
closed figure. So, two
line segments cannot
form a polygon.

A polygon is a
closed plane figure
formed by three or
more line segments.

Look at the figures.
Then answer the question.

4. Which figures are polygons? Figures ⬜

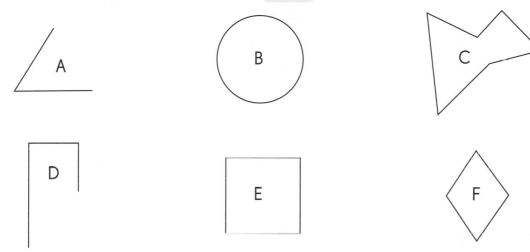

A

B

C

D

E

F

🔍 Let's Explore!

Use craft sticks. Make the following figures.

1. Use two sticks and form a figure.

2. Use 5 sticks and form two figures.
   One is closed and the other open.

3. Use 6 sticks and form two figures.
   One is closed and the other open.

Recall what open and closed figures, and polygons are.

Which figures are polygons?
Draw them on a piece of paper.

Which figures are not polygons?
Draw them on a piece of paper.

Identify special polygons and their names.

Polygons can be classified according to the number of sides they have.
These are some polygons and their names.

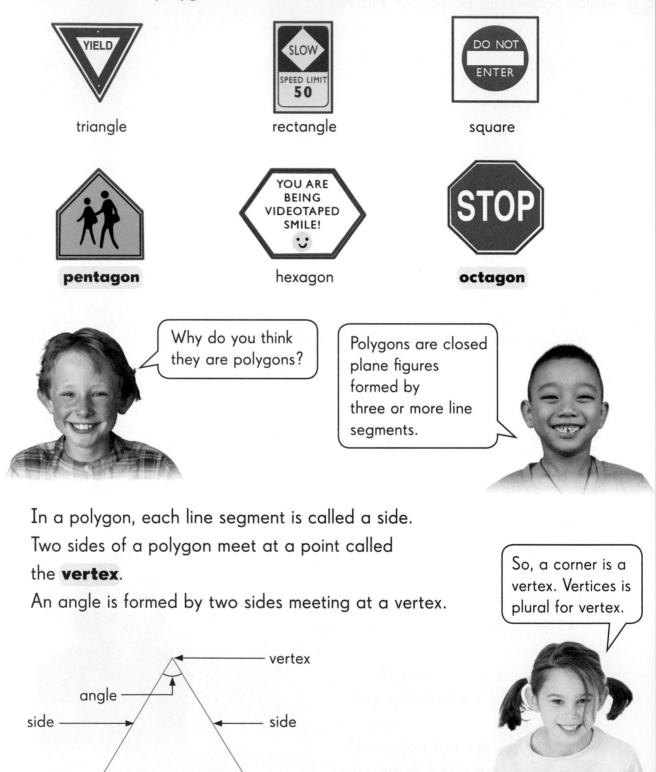

triangle

rectangle

square

pentagon

hexagon

octagon

Why do you think they are polygons?

Polygons are closed plane figures formed by three or more line segments.

In a polygon, each line segment is called a side.
Two sides of a polygon meet at a point called
the **vertex**.
An angle is formed by two sides meeting at a vertex.

So, a corner is a vertex. Vertices is plural for vertex.

vertex

angle

side

side

triangle

Guided Practice

Identify the angles. Label the parts of this pentagon.

5

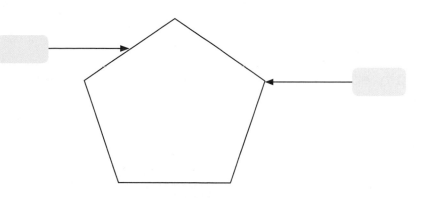

pentagon

Complete.

6 Count the number of vertices.

7 Count the number of sides.

8 Count the number of angles.

Choose true or false for each statement.

9 An octagon has eight sides and eight angles.

10 A hexagon has seven vertices and six sides.

11 A square and a rectangle have four vertices and four angles each.

12 All polygons have four sides.

Hands-On Activity

WORK IN PAIRS

Materials:
• polygons

1. Identify each polygon and find the number of sides, angles, and vertices.

Record the information in the table.

Polygons	Number of Sides	Number of Angles	Number of Vertices

What can you say about the number of sides, angles, and vertices of a polygon?

2. Walk around your school or classroom.
   Look for objects that have the shapes listed in the table.

Polygons	Objects
Triangle	
Square	
Rectangle	
Pentagon	
Hexagon	
Octagon	

Identify quadrilaterals.

These are **quadrilaterals**.

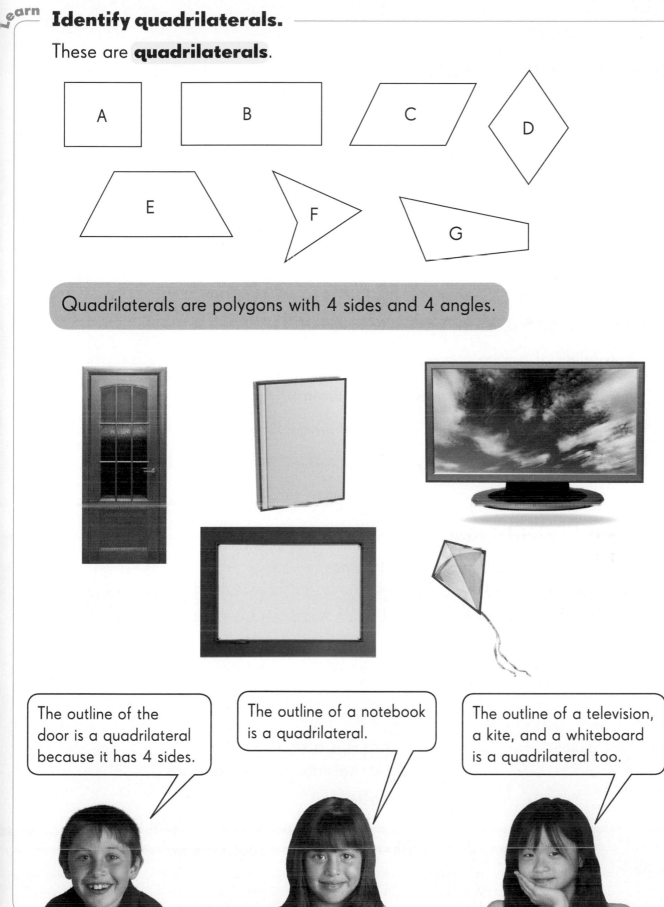

> Quadrilaterals are polygons with 4 sides and 4 angles.

The outline of the door is a quadrilateral because it has 4 sides.

The outline of a notebook is a quadrilateral.

The outline of a television, a kite, and a whiteboard is a quadrilateral too.

Guided Practice

Choose the quadrilaterals.

13

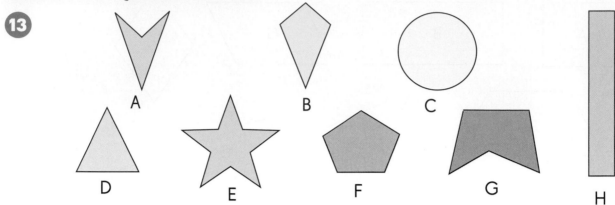

Choose true or false for each statement.

14 The outline of a ruler is a quadrilateral.

15 The outline of a bottle cap is a quadrilateral.

16 The outline of a postcard is a quadrilateral.

17 The outline of an envelope is a quadrilateral.

Learn — Identify quadrilaterals and their properties.

Some quadrilaterals have special names.
They are classified by

a pairs of sides that are parallel.

b sides that are of equal length.

c angles that are right angles.

Figure A is a square.
Opposite sides of a square are **parallel**.
All sides of a square are of equal length.
All 4 angles of a square are right angles.

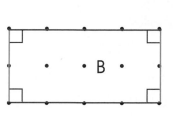

Figure B is a rectangle.
Opposite sides of a rectangle are parallel.
Only the opposite sides of a rectangle need to be of equal length.
All 4 angles of a rectangle are right angles.

Figure C is a **parallelogram**.
Opposite sides of a parallelogram are parallel.
Only the opposite sides of a parallelogram need to be of equal length.
There are 4 angles in a parallelogram.

Figure D is a **rhombus**.
Opposite sides of a rhombus are parallel.
All sides of a rhombus are of equal length.
There are 4 angles in a rhombus.

Both figures E and F are trapezoids.
Only one pair of opposite sides are parallel.
There are 4 angles in a trapezoid.
A trapezoid can have 2 right angles as in figure F.

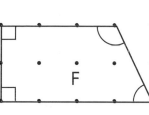

Squares, rectangles, parallelograms, and rhombuses have two pairs of opposite sides that are parallel.

I can think of the rhombus as a parallelogram with four sides that are of equal length.

 **Hands-On Activity**

Materials:
- a geoboard
- rubber bands
- square grid paper

WORK IN PAIRS

Make the five quadrilaterals with special names on the geoboard.
Then draw them on a square grid paper and identify them.
Partners can take turns making a quadrilateral.
Then draw and name it.

Example:

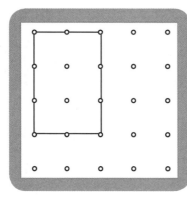

Discuss how the quadrilaterals are the same and how they are different.

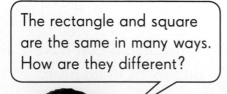 The rectangle and square are the same in many ways. How are they different?

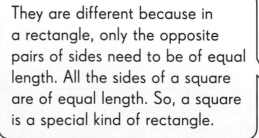 They are different because in a rectangle, only the opposite pairs of sides need to be of equal length. All the sides of a square are of equal length. So, a square is a special kind of rectangle.

Guided Practice

Complete.

18 Identify each rhombus. Figure [   ]

19 Identify each trapezoid. Figures [   ]

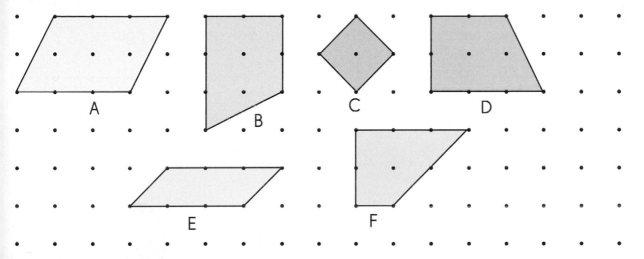

Fill in the blanks.

20 A rectangle has [   ] pairs of parallel sides, [   ] pairs of sides that are of equal length, and [   ] right angles.

21 A rhombus has [   ] pairs of parallel sides, [   ] sides that are of equal length, and [   ] angles.

22 A trapezoid has [   ] pair of parallel sides and [   ] angles. Sometimes, a trapezoid has [   ] right angles.

23 A parallelogram has [   ] pairs of parallel sides, [   ] pairs of sides that are of equal length, and [   ] angles.

Choose true or false for each statement. Explain your thinking.

24 A parallelogram is not a square.
[   ]

25 A square is a special type of rectangle. [   ]

26 A rectangle may or may not be a square. [   ]

27 A trapezoid is a parallelogram. [   ]

28 A rectangle has four right angles.

29 A rhombus has four equal sides.

30 A parallelogram has only one set of parallel sides.

 Learn

Combine and break apart polygons.

Combine the polygons on the left to make other polygons and figures.

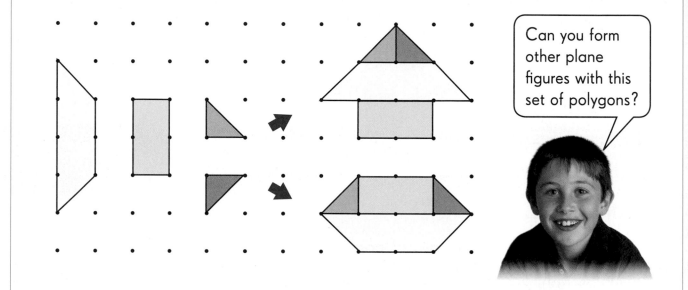

Can you form other plane figures with this set of polygons?

Break apart the polygon on the left. Use the pieces to make different smaller polygons.

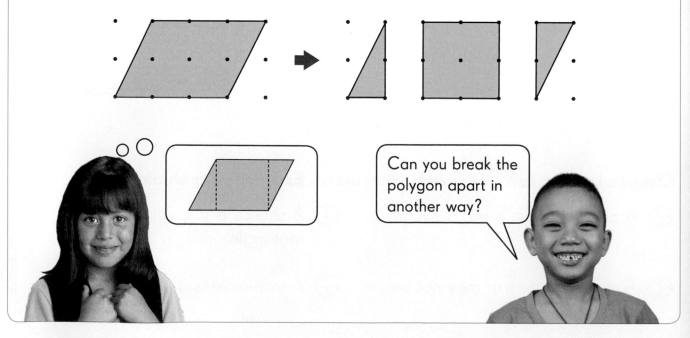

Can you break the polygon apart in another way?

Hands-On Activity

Materials:
- a geoboard
- rubber bands

WORK IN PAIRS

1. Use a geoboard and rubber bands to make shapes.
   Use two or more of these quadrilaterals:
   square, rectangle, parallelogram, rhombus, and trapezoid.
   List the polygons used to make your figure.

Example:

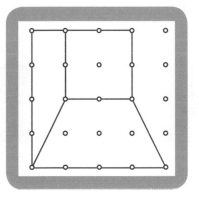

Polygons used: square and trapezoid

2. This is a **tangram**.
   It is made up of 7 polygons that can be put together to make a square.

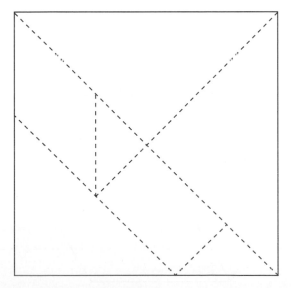

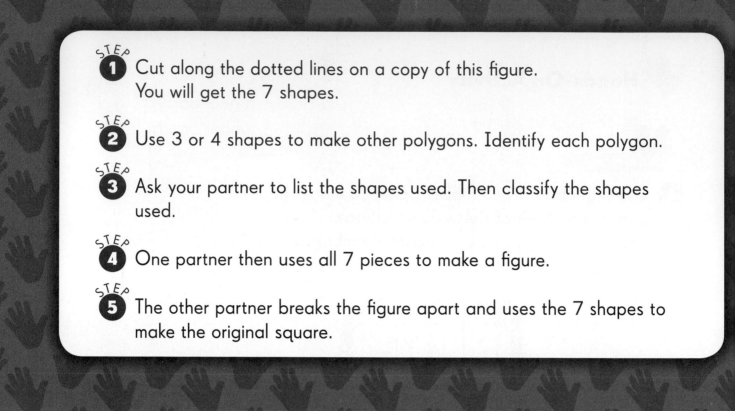

STEP 1 Cut along the dotted lines on a copy of this figure. You will get the 7 shapes.

STEP 2 Use 3 or 4 shapes to make other polygons. Identify each polygon.

STEP 3 Ask your partner to list the shapes used. Then classify the shapes used.

STEP 4 One partner then uses all 7 pieces to make a figure.

STEP 5 The other partner breaks the figure apart and uses the 7 shapes to make the original square.

Guided Practice

Trace and cut out the polygons to make other polygons. You may use more than one of each type of polygon.

31

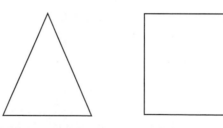

32 **Find how many polygons are in the figure. List them.**

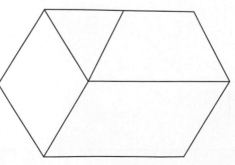

Let's Practice

Complete the table. Choose yes or no.

1

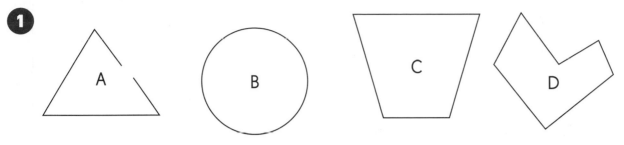

Property	Figure A	Figure B	Figure C	Figure D
It is a closed figure.				
There are 3 or more line segments.				

Fill in the blanks.

2 Figures [ ] and [ ] are polygons.

Complete the table.

3

Figures	Name	Number of Sides	Number of Angles	Number of Vertices
			3	3
		4		
	Pentagon		5	5
		6	6	
				8

Solve.

4 I am a polygon. I have 1 more vertex than a square has. What am I?

5 Draw one polygon in the shape below to make it an octagon.

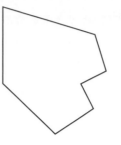

6 Draw dotted lines to divide the figure into smaller polygons.
Then list the polygons.

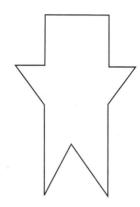

Choose the answer.

7 A polygon with four sides is a quadrilateral / triangle / hexagon .

8 A quadrilateral with four sides of equal length and four right angles is a rectangle / square / rhombus .

9 A rectangle / square/ rhombus is a quadrilateral that has two pairs of parallel sides, two pairs of sides that are of equal length and four right angles.

10 A parallelogram / trapezoid / triangle is a quadrilateral with two pairs of sides that are also of equal length.

11 A parallelogram with all sides of equal length is a rhombus / trapezoid /pentagon.

12 A rhombus / trapezoid / square is a quadrilateral with two sides that are parallel but not of equal length.

ON YOUR OWN

Go to Workbook B:
Practice 1, pages 199–206

1 Explain why these figures are not polygons.

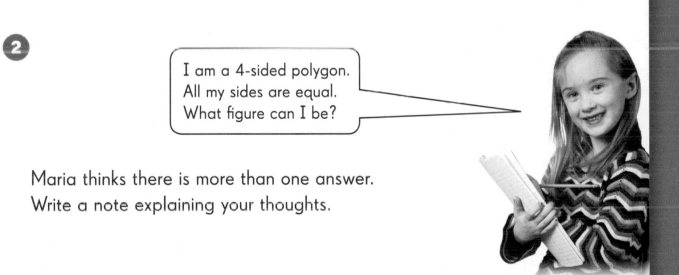

A

B

2

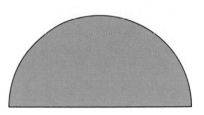

I am a 4-sided polygon.
All my sides are equal.
What figure can I be?

Maria thinks there is more than one answer.
Write a note explaining your thoughts.

Lesson 18.2 Congruent Figures

Lesson Objectives

- Identify a slide, flip, and turn.
- Slide, flip, and turn shapes to make congruent figures.
- Identify congruent figures.

Vocabulary

slide

flip

turn

rotate

congruent

Learn

Plane figures can slide, flip, and turn.

You can move figures in different ways.

Imagine pushing this figure from here to there. You slide it along.

The figure of the dog has been slid along from left to right.

To **slide** a figure is to move it along in any direction.

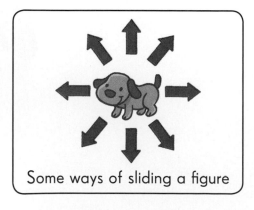

Some ways of sliding a figure

When I hold the letter D in front of a mirror, the image in the mirror is like the back side of the letter D.

front side   back side

back side

After flip

Before flip

Before flip   After flip

front side

The letter D has been flipped over a line.
To **flip** a figure is to turn it front to back over a line.

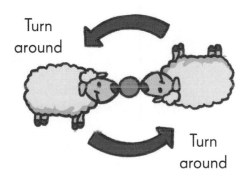

Turn around

Turn around

The figure of the sheep has been turned through a half turn.
To **turn** a figure is to **rotate** it about a point.

Flips, slides, and turns are movements that change the position of figures.

But the shape and size of the figures remain unchanged.

Two figures that have the same shape and size are **congruent**.

Guided Practice

Trace one of the two figures. Cut it out and place it on top of the other figure. Decide which sets of shapes have been slid along in any direction and are congruent.

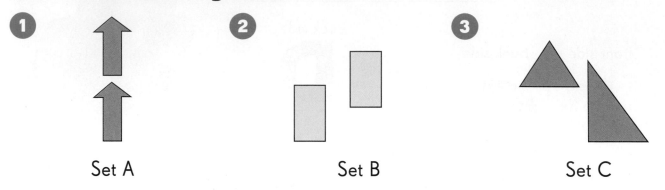

1

Set A

2

Set B

3

Set C

Trace one of the two figures. Cut it out and place it on top of the other figure. Decide which sets of shapes are flipped and congruent.

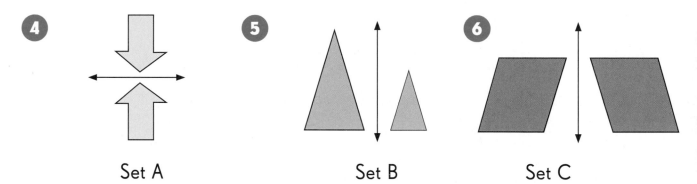

4

Set A

5

Set B

6

Set C

Trace one of the two figures. Cut it out and place it on top of the other figure. Decide which sets of shapes have been turned about a point and are congruent.

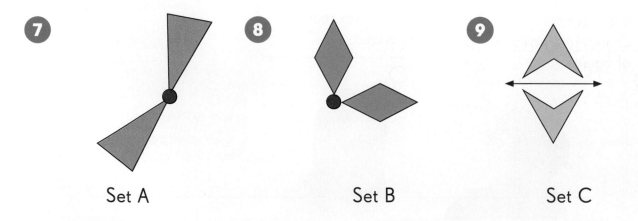

7

Set A

8

Set B

9

Set C

Identify pairs of congruent figures.

Congruent figures have the same shape and size.

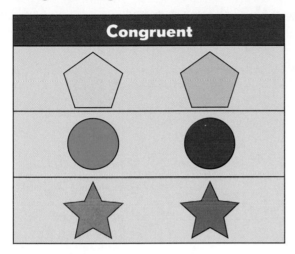

Congruent

How can you be sure that these figures are congruent figures?

Put one on top of the other to see if they fit exactly.

Can two figures appear in different positions and be congruent?

Yes, if they are the same shape and size. You could show it by placing one figure on top of the other figure.

Not Congruent			
Reason	• Same shape • Not the same size	• Not the same shape • Not the same size	• Not the same shape

Guided Practice

Trace one of the two figures. Cut it out and place it on top of the other figure. Decide whether the shapes are congruent. Choose yes or no.

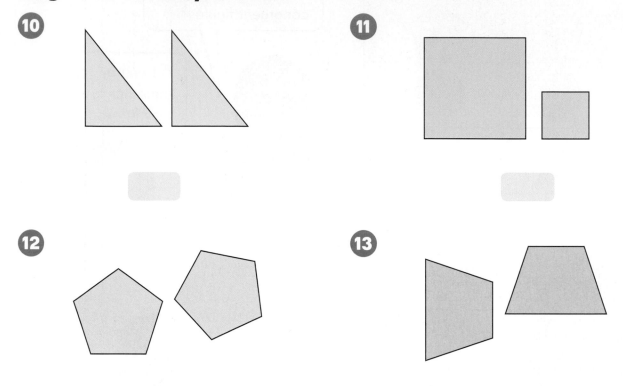

10

11

12

13

Complete. Use dot paper or grid paper to help you.

14 Draw two congruent hexagons. Draw a third hexagon that is not congruent.

A hexagon is a six-sided polygon.

15 Draw two congruent shapes. Then draw a third shape having the same shape but not congruent.

16 Draw two congruent parallelograms. Then draw a third parallelogram that is not congruent.

Look at the U.S. flag.

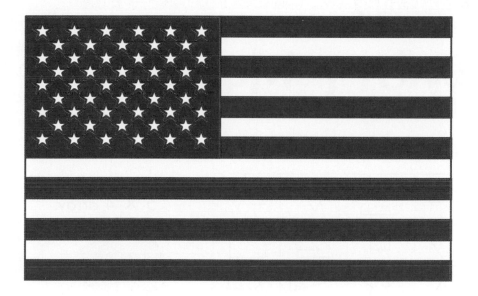

17 How many stars are there? [   ]

18 Are all the stars congruent? [   ]

19 Identify the stripes that are congruent. [   ]

Hands-On Activity

Materials:
- a geoboard
- rubber bands

Use a geoboard and some rubber bands.

1 Make two figures that are congruent.
Explain to your partner why the figures are congruent.

2 Make two figures that are not congruent.
Explain to your partner why the figures are not congruent.

 WORKING TOGETHER **Game**

Memory Match!

Players: 2
Materials:
• 20 conguent shape cards.

STEP 1 Use these 20 cards.

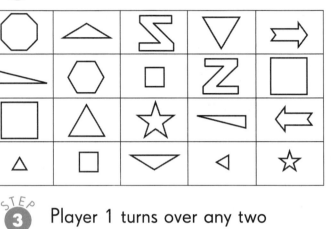

STEP 2 Mix up the cards and place them face-down in a 5 × 4 array.

STEP 3 Player 1 turns over any two cards. If they are congruent, the player keeps the cards and picks another two cards. If the cards are not congruent, the player turns the cards over in their same position. The next player takes a turn.

STEP 4 Repeat Step 3 until all matches are made.

The player with the most matches wins!

Let's Practice

Fill in the blanks.

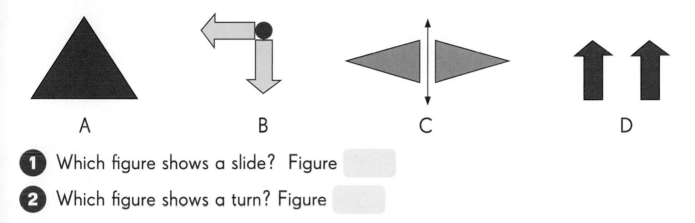

A   B   C   D

1 Which figure shows a slide? Figure [   ]

2 Which figure shows a turn? Figure [   ]

Choose the answer.

3 This is a pattern. The triangles going from left to right is an illustration of a slide/flip/turn.

Choose the figure that shows a turn.

4

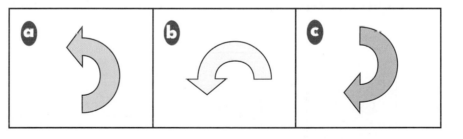

5

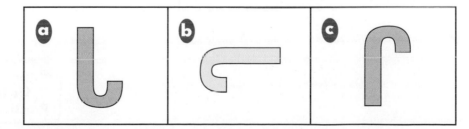

Trace the first figure A. Cut it out and place it on top of figure B.

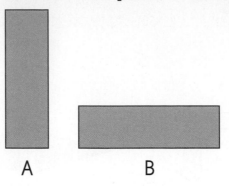

A   B

6 **Choose true or false. Use your figures to help you.**

Statements	True	False
The two rectangles are congruent.		
Rectangle A was flipped to make rectangle B.		
Rectangle A was slid to make rectangle B.		
Rectangle was turned to make rectangle B.		

Trace the first figure. Cut it out and place it on top of the other figures. Then choose a figure which is congruent.

5

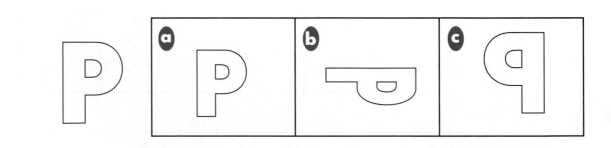

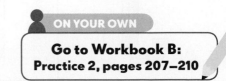

ON YOUR OWN

Go to Workbook B:
Practice 2, pages 207–210

1. Rachel drew a pentagon with 5-inch sides. Tom drew an octagon with 5-inch sides. Tom says his figure is congruent to Rachel's.

   Is Tom correct? Explain why or why not.

   > Two figures are congruent when they have the same shape and size.

2. Kelly and Kelvin each drew a trapezoid. Kelly says that her figure is congruent to Kevin's. Explain how you will check whether the two figures are congruent.

18.3 Symmetry

Vocabulary
symmetry
line of symmetry

Lesson Objectives

- Identify symmetric figures.
- Use folding to find a line of symmetry.

Learn **Recognizing symmetric figures.**

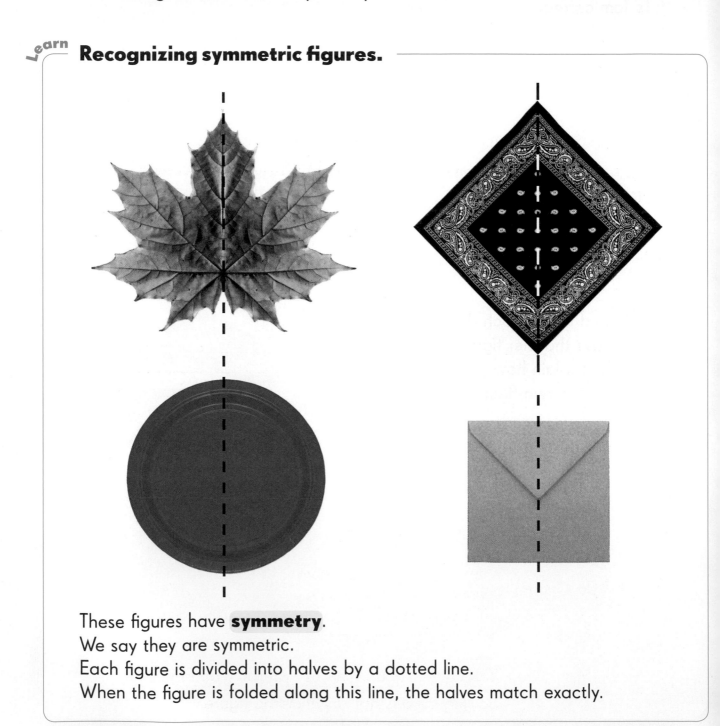

These figures have **symmetry**.
We say they are symmetric.
Each figure is divided into halves by a dotted line.
When the figure is folded along this line, the halves match exactly.

Use folding to find a line of symmetry to identify symmetric figures.

Fold Figure A along the dotted line.

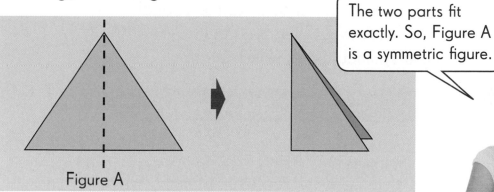

The two parts fit exactly. So, Figure A is a symmetric figure.

Figure A

The figure is divided into congruent halves by the dotted line.
The congruent halves fit exactly when folded along the dotted line. The dotted line is called a **line of symmetry**.

Fold Figure B along the dotted line as shown.

Figure B

The two parts do not fit exactly.

The dotted line is **not** a line of symmetry.

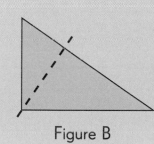

Trace Figure B and cut it out. Then fold it in different ways to find if it still has a line of symmetry.

You cannot find a line of symmetry on Figure B.
So, Figure B is not a symmetric figure.

 **Hands-On Activity**

Use the drawing tool in your computer to write the capital letters of the alphabet from A to Z. Then print them. Decide which letters are symmetric and which are not.

Symmetric	Not Symmetric
X	R

Compare your answers with those of your friends.

Compare your answers with those of your friends.

Guided Practice

Choose the symmetric figures. Figures [ ]

1

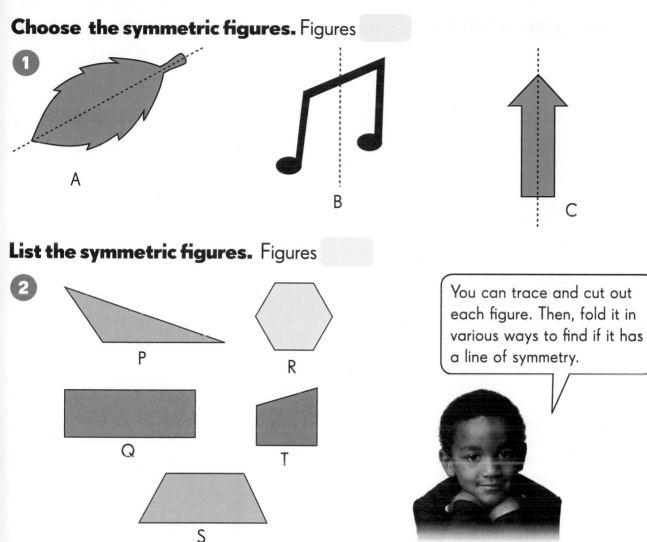

A

B

C

List the symmetric figures. Figures [ ]

2

P

R

Q

T

S

> You can trace and cut out each figure. Then, fold it in various ways to find if it has a line of symmetry.

Decide which of the dotted lines are lines of symmetry.

3

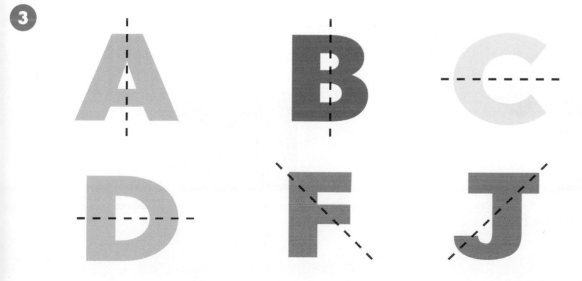

A B C

D F J

Complete.

 Find the symmetric figures. Figures [   ]

Figure A

Figure B

Figure C

Figure D

Figure E

Figure F

Rita drew this picture below using the drawing tools in her computer.

Name the symmetric figures.

2

3 Draw a picture showing at least 5 symmetric figures.

4 Make a list of objects around you that are symmetric.

A leaf, a kite, a scarf, and an envelope are some objects that might be symmetric.

ON YOUR OWN

Go to Workbook B:
Practice 3, pages 211–212

The letters P and Q are not symmetric figures.

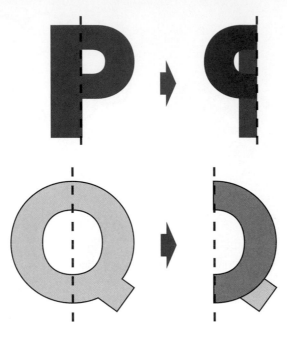

1. Explain why are these not symmetric figures.

First, recall what makes a symmetric figure. Then, check for symmetry in a figure by identifying a line of symmetry.

2. How would you check for symmetry in a figure?

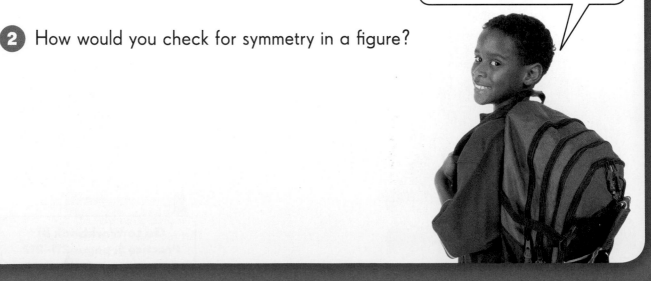

Put On Your Thinking Cap!

PROBLEM SOLVING

How many kinds of triangles can you find?

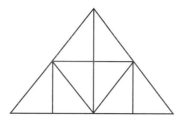

Use square grid paper to draw each triangle you find.
Then find the total number of triangles.
Are there any congruent triangles?
If yes, how many sets of congruent triangles are there?

First, find how many kinds
of triangles there are. Then,
count the total number of
each kind of triangle.

ON YOUR OWN

**Go to Workbook B:
Put on Your Thinking Cap!
pages 213–214**

Chapter Wrap Up

Study Guide
You have learned...

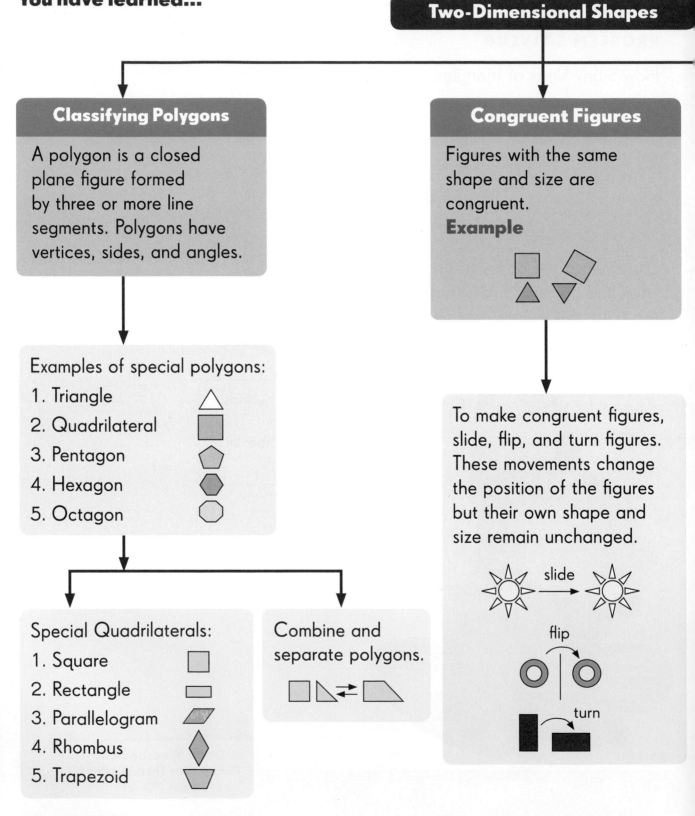

Two-Dimensional Shapes

Classifying Polygons

A polygon is a closed plane figure formed by three or more line segments. Polygons have vertices, sides, and angles.

Examples of special polygons:

1. Triangle
2. Quadrilateral
3. Pentagon
4. Hexagon
5. Octagon

Special Quadrilaterals:

1. Square
2. Rectangle
3. Parallelogram
4. Rhombus
5. Trapezoid

Combine and separate polygons.

Congruent Figures

Figures with the same shape and size are congruent.
Example

To make congruent figures, slide, flip, and turn figures. These movements change the position of the figures but their own shape and size remain unchanged.

slide

flip

turn

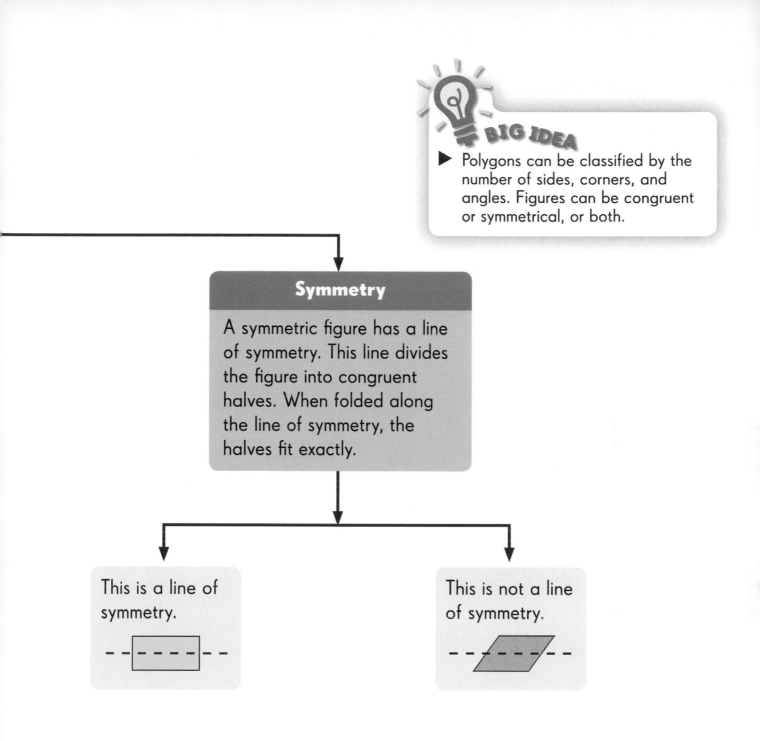

▶ Polygons can be classified by the number of sides, corners, and angles. Figures can be congruent or symmetrical, or both.

Symmetry

A symmetric figure has a line of symmetry. This line divides the figure into congruent halves. When folded along the line of symmetry, the halves fit exactly.

This is a line of symmetry.

This is not a line of symmetry.

Chapter Review/Test

Vocabulary

Complete the sentences with words from the box.

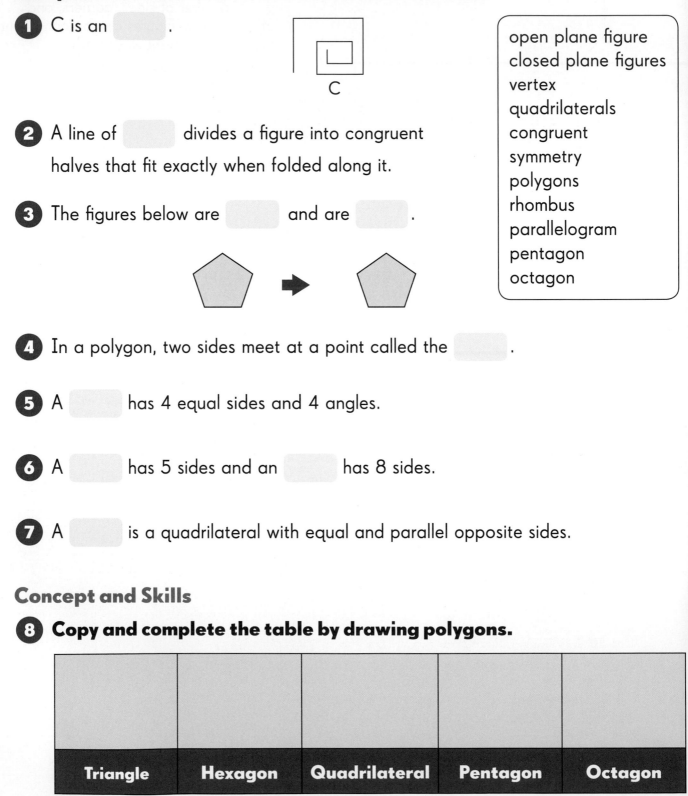

1 C is an ____ .

C

2 A line of ____ divides a figure into congruent halves that fit exactly when folded along it.

3 The figures below are ____ and are ____ .

| open plane figure |
| closed plane figures |
| vertex |
| quadrilaterals |
| congruent |
| symmetry |
| polygons |
| rhombus |
| parallelogram |
| pentagon |
| octagon |

4 In a polygon, two sides meet at a point called the ____ .

5 A ____ has 4 equal sides and 4 angles.

6 A ____ has 5 sides and an ____ has 8 sides.

7 A ____ is a quadrilateral with equal and parallel opposite sides.

Concept and Skills

8 **Copy and complete the table by drawing polygons.**

Triangle	**Hexagon**	**Quadrilateral**	**Pentagon**	**Octagon**

Identify the angles. Label the parts of the shapes.

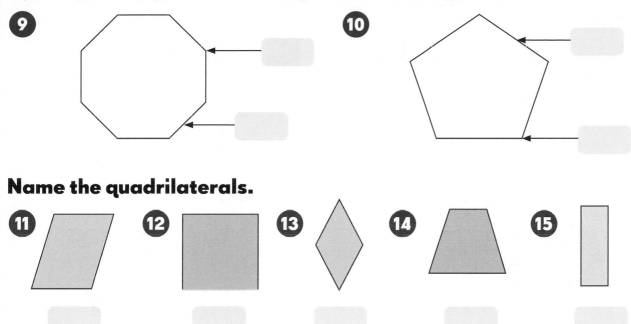

9

10

Name the quadrilaterals.

11 **12** **13** **14** **15**

Choose true or false for each statement.

16 The outline of an envelope is a quadrilateral.

17 The outline of a star is a quadrilateral.

18 A square is a special type of rectangle.

19 A rhombus has 4 sides of equal length and 4 right angles.

20 A trapezoid has 1 pair of parallel lines and 4 angles.

21 A parallelogram has 2 pairs of parallel sides that are of equal length and 4 right angles.

Are these shapes congruent? Choose yes or no.

22

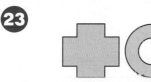

23

24

For each pair of figures, tell how the figure was moved. Choose slide, flip, or turn.

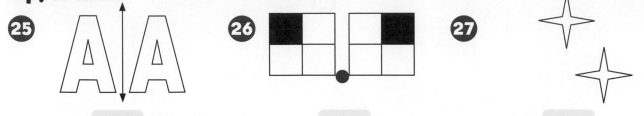

25

26

27

Are the figures symmetrical? Choose yes or no.

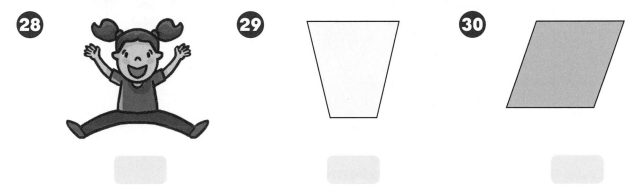

28

29

30

Decide which line is a line of symmetry. Figure

31

A

32

B

33

C

Problem Solving

34 Kyle drew 4 polygons labeled A, B, C, and D. Figure A
has twice as many sides as Figure B. Figure B has 3 vertices.
Figure C has half as many sides as Figure D. Figure D
has 8 vertices. Name each polygon Kyle draw.

Area and Perimeter

The basketball court is smaller than the soccer field. It has a smaller area.

The man drawing the line around the soccer field needs more paint.

Lessons

BIG IDEA

▶ Explore and understand units used to find perimeter and area of figures and analyze the relationship between them.

343

Recall Prior Knowledge

Using an area model to multiply

3 rows of apples

7 apples in each row

3 × 7

$$3 × 7 = 7 + 7 + 7$$
$$= 21$$

Showing a shape on a dot paper and a square grid paper

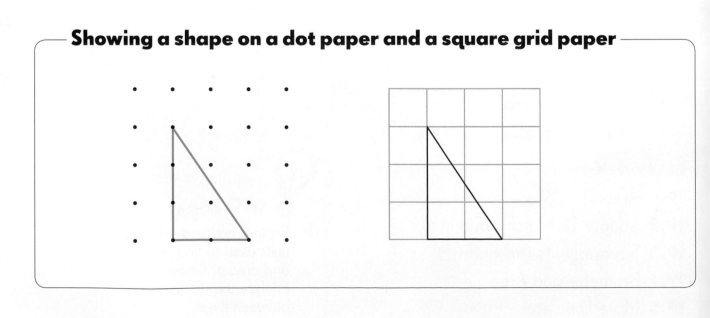

Measuring length with a ruler

Measure the lengths of the line segments and curves.

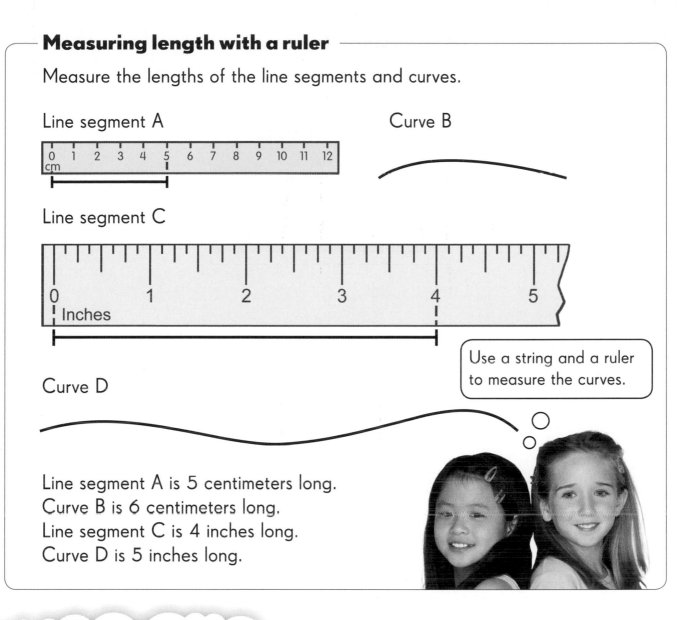

Line segment A

Curve B

Line segment C

Curve D

Use a string and a ruler to measure the curves.

Line segment A is 5 centimeters long.
Curve B is 6 centimeters long.
Line segment C is 4 inches long.
Curve D is 5 inches long.

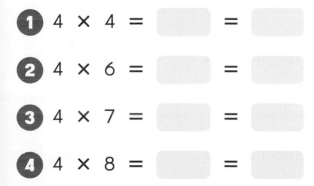

✔ Quick Check

Express each multiplication fact as an addition fact.
Then find the product.

1 4 × 4 = [　　] = [　　]

2 4 × 6 = [　　] = [　　]

3 4 × 7 = [　　] = [　　]

4 4 × 8 = [　　] = [　　]

Look at the area model and complete.

5

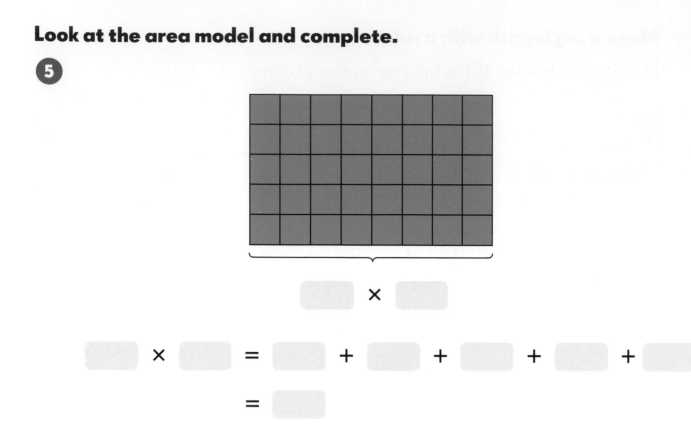

[ ] × [ ]

[ ] × [ ] = [ ] + [ ] + [ ] + [ ] + [ ]

= [ ]

Draw an identical trapezoid on square grid paper.

6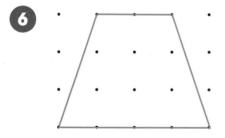

7 **Find the length of each line segment.**
Use a ruler to help you.

Line segment A

├───────────────────────┤ Line segment A is [ ] inches long.

Line segment B

├───────────────────┤ Line segment B is [ ] centimeters long.

19.1 Area

Lesson Objectives

- Understand the meaning of area.
- Use square units to find the area of plane figures made of squares and half squares.
- Compare areas of plane figures and make plane figures of the same area.

Learn

Count whole square tiles to find area.

Look at the figures.

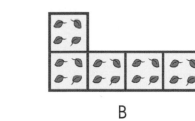

A   B   C

Count the number of square tiles in each figure.

Figure A is made up of 4 square tiles.

Figure B is made up of 5 square tiles.

Figure C is made up of 6 square tiles.

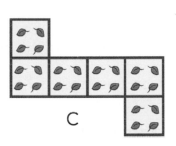

Let each square tile stand for 1 unit.
Figure B is made up of 5 square tiles. So, its area is 5 square units.
Figure C has the largest area.
Figure A has the smallest area.

The amount of surface covered by the tiles is the area of each figure.

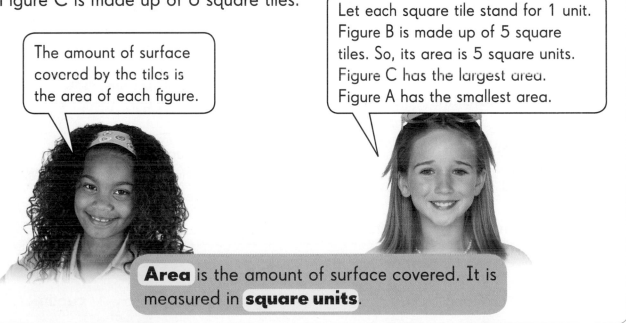

Area is the amount of surface covered. It is measured in **square units**.

Guided Practice

Look at the figures and answer the questions.

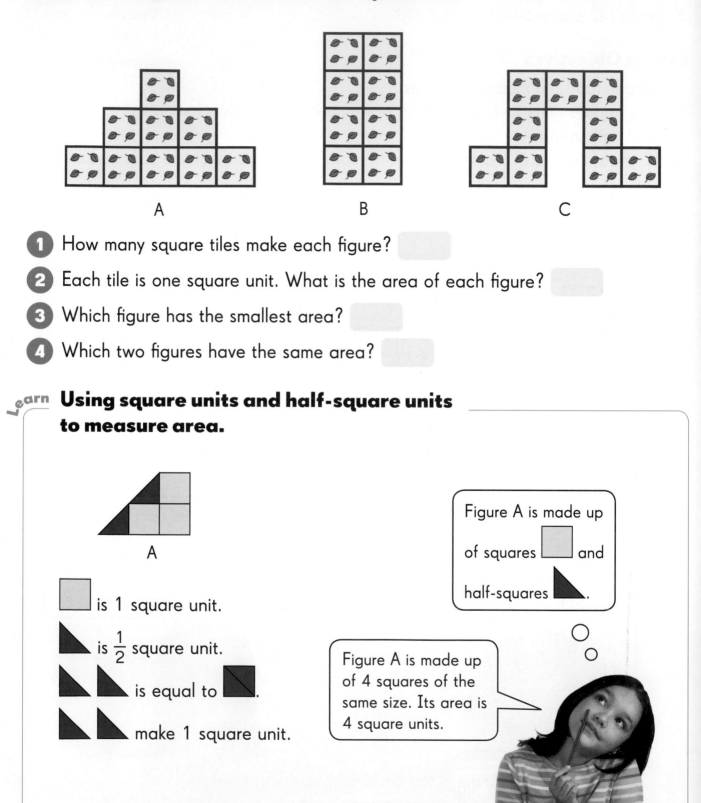

A

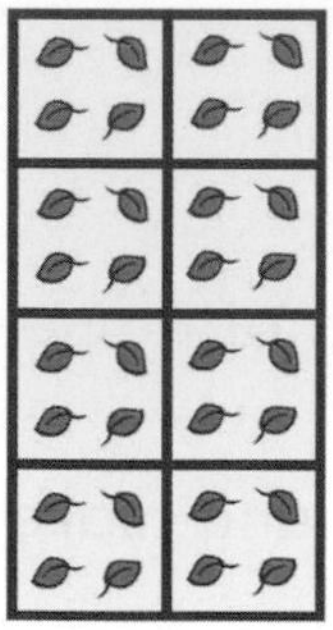

B

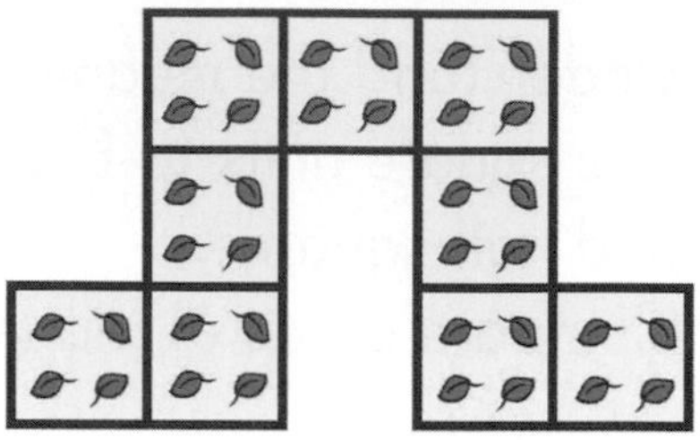

C

1. How many square tiles make each figure?
2. Each tile is one square unit. What is the area of each figure?
3. Which figure has the smallest area?
4. Which two figures have the same area?

Learn **Using square units and half-square units to measure area.**

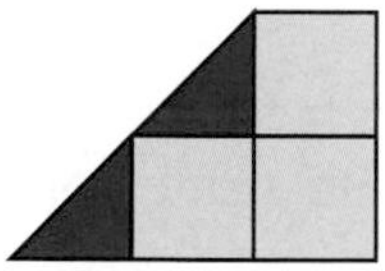

A

Figure A is made up of squares and half-squares.

■ is 1 square unit.

◣ is $\frac{1}{2}$ square unit.

◣ ◣ is equal to ■.

◣ ◣ make 1 square unit.

Figure A is made up of 4 squares of the same size. Its area is 4 square units.

Guided Practice

The figure is made up of square and half-square tiles. Express the area in square units.

5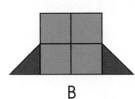

B

Each square is one square unit.

Figure B is made up of [　] squares of the same size.

The area of Figure B is [　] square units.

 **Hands-On Activity**

WORKING IN GROUPS

Work in groups of four.

Materials:
- 10 squares tiles
- 10 half-square tiles

1 Make four different figures.
Use 4 squares and 2 half-squares for each figure.
Find the area of each figure in square units.

2 Make four different figures, each with an area of 6 square units.
How many squares and half-squares did you use for each figure?

3 Make your own figure.
Then work with your group to complete the description.

The figure is made up of [　] squares and [　] half-squares.

The area of the figure is [　] square units.

Continued on next page

Materials:
• red paper
• blue paper

4 Work with a partner.
Use a few pieces of red and blue paper.
Trace the red shape and blue shape and cut them out.
Make forty pieces of the red shape and twenty pieces of
the blue shape.

red shape

blue shape

Follow the directions and complete.

STEP **1** Place red shapes over the cover of your Mathematics book.

How many did you use? [   ] red shapes.

The area of the cover of the book is about [   ] red shapes.

STEP **2** Place blue shapes over the cover of your Mathematics book.

How many did you use? [   ] blue shapes.

The area of the cover of the book is about [   ] blue shapes.

STEP **3** Discuss your findings.

Solve. The figures are made up of square and half-square tiles.

Find the area of each figure.
Give your answer in square units.

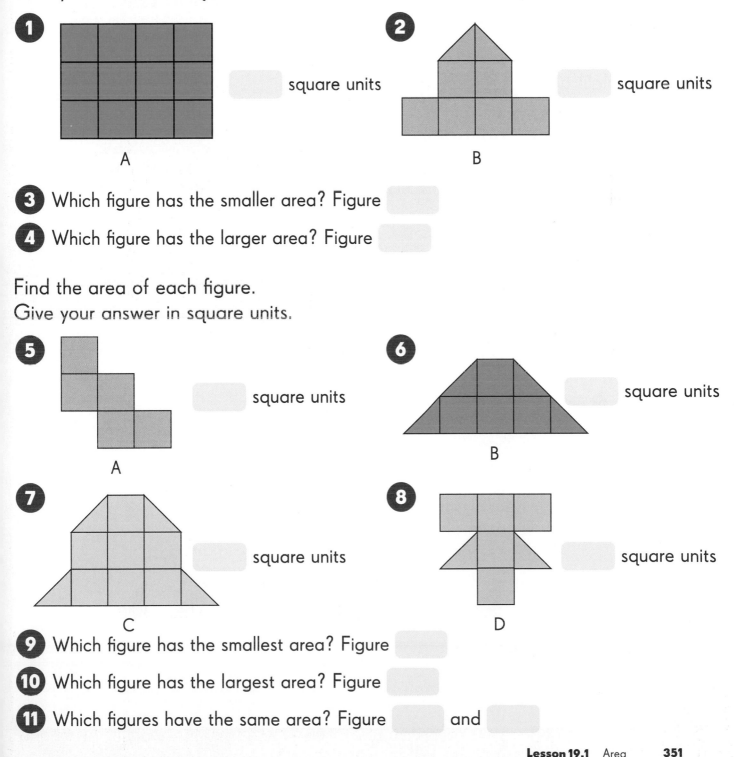

1 [   ] square units

A

2 [   ] square units

B

3 Which figure has the smaller area? Figure [   ]

4 Which figure has the larger area? Figure [   ]

Find the area of each figure.
Give your answer in square units.

5 [   ] square units

A

6 [   ] square units

B

7 [   ] square units

C

8 [   ] square units

D

9 Which figure has the smallest area? Figure [   ]

10 Which figure has the largest area? Figure [   ]

11 Which figures have the same area? Figure [   ] and [   ]

12 Which two figures have the same area? Figures [ ] and [ ]

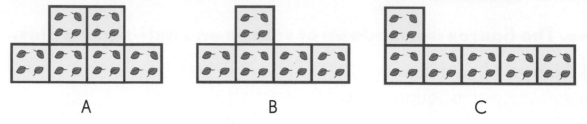

A   B   C

13 You want Figures A, B, and C to have the same area.
Explain two ways of doing this.

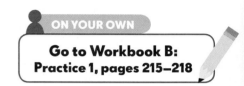
ON YOUR OWN

**Go to Workbook B:
Practice 1, pages 215–218**

Let's Explore!

WORK IN PAIRS

You have nine half-square tiles. Use all the tiles to make three figures.
Compare your figures with those made by your classmates.

What do you notice about the areas of the figures?

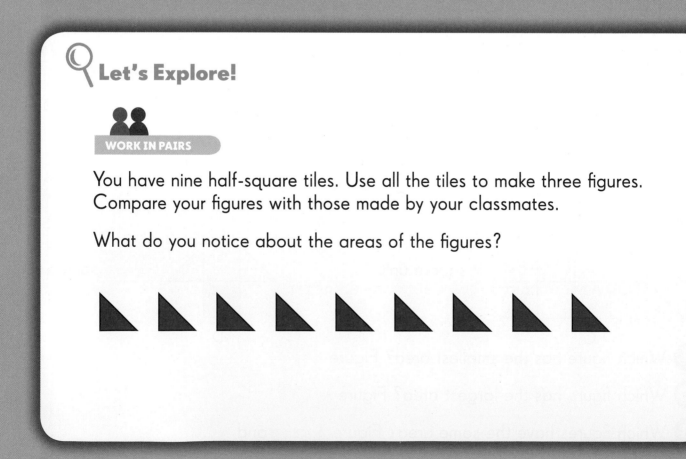

# Square Units (cm² and in.²)

Lesson Objective

- Use square centimeter and square inch to find and compare the area of figures.

Learn **Find the area of plane figures in square centimeters.**

This is a 1-centimeter square.

Each side of the square is 1 centimeter long.

Its area is 1 **square centimeter**.

You can write this as 1 cm².

1 cm
1 cm

a 1-cm square

The square centimeter (cm²) is a metric unit of measure for area.

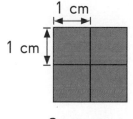

1 cm
1 cm

a 2-cm square

A 2-centimeter square is made up of four 1-centimeter squares.

Its area is 4 square centimeters (cm²).

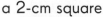
Continued on next page

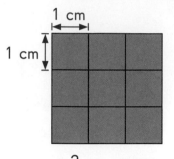

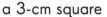

a 3-cm square

Count the number of 1 centimeter squares.

A 3-centimeter square is made up of nine 1-centimeter squares.

The area of each 1-centimeter square is 1 square centimeter.

So, the area of the 3-centimeter square is 9 square centimeters.

Guided Practice

Complete.

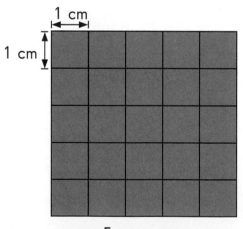

a 5-cm square

1 A 5-centimeter square is made up of ⬚ 1-centimeter squares.

2 The area of each 1-centimeter square is ⬚ square centimeter.

3 So, the area of the 5-centimeter square is ⬚ square centimeters.

Solve. The figures are made up of square and half-square tiles.

4 Find the area of this figure.

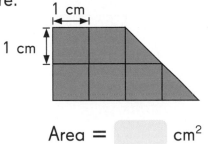

1 cm

1 cm

Area = [ ] cm²

5 Find the area of each figure.

1 cm

1 cm

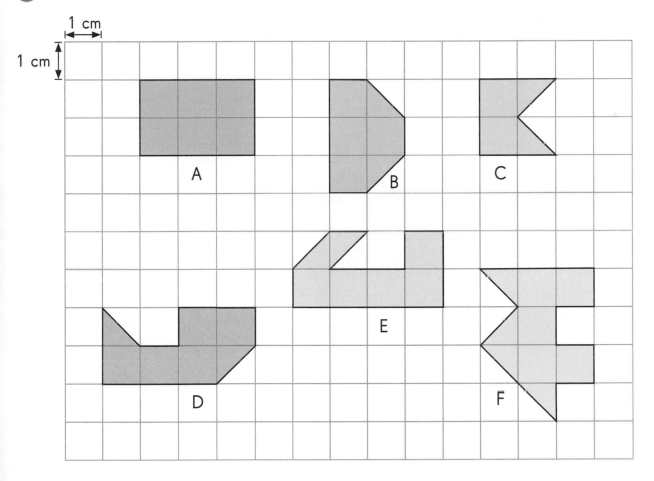

A

B

C

E

D

F

6 Which figure has the smallest area? Figure [ ]

7 Which figure has the largest area? Figure [ ]

8 Which figures have the same area? Figures [ ] , [ ] , and [ ]

Find the area of plane figures in square inches.

This is a 1-inch square.
Each side of the square is 1 inch long.
Its area is 1 square inch (in.²).

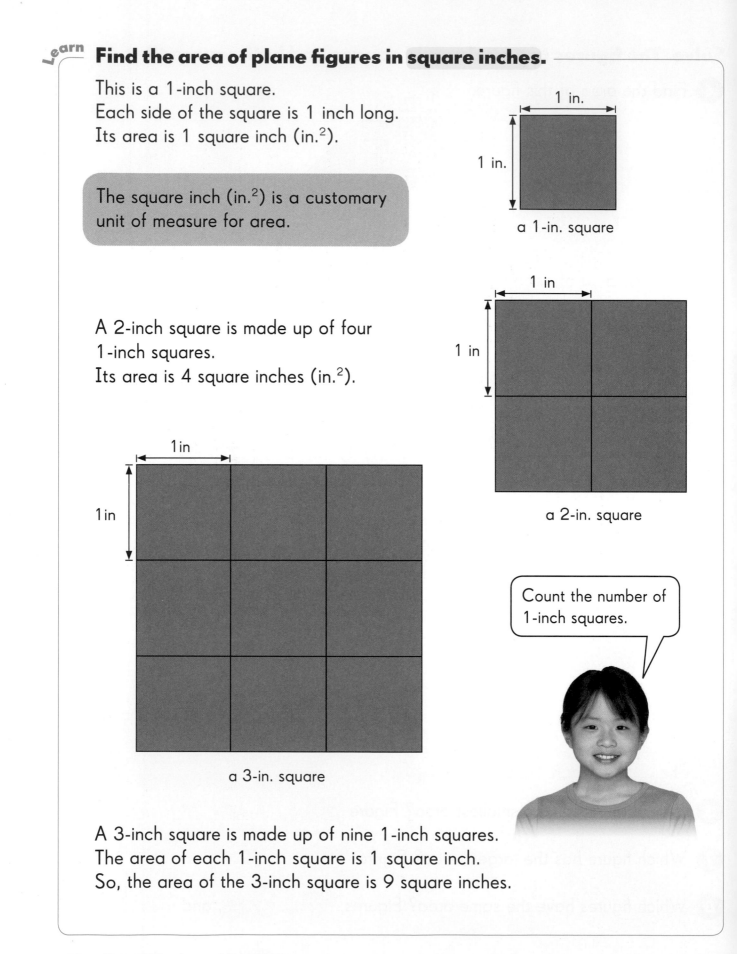

a 1-in. square

The square inch (in.²) is a customary unit of measure for area.

A 2-inch square is made up of four 1-inch squares.
Its area is 4 square inches (in.²).

a 2-in. square

a 3-in. square

Count the number of 1-inch squares.

A 3-inch square is made up of nine 1-inch squares.
The area of each 1-inch square is 1 square inch.
So, the area of the 3-inch square is 9 square inches.

Guided Practice

Complete.

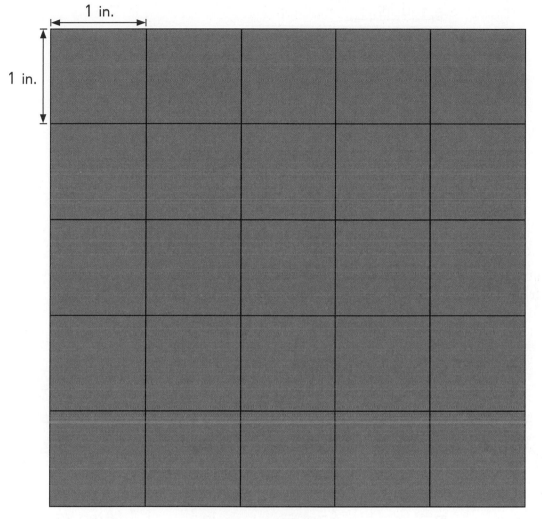

1 in.

1 in.

a 5-in. square

9 A 5-inch square is made up of [   ] 1-inch squares.

10 The area of each 1-inch square is [   ] square inch.

11 So, the area of the 5-inch square is [   ] square inches.

The figures are made up of square and half-square tiles.

12 Find the area of this figure.

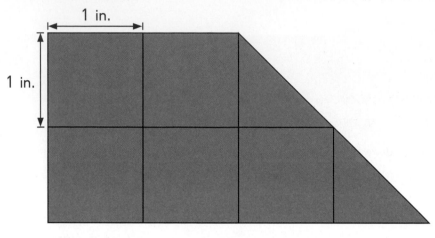

Area = [   ] in.²

What is the area of each figure?

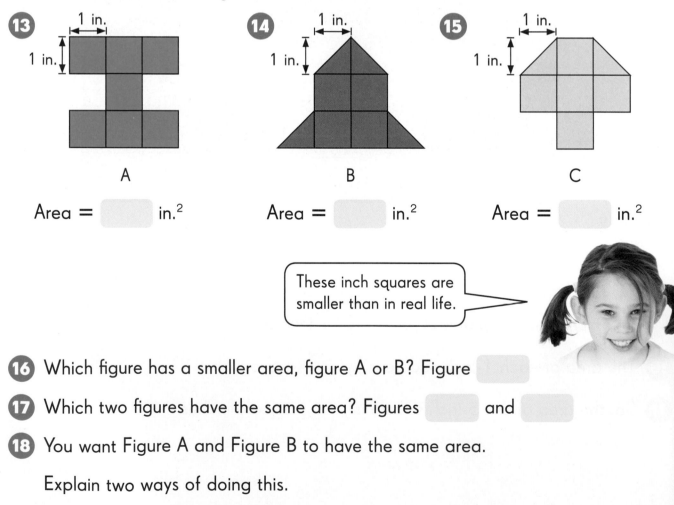

13 1 in. / 1 in.

A

Area = [   ] in.²

14 1 in. / 1 in.

B

Area = [   ] in.²

15 1 in. / 1 in.

C

Area = [   ] in.²

These inch squares are smaller than in real life.

16 Which figure has a smaller area, figure A or B? Figure [   ]

17 Which two figures have the same area? Figures [   ] and [   ]

18 You want Figure A and Figure B to have the same area.

Explain two ways of doing this.

Hands-On Activity

WORKING TOGETHER

Use a computer program that allows you to draw figures on a grid. Resize the grid to match each unit of measure.

The figures are made up of square and half-square tiles.
Draw these figures and color them.
Print your shapes and share them with your classmates.

Tech Connection

These inch squares are smaller than in real life.

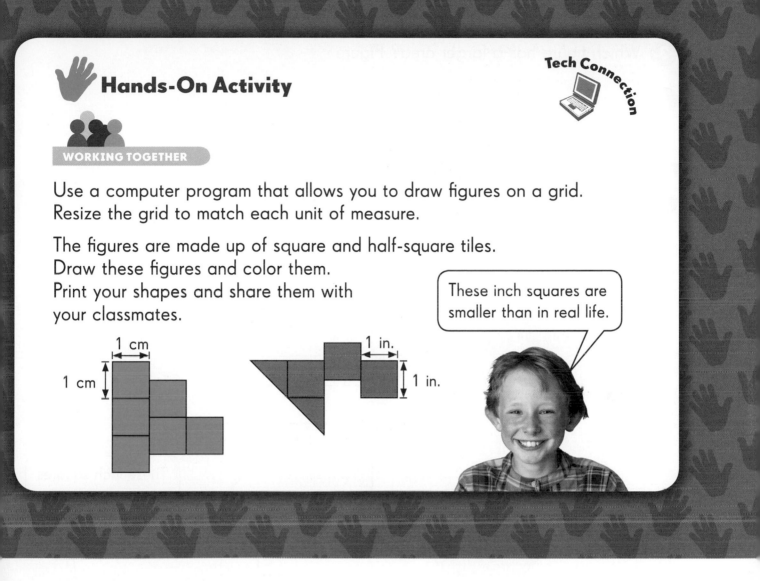

Let's Practice

Solve. The figures are made up of square and half-square tiles.

Find the area of each figure.

1

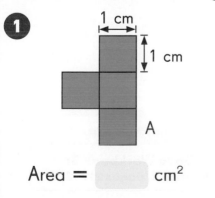

Area = [   ] cm²

2

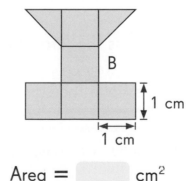

Area = [   ] cm²

3 Which figure has a larger area? Figure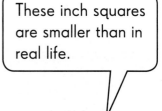

4 You want both figures to have the same area.
Explain two ways of doing this.

Find the area of each figure.

5 1 in.

1 in.

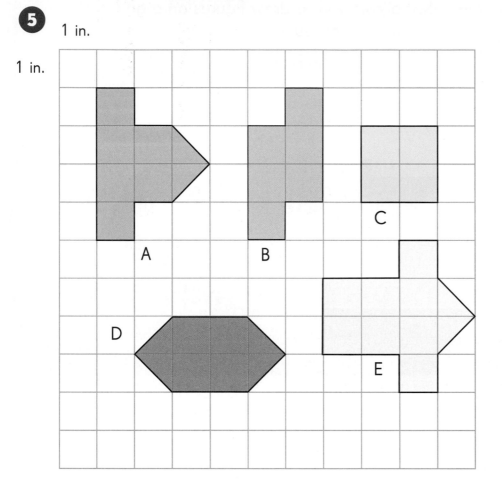

These inch squares are smaller than in real life.

6 Which figure has the smallest area? Figure

7 Which figure has the largest area? Figure

8 Which figures have the same area? Figures   and

ON YOUR OWN

Go to Workbook B:
Practice 2, pages 219–222

Math Journal

> Is 4-centimeter square the same as 4 square centimeters?

Choose the statements that explain the answer to the girl's question.

1 4 square centimeters is another way of saying 4-centimeter square.

2 A 4-centimeter square refers to a square with sides 4 centimeters long.

3 4 square centimeters is an area measurement.

4 A 2-centimeter square has an area of 4 square centimeters.

5 A 4-centimeter square has an area of 16 square centimeters.

Draw figure(s) to show 4-centimeter square and 4 square centimeters.

19.3 Square Units (m² and ft²)

Lesson Objectives

Vocabulary
square meter (m²)
square foot (ft²)

- Use square meters and square feet to find and compare the area of plane figures.
- Estimate the area of small and large surfaces.

Learn

Find the number of square meters that cover a surface.

Each side of this table top is 1 meter long.
Its area is 1 **square meter** (m²).

1 m

1 m

Which do you think is larger,
1 square centimeter or
1 square meter? Why?

The square meter (m²) is also a metric unit of measure for area.
1 square meter (m²) is larger than 1 square centimeter (cm²).

A table top is about 1 square meter.

The sticker has an area of 1 square centimeter.

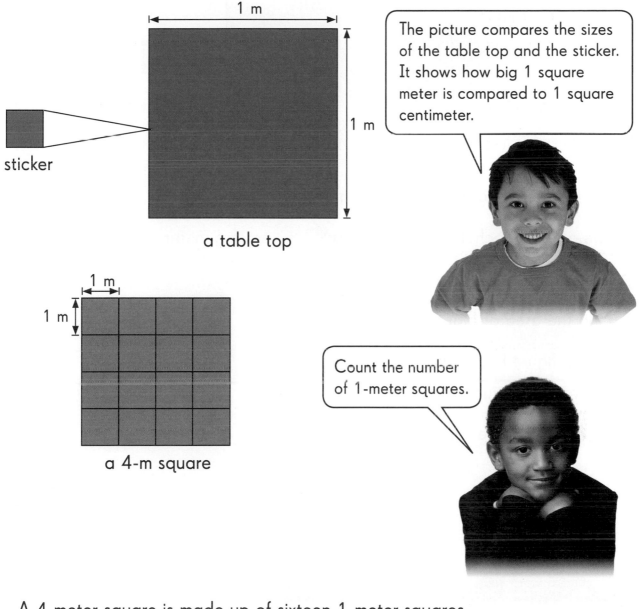

1 m

1 m

sticker

a table top

The picture compares the sizes of the table top and the sticker. It shows how big 1 square meter is compared to 1 square centimeter.

1 m

1 m

a 4-m square

Count the number of 1-meter squares.

A 4-meter square is made up of sixteen 1-meter squares.

The area of each 1-meter square is 1 square meter.

So, the area of the 4-meter square is 16 square meters.

Guided Practice

Complete. The figures are made up of square and half-square tiles.

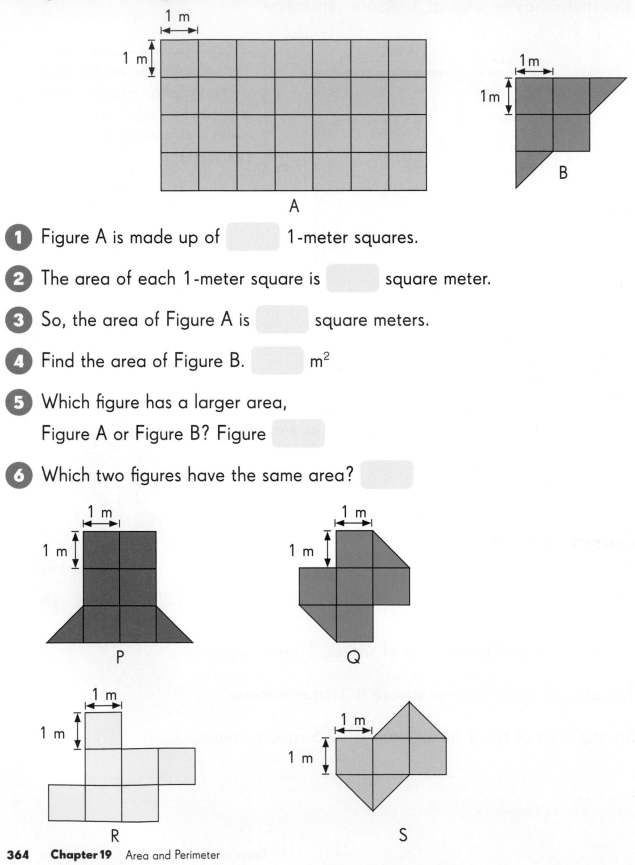

1 Figure A is made up of ___ 1-meter squares.

2 The area of each 1-meter square is ___ square meter.

3 So, the area of Figure A is ___ square meters.

4 Find the area of Figure B. ___ m²

5 Which figure has a larger area,
Figure A or Figure B? Figure ___

6 Which two figures have the same area? ___

Find the number of square feet that cover a plane surface.

Each side of this floor tile is 1 foot long.
Its area is 1 **square foot** (ft²).

1 ft

1 ft

Which do you think is larger, 1 square inch or 1 square foot? Why?

The square foot (ft²) is also a customary unit of measure for area.
1 square foot is larger than 1 square inch.

The floor tile is 1 square foot.
The stamp has an area of 1 square inch.

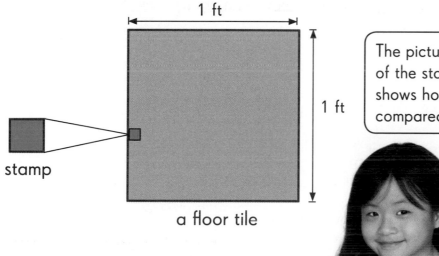

1 ft

1 ft

stamp

a floor tile

The picture compares the sizes of the stamp and the floor tile. It shows how small 1 square inch is compared to 1 square foot.

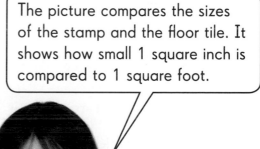

Continued on next page

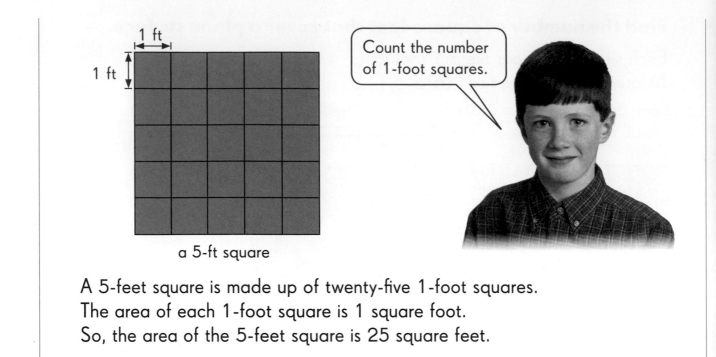

a 5-ft square

Count the number of 1-foot squares.

A 5-feet square is made up of twenty-five 1-foot squares.
The area of each 1-foot square is 1 square foot.
So, the area of the 5-feet square is 25 square feet.

Guided Practice

Complete. The figures are made up of square and half-square tiles.

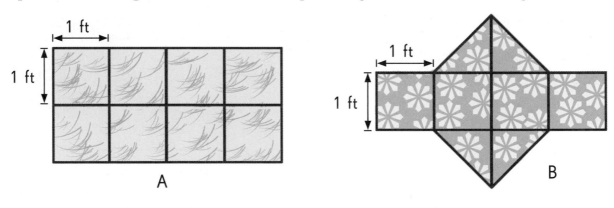

A

B

7 Figure A is made up of ▢ 1-foot tiles.

8 The area of each 1-foot tile is ▢ square foot.

9 So, the area of Figure A is ▢ square feet.

10 The area of Figure B is ▢ square feet.

11 Which figure has a smaller area,

Figure A or Figure B? Figure ▢

Hands-On Activity

Look around your classroom and home. Identify objects that have an area of about 1 square centimeter, 1 square inch, 1 square foot, and 1 square meter.

Area	Objects I found in school	Objects I found at home
About 1 cm²		
About 1 m²		
About 1 in.²		
About 1 ft²		

Use gift wrap and tape to make a square piece of paper with an area of 1 square meter and 1 square foot.

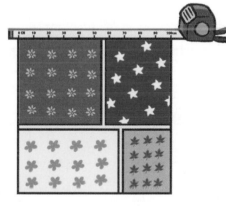 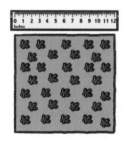

Use both pieces of papers to estimate the area of these objects in your classroom.

| Objects | Estimated Area | |
	Square meter (m²)	Square feet (ft²)
Door		
Your Table		

Let's Practice

Solve. The figures are made up of square and half-square tiles.

Find the area of each figure.

1

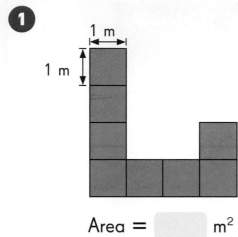

1 m

1 m

Area = ⬚ m²

2

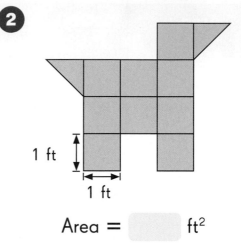

1 ft

1 ft

Area = ⬚ ft²

Find the area of each figure.

3

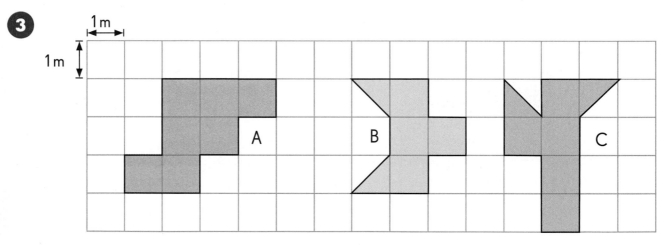

1 m

1 m

A   B   C

4 Which figure has the smallest area? Figure ⬚

5 Which figure has the largest area? Figure ⬚

6 Which figure has an area 1 m² less than Figure A? Figure ⬚

Find the area of each figure.

7

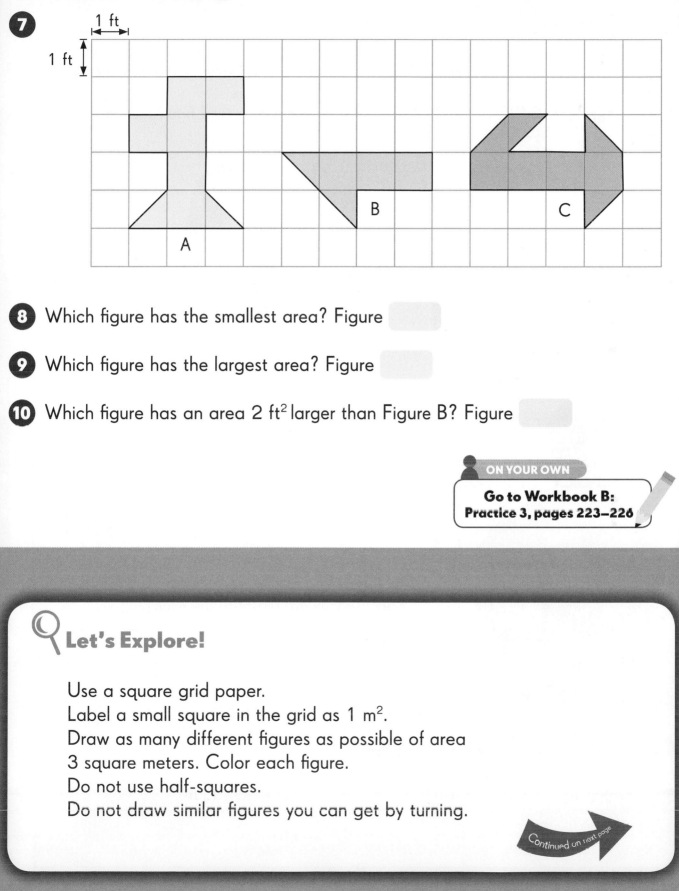

8 Which figure has the smallest area? Figure ▢

9 Which figure has the largest area? Figure ▢

10 Which figure has an area 2 ft² larger than Figure B? Figure ▢

ON YOUR OWN

Go to Workbook B:
Practice 3, pages 223–226

Let's Explore!

Use a square grid paper.
Label a small square in the grid as 1 m².
Draw as many different figures as possible of area
3 square meters. Color each figure.
Do not use half-squares.
Do not draw similar figures you can get by turning.

Continued on next page

Example

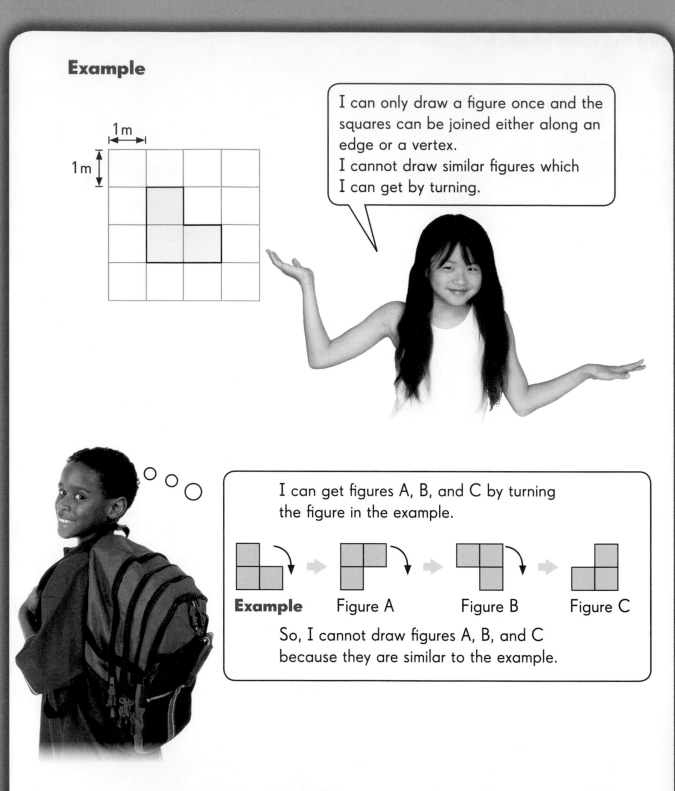

1 m

1 m

I can only draw a figure once and the squares can be joined either along an edge or a vertex.
I cannot draw similar figures which I can get by turning.

I can get figures A, B, and C by turning the figure in the example.

Example   Figure A   Figure B   Figure C

So, I cannot draw figures A, B, and C because they are similar to the example.

How many other figures can you draw?

19.4 Perimeter and Area

Lesson Objectives

- Understand the meaning of perimeter.
- Find the perimeter of figures formed using small squares.
- Compare the area and perimeter of two figures.

Vocabulary
perimeter

Learn Find the perimeter and area of a figure.

Look at the rectangle on the geoboard.

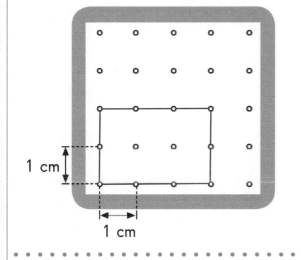

The **perimeter** of the rectangle is the distance around it. To find the perimeter, you find the length of each side of the rectangle in centimeters and add them.

3 + 2 + 3 + 2 = 10

So, the perimeter of the rectangle is 10 centimeters.

The area of the rectangle is 6 square centimeters.

Look at the figure.

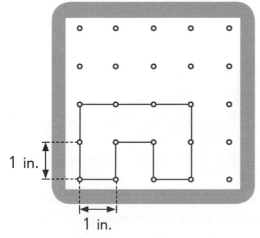

You can also measure perimeter in meters and feet.

The perimeter of this figure is 12 inches.
Its area is 5 square inches.

Continued on next page

Perimeter can be measured in centimeters (cm), inches (in.), meters (m), and feet (ft).
Area can be measured in square centimeters (cm²), square inches (in.²), square meters (m²), and square feet (ft²).

Guided Practice

Complete.

Look at the two figures on the geoboard.

They have the same perimeter.

1 The perimeter of each figure is [ ] centimeters.

They do not have the same area.

2 The area of Figure A is [ ] square centimeters.

3 The area of Figure B is [ ] square centimeters.

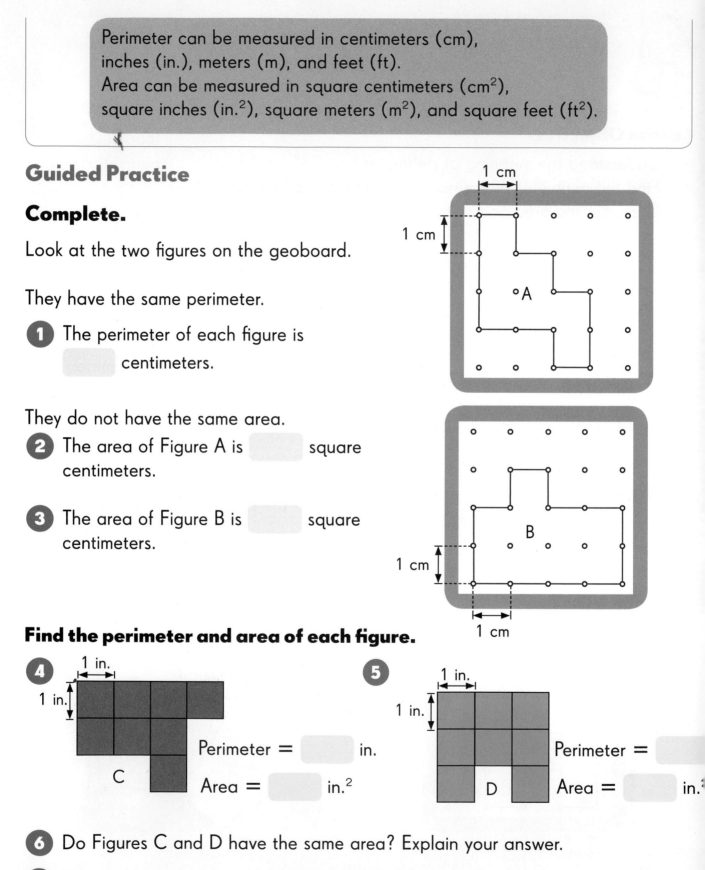

Find the perimeter and area of each figure.

4 1 in. 1 in.

C

Perimeter = [ ] in.

Area = [ ] in.²

5 1 in. 1 in.

D

Perimeter = [ ]

Area = [ ] in.²

6 Do Figures C and D have the same area? Explain your answer.

7 Do they have the same perimeter? Explain your answer.

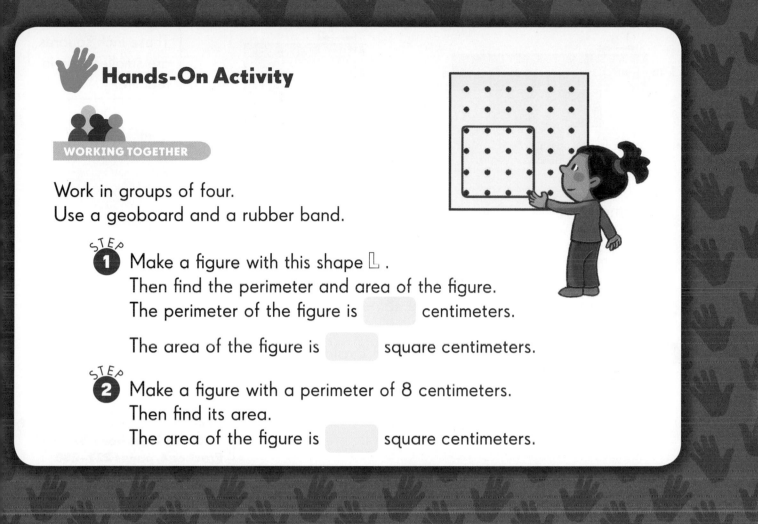

Hands-On Activity

WORKING TOGETHER

Work in groups of four.
Use a geoboard and a rubber band.

STEP 1 Make a figure with this shape L .
Then find the perimeter and area of the figure.
The perimeter of the figure is [ ] centimeters.

The area of the figure is [ ] square centimeters.

STEP 2 Make a figure with a perimeter of 8 centimeters.
Then find its area.
The area of the figure is [ ] square centimeters.

Let's Practice

Complete.

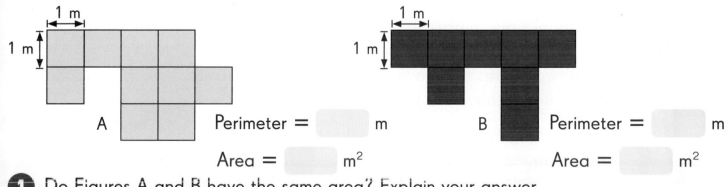

A   Perimeter = [ ] m

Area = [ ] m²

B   Perimeter = [ ] m

Area = [ ] m²

1 Do Figures A and B have the same area? Explain your answer.

2 Do they have the same perimeter? Explain your answer.

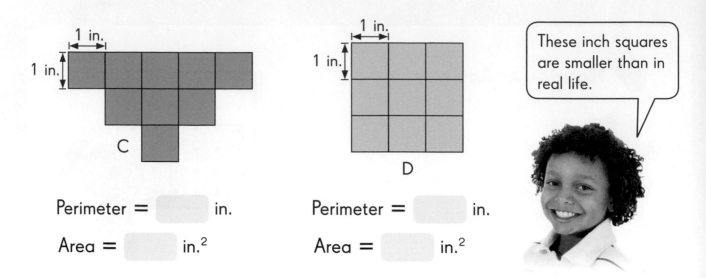

Perimeter = [ ] in. Perimeter = [ ] in.

Area = [ ] in.² Area = [ ] in.²

3 Do Figures C and D have the same area? Explain your answer.

4 Do they have the same perimeter? Explain your answer.

ON YOUR OWN

Go to Workbook B:
Practice 4, pages 227–230

Let's Explore!

Use a geoboard and rubber band to make these figures.

1 Make two figures that have an area of 8 square units.
Do the figures have the same perimeter?

2 Make two figures that have a perimeter of 12 units.
Do the figures have the same area?

3 Make a square with sides of 4 units each.
What do you notice about its area and perimeter?

More Perimeter

Lesson Objectives

- Find the perimeter of a figure by adding up all its sides.
- Choose the appropriate tool and units of length to measure perimeter.
- Measure the perimeter of surfaces of objects and places.

Learn **Find the perimeter of figures.**

Each side of the square is 6 centimeters long.
Find its perimeter.

Perimeter = 6 + 6 + 6 + 6

           = 24 cm

The perimeter is
24 centimeters.

6 cm

6 cm

How many sides does
the square have?

Guided Practice

Complete.

1 Measure the sides of the rectangle in centimeters. Find its perimeter.

Perimeter = ☐ + ☐ + ☐ + ☐

           = ☐

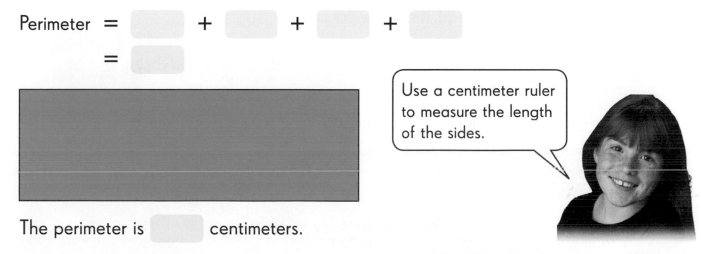

Use a centimeter ruler
to measure the length
of the sides.

The perimeter is ☐ centimeters.

2 Find the perimeter of the figure.

Perimeter = ☐ + ☐ + ☐ + ☐ + ☐

= ☐ in.

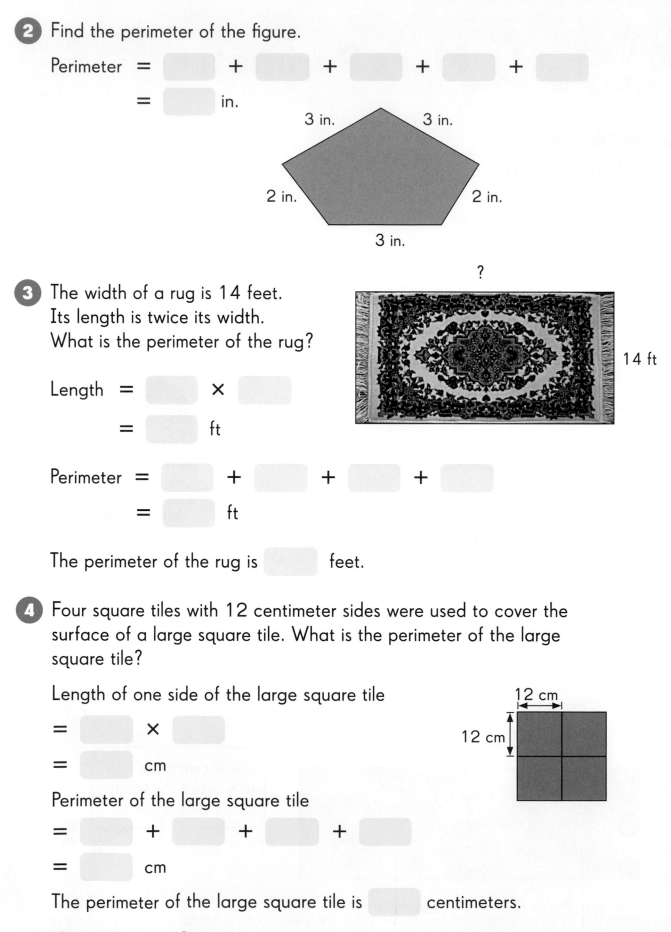

3 in.　　　　3 in.

2 in.　　　　　　2 in.

3 in.

3 The width of a rug is 14 feet.
Its length is twice its width.
What is the perimeter of the rug?

?

14 ft

Length = ☐ × ☐

= ☐ ft

Perimeter = ☐ + ☐ + ☐ + ☐

= ☐ ft

The perimeter of the rug is ☐ feet.

4 Four square tiles with 12 centimeter sides were used to cover the surface of a large square tile. What is the perimeter of the large square tile?

Length of one side of the large square tile

= ☐ × ☐

= ☐ cm

12 cm

12 cm

Perimeter of the large square tile

= ☐ + ☐ + ☐ + ☐

= ☐ cm

The perimeter of the large square tile is ☐ centimeters.

5 The width of a rectangular field is 35 meters long.
Its length is three times as long as its width. Ian ran around the field once.
How far did he run?

Length of field = [ ] × [ ]   35 m

= [ ] m

Perimeter = [ ] + [ ] + [ ] + [ ]

= [ ] m

Ian ran [ ] meters.

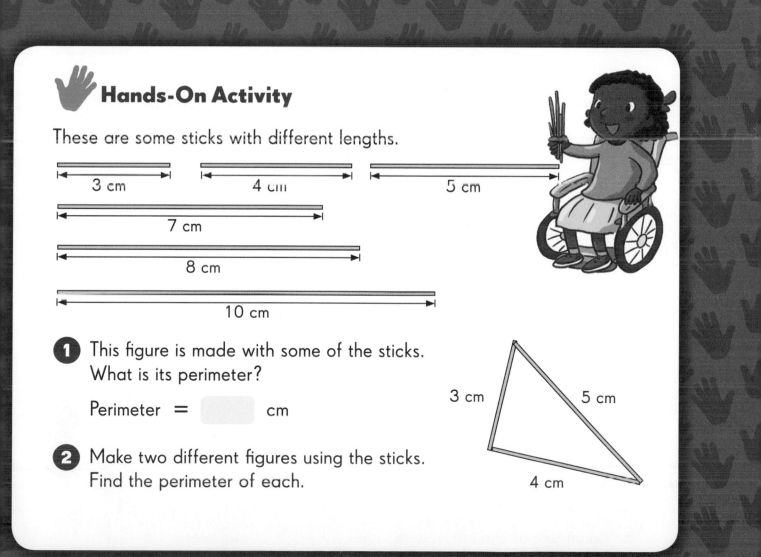

Hands-On Activity

These are some sticks with different lengths.

|← 3 cm →|

|← 4 cm →|

|← 5 cm →|

|← 7 cm →|

|← 8 cm →|

|← 10 cm →|

1 This figure is made with some of the sticks.
What is its perimeter?

Perimeter = [ ] cm

3 cm   5 cm

4 cm

2 Make two different figures using the sticks.
Find the perimeter of each.

1 Write how you would find the perimeter of your classroom. Include each step.

> What lengths do I have to measure?
> What tools do I use to measure?
> How do I find the perimeter from my measurements?

2 Your best friend was absent from class and missed the lesson on perimeter. Write a letter to him explaining the term. Use diagrams to help you.

> First, think of an example to illustrate the term. Then think of a unit of measure to be used in the example.

Let's Practice

Solve.
Measure the sides of the figure with a centimeter ruler.
Then find the perimeter.

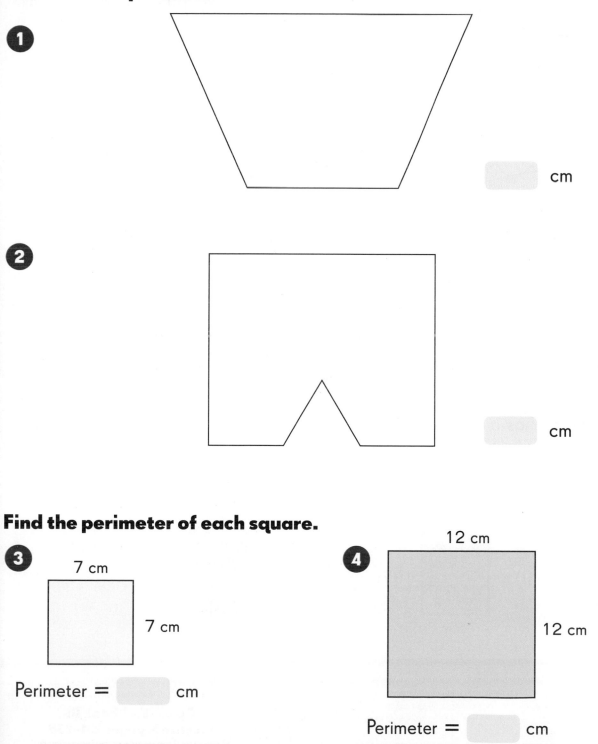

1 ___ cm

2 ___ cm

Find the perimeter of each square.

3

7 cm

7 cm

Perimeter = ___ cm

4

12 cm

12 cm

Perimeter = ___ cm

5 Each side of a square is 8 meters.
Find the perimeter of the square.

Find the perimeter of each rectangle.

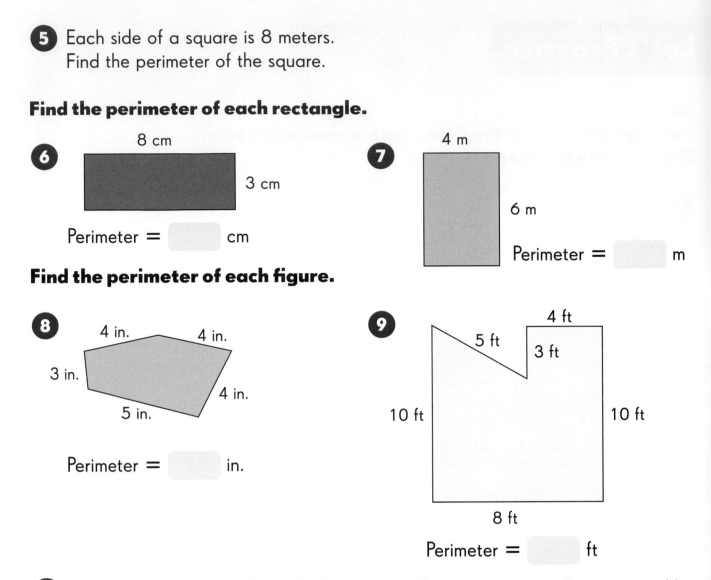

6

8 cm

3 cm

Perimeter = ⬚ cm

7

4 m

6 m

Perimeter = ⬚ m

Find the perimeter of each figure.

8

4 in.   4 in.

3 in.

4 in.

5 in.

Perimeter = ⬚ in.

9

4 ft

5 ft

3 ft

10 ft   10 ft

8 ft

Perimeter = ⬚ ft

10 Mr. Carlson has a garden with these sides. He wants to put a fence around his garden. Find the length of fencing he needs.

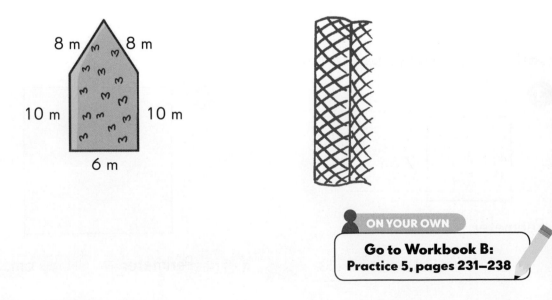

8 m   8 m

10 m   10 m

6 m

ON YOUR OWN

Go to Workbook B:
Practice 5, pages 231–238

Put On Your Thinking Cap!

PROBLEM SOLVING

1 How many squares of different sizes can you find in this figure?

Use the chart to help you find the answer.

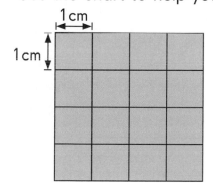

Size of Square	Number of Squares
1-cm	
2-cm	
3-cm	
4-cm	

2 How many 1-centimeter squares are in each figure?

 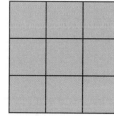

The squares may overlap.

Figure	Number of Squares		
1	1		
2	1 + ___ = ___		
3	1 + ___ + ___ = ___		

3 What pattern do you see? Describe it.

4 How many squares would there be in Figure 10?

ON YOUR OWN

**Go to Workbook B:
Put on Your Thinking Cap!
pages 239–242**

Chapter Wrap Up

Study Guide
You have learned...

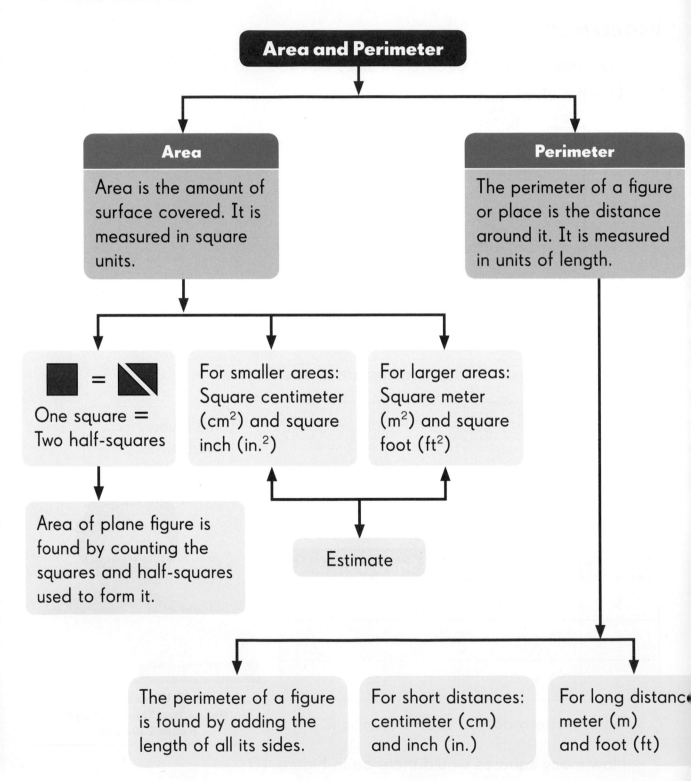

Area and Perimeter

Area

Area is the amount of surface covered. It is measured in square units.

Perimeter

The perimeter of a figure or place is the distance around it. It is measured in units of length.

One square = Two half-squares

For smaller areas: Square centimeter (cm^2) and square inch (in.^{2})

For larger areas: Square meter (m^2) and square foot (ft^2)

Area of plane figure is found by counting the squares and half-squares used to form it.

Estimate

The perimeter of a figure is found by adding the length of all its sides.

For short distances: centimeter (cm) and inch (in.)

For long distance: meter (m) and foot (ft)

BIG IDEA

▶ Explore and understand units used to find perimeter and area of figures and analyze the relationship between them.

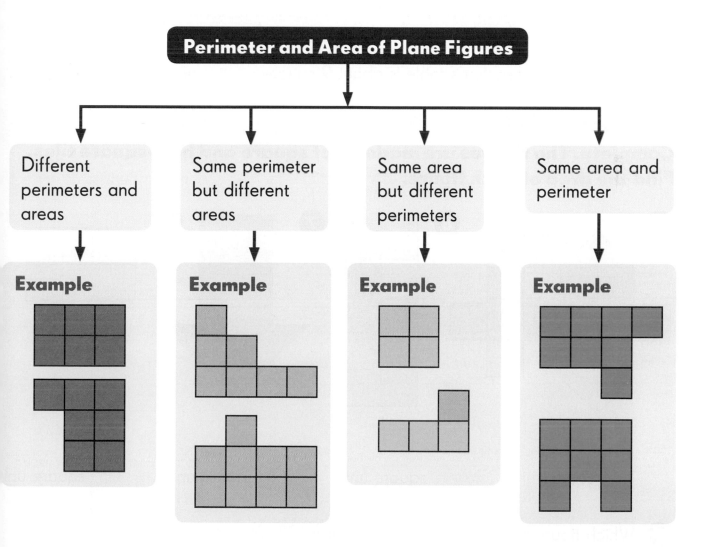

Perimeter and Area of Plane Figures

- Different perimeters and areas
  - **Example**
- Same perimeter but different areas
  - **Example**
- Same area but different perimeters
  - **Example**
- Same area and perimeter
  - **Example**

Chapter Review/Test

Vocabulary
Complete the sentences.

area
perimeter
centimeters
meter
inches
feet

1 The amount of surface covered is the _____ .

2 The distance around a figure or place is its _____ .

3 The perimeter of a stamp is about 8 _____ or 4 _____ .

4 The area of a teacher's table is about 9 square _____ or 1 square _____ .

Concept and Skills
Complete. The figures are made up of square and half-square tiles. Find the area of each figure.

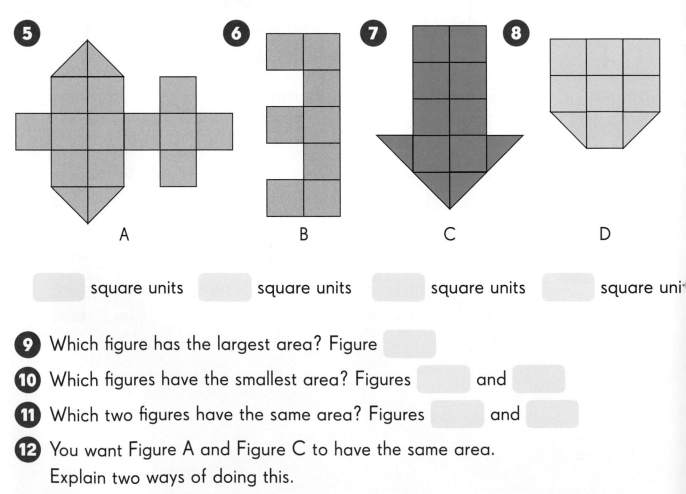

5 A

6 B

7 C

8 D

_____ square units _____ square units _____ square units _____ square uni

9 Which figure has the largest area? Figure _____

10 Which figures have the smallest area? Figures _____ and _____

11 Which two figures have the same area? Figures _____ and _____

12 You want Figure A and Figure C to have the same area.
Explain two ways of doing this.

The figures are made up of square and half-square tiles.
Find the area of each figure.

13
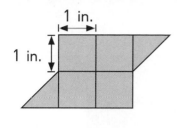

Area = ⬚ in.²

14
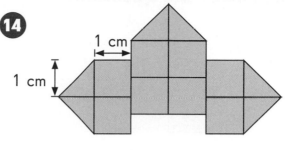

Area = ⬚ cm²

15
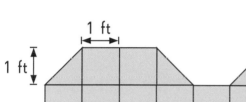

Area = ⬚ ft²

16

Area = ⬚ m²

Find the perimeter and area of each figure.

17

Perimeter = ⬚ in.

Area = ⬚ in.²

18

Perimeter = ⬚ cm

Area = ⬚ cm²

These inch squares are smaller than in real life.

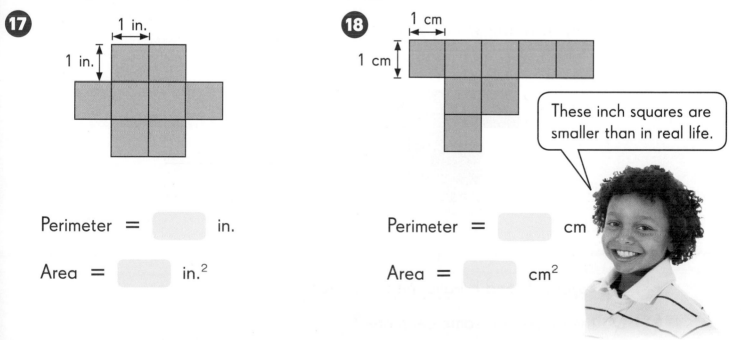

Find the perimeter and area of each figure. Then answer the questions.

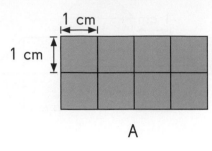

A

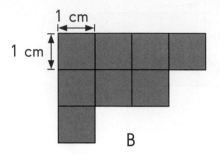

B

19 Do Figures A and B have the same area?

20 Do they have the same perimeter?

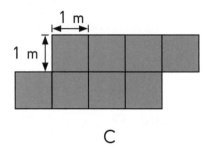

C

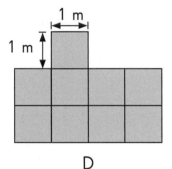

D

21 Do Figures C and D have the same area?

22 Do they have the same perimeter?

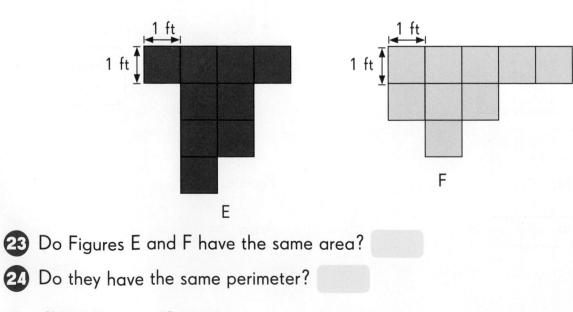

E

F

23 Do Figures E and F have the same area?

24 Do they have the same perimeter?

Measure the sides of the parallelogram. Find its perimeter.

25

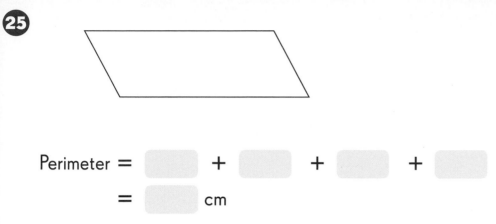

Perimeter = [ ] + [ ] + [ ] + [ ]

= [ ] cm

Problem Solving

26 A rectangular field is 10 meters by 5 meters. A fence is put around it. How long must the fence be?

27 Two square tiles each with a side length of 6 centimeters are placed side by side to form a rectangle. What is the perimeter of the rectangle?

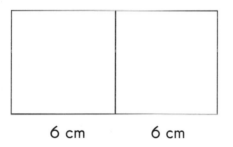

6 cm   6 cm

28 The diagram below shows a kitchen floor.

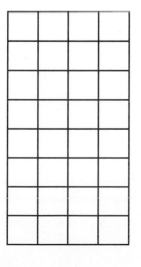

Mr. Thompson needs alternating white and blue tiles to cover the kitchen floor. How many tiles of each color should he buy?

Blank

 **Focus Lessons**

**COMMON
CORE**

**3.NF.3.c. Express whole numbers
as fractions, and recognize
fractions that are equivalent to
whole numbers.**

Lesson Objectives

- Express whole numbers as fractions.
- Recognize fractions that are equal to whole numbers.

Let's Explore!

Whole numbers can be written as fractions.

The number $1 = \dfrac{1}{1}$ $1 \div 1 = 1$

1 $3 = \dfrac{3}{1}$, $4 =$ _____   **2** $5 =$ _____

Whole numbers can be written as other fractions.

The number 1 can also be written as $\dfrac{2}{2}$ because $2 \div 2 = 1$.

3 Write another fraction for 1.

What do you notice about these fractions $\dfrac{4}{2}$, $\dfrac{8}{4}$, and $\dfrac{6}{3}$?

4 Write another fraction for 2.

Write two fractions to show each of these numbers.

5 5   **6** 6

What numbers are shown by these fractions?

7 $\dfrac{7}{1}$ **8** $\dfrac{10}{2}$

9 $\dfrac{21}{7}$ **10** $\dfrac{111}{111}$

15.1.a Measuring Length

3.MD.4. Generate measurement data by measuring lengths using rulers marked with halves and fourths of an inch. Show the data by making a line plot, where the horizontal scale is marked off in appropriate units — whole numbers, halves, or quarters.

Lesson Objectives

- Estimate and measure lengths in halves and fourths of an inch.
- Estimate and show measurements in a line plot with a scale of whole numbers and fractions.

Vocabulary
quarter-inch
three quarter-inch

Estimate and measure length to the nearest quarter-inch.

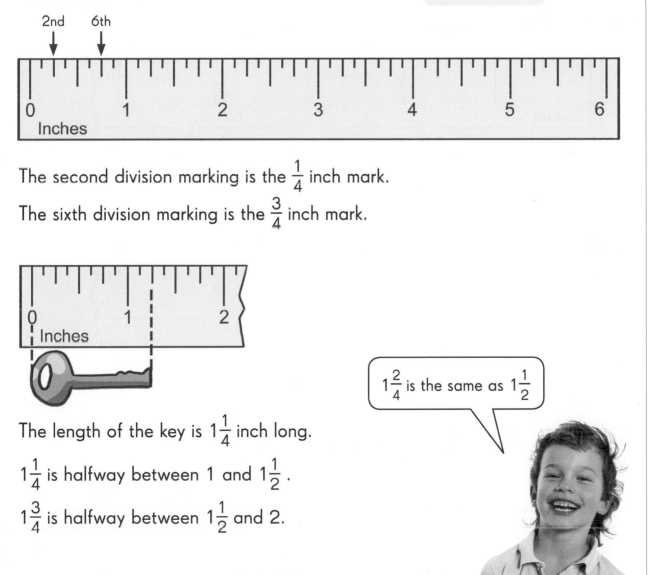

The second division marking is the $\frac{1}{4}$ inch mark.

The sixth division marking is the $\frac{3}{4}$ inch mark.

The length of the key is $1\frac{1}{4}$ inch long.

$1\frac{1}{4}$ is halfway between 1 and $1\frac{1}{2}$.

$1\frac{3}{4}$ is halfway between $1\frac{1}{2}$ and 2.

$1\frac{2}{4}$ is the same as $1\frac{1}{2}$

Let's Practice

Measure the length.

1 The length of the scissors is _____ inches long.

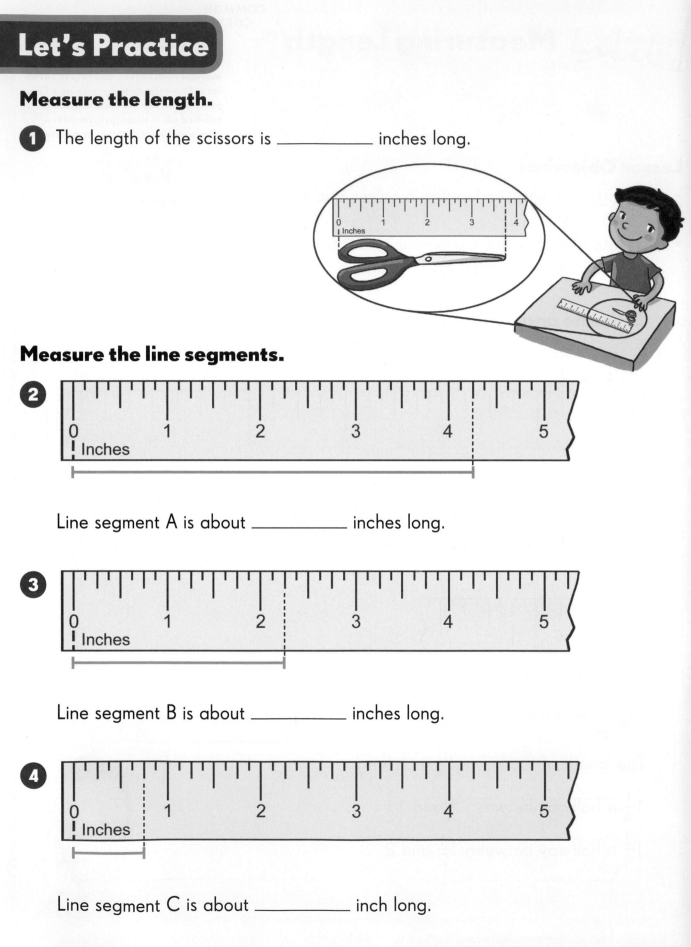

Measure the line segments.

2

Line segment A is about _____ inches long.

3

Line segment B is about _____ inches long.

4

Line segment C is about _____ inch long.

Hands-On Activity

WORKING TOGETHER

Find objects in and around your desk that have lengths from 1 to 3 inches. Meaure the length to the nearest quarter-inch.

Object	Measured Length (in.)

Ask 2 friends for their measurements. Record all your data in a tally chart. Then show the data on a line plot.

Number of Objects at Each Length

Length (in.)	Tally	Number of Items
1		
$1\frac{1}{4}$		
$1\frac{1}{2}$		
$1\frac{3}{4}$		
2		
$2\frac{1}{4}$		
$2\frac{1}{2}$		
$2\frac{3}{4}$		
3		

Lesson 19.4.a Real-World Problems: Area

COMMON CORE

3.MD.7.b. Multiply side lengths to find areas of rectangles with whole-number side lengths in the context of solving real world and mathematical problems, and represent whole-number products as rectangular areas in mathematical reasoning.

3.MD.7.d. Recognize area as additive. Find areas of rectilinear figures by decomposing them into non-overlapping rectangles and adding the areas of the non-overlapping parts, applying this techique to solve real world problems.

Lesson Objectives

• Multiply the side lengths of rectangles to find the area to solve real-world problems.

• Represent whole-number products as rectangular areas.

• Find the area of figures by separating them into two rectangles and adding their areas.

Learn Find the area of a rectangle using multiplication to solve word problems.

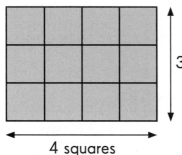

3 squares

4 squares

If you know the length and width of a rectangle, you can use multiplication to find its area.

The area of a rectangle is length × width.

$4 \times 3 = 12$

The area of this rectangle is 12 square units.

Carla's doll's quilt is made up of 1-inch squares of cloth.

The length is 6 inches.

The width is 4 inches.

What is the area of her doll's quilt?

$6 \times 4 = 24$

The area of her doll's quilt is 24 square inches.

4 inches

6 inches

Let's Practice

Solve.

1 The fish pond at the park has a length of 8 meters and a width of 6 meters. What is the area of the fish pond?

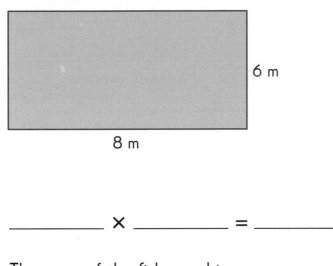

6 m

8 m

_____ × _____ = _____

The area of the fish pond is _____ m².

2 Matt needs a piece of cloth with a length of 6 meters and a width of 5 meters to sew an apron for his Grandmother.
What is the area of the piece of cloth?

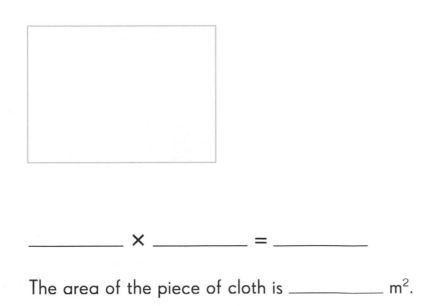

_____ × _____ = _____

The area of the piece of cloth is _____ m².

Let's Explore!

Use a geoboard and rubber bands to make these figures.

 Make as many different rectangles as you can with an area of 12 square units, and record their lengths and widths in the table.

 Write their area as a multiplication fact.

Area (square units)	Length	Width	Multiplication Fact
12			
12			
12			

Draw area models to represent these rectangles.
Then, write their areas as multiplication facts.

 8 square units

4 10 square units

5 14 square units

Find the area of a figure by separating it into two rectangles, then add the area of both rectangles to solve real-word problems.

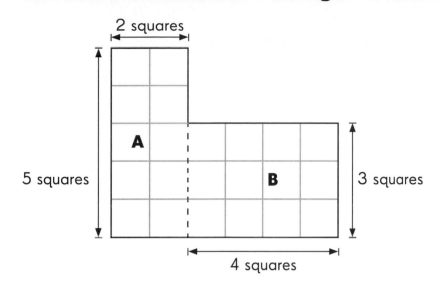

To find the area of the figure, first you separate the figure into two rectangles.
Then, use multiplication to find the area of each rectangle.
Now, add the two areas together.

The area of a rectangle = length × width.

Area of rectangle A = 5 × 2 = 10 square units

Area of rectangle B = 4 × 3 = 12 square units

Area of the figure = 10 + 12
                            = 22 square units

The area of the figure is 22 square units.

Jermain buys square-foot tiles for his driveway.
What is the area of his driveway?

Area of rectangle C
= 3 × 2 = 6

Area of rectangle D
= 4 × 2 = 8

The area of the driveway is
6 + 8 = 14 square feet.

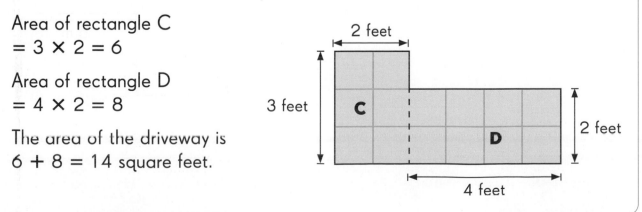

Draw a line to separate the figure. Then solve.

1 The Campo family has a "L" shaped swimming pool in their backyard. What is the total area of the swimming pool?

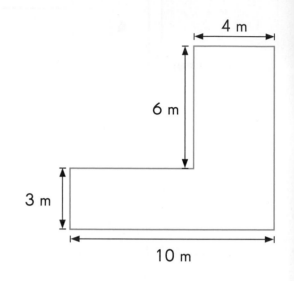

2 Two neighbours Kim and Mario, share a vegetable garden at a community farm. The farm's rule is that no garden can occupy more than 50 square meters. What is the total area of their vegetable garden? Did they follow the rule?

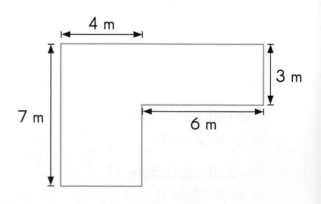

Glossary

A

- **angle**

  When two line segments share the same endpoint, they form an angle.

     This is angle *H*.

- **area**

  Area is the number of square units needed to cover the surface of each figure.

  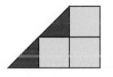   The area of this figure is 4 square units.

- **axis**

  An axis is a grid line that can be either vertical or horizontal. See **horizontal axis** and **vertical axis**.

B

- **benchmark**

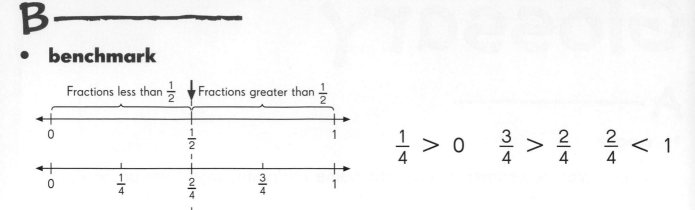

The common benchmarks for comparing fractions are 0, $\frac{1}{2}$, and 1.

- **break apart polygon**

This is an example of how to break a polygon apart.

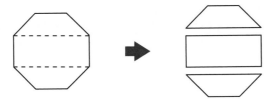

An octagon can be broken apart into one rectangle and two trapezoids. See **polygon**.

C

- **capacity**

  Capacity is the amount of liquid that a container can hold.

- **centimeter (cm)**

  Centimeter is a metric unit of length. It is used to measure shorter lengths. Write cm for centimeter.

  100 cm = 1 m

  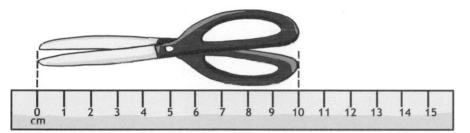

  The pair of scissors is 10 centimeters long.

- **closed plane figure**

    A plane figure that starts and ends at the same point.

    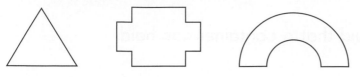

    These are examples of closed plane figures.

- **cold**

    Use cold, cool, warm, and hot as referents to estimate temperature. When the temperature outside is 32°F, it is cold.

- **combine polygons**

    A triangle and a trapezoid can be joined to form a pentagon. This is an example of how polygons can be combined. See **polygon**.

- **congruent**

    Identical figures are congruent. They have the same shape and size.

    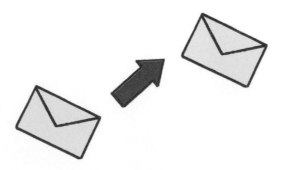

- **convert**

  You can convert units of measurement.

  For example, these conversions express time in minutes or hours and minutes.

  $$1 \text{ h } 10 \text{ min} = 60 \text{ min} + 10 \text{ min}$$
  $$= 70 \text{ min}$$

  $$135 \text{ min} = 120 \text{ min} + 15 \text{ min}$$
  $$= 2 \text{ h } 15 \text{ min}$$

- **cool**

  When the temperature outside is 50°F, it is cool.

  See **cold**.

- **cup (c)**

  Cup is a customary unit of capacity. Write c for cup.

D

- **degrees Fahrenheit (°F)**

  This is the customary unit of measurement for temperature.

- **denominator**

  It is the number below the line in a fraction. It shows the number of equal parts into which the whole is divided.

  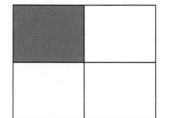

  $\frac{1}{4}$ of the rectangle is shaded.

  In the fraction $\frac{1}{4}$, 4 is the denominator.

- **distance**

  Distance is the length between one place and another.

  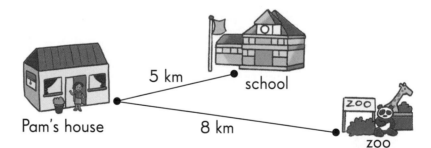

  The distance between Pam's house and the zoo is 8 kilometers.

E

- ## elapsed time

  The amount of time that has passed between the start and the end of an activity.

  Start:

  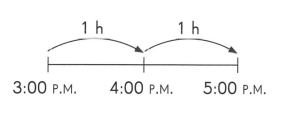

  1 h   1 h

  3:00 P.M.   4:00 P.M.   5:00 P.M.

  End:

  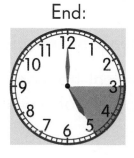

  Tom's soccer practice lasted 2 hours.
  2 hours is the elapsed time between 3:00 P.M. and 5:00 P.M.

- ## endpoint

  It is the end of a line segment.

  endpoint

  See **line segment**.

- **equal parts**

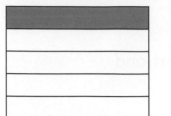

This whole is made up of 5 equal parts. $\frac{1}{5}$ is 1 out of the 5 equal parts.

- **equivalent fractions**

Equivalent fractions are two or more fractions that name the same parts of a whole.

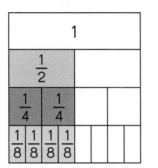

$\frac{1}{2}$, $\frac{2}{4}$, and $\frac{4}{8}$ name the same parts of a whole.

F ─────

- ## Fahrenheit (°F)

  See **degrees Fahrenheit**.

- ## flip

  Turn a shape front to back over a line.

front side   back side

before flip   after flip

back side

after flip

before flip

front side

- ## foot (ft)

  Foot is a customary unit of length.
  Write ft for foot.
  1 ft = 12 in.

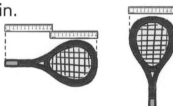

  The length of the tennis racket is 2 feet.
  The width of the tennis racket is 1 foot.

G

- **gallon (gal)**

  Gallon is a customary unit of capacity. Write gal for gallon.
  1 gal = 4 qt

  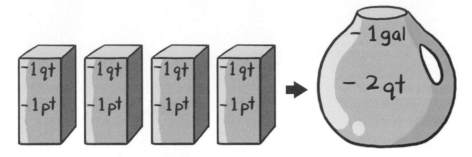

- **gram (g)**

  Gram is the metric unit of mass. It is used to measure the mass of lighter objects. Write g for gram.
  1,000 g = 1 kg

  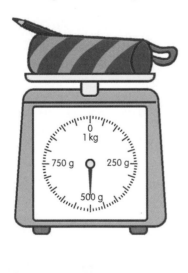

  The mass of the pencil case is 500 grams.

- **greater than (>)**

  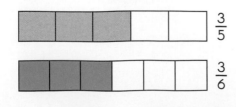

  $\frac{3}{5}$ is greater than $\frac{3}{6}$.

- **greatest**

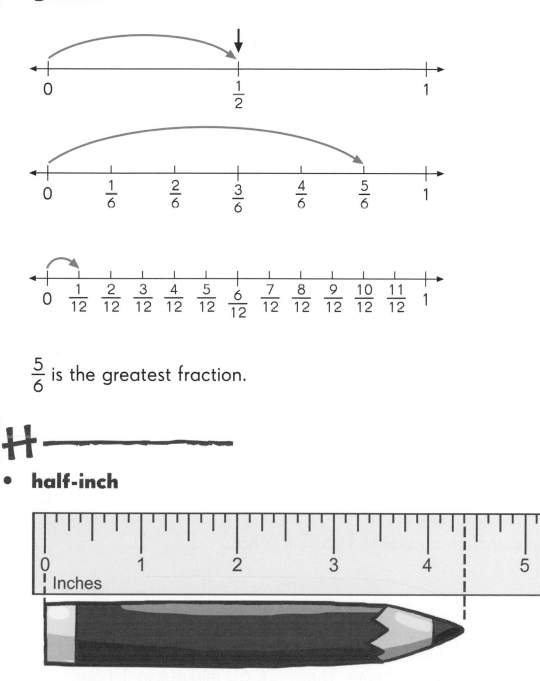

$\frac{5}{6}$ is the greatest fraction.

- **half-inch**

The length of the pencil is $4\frac{1}{2}$ inches, measured to the nearest half-inch.
See **inch**.

- **horizontal axis**

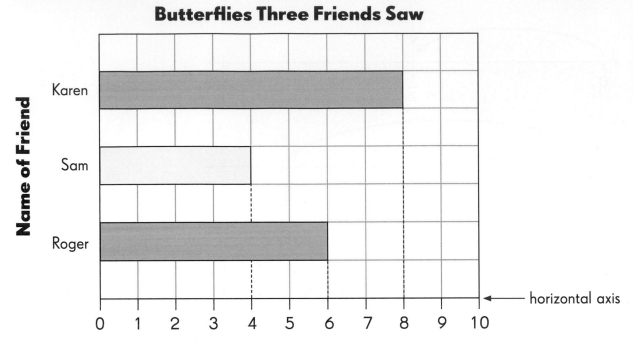

The value of each bar can be read from the horizontal axis, which is marked 0 through 10.

See **axis**.

- **hot**

When the temperature outside is 105°F, it is hot.

See **cold**.

- **hour (h)**

It is a unit of measurement of time. There are 60 minutes in 1 hour. Write h for hour.

60 min = 1 h

See **minute**.

- **inch (in.)**

  Inch is a customary unit of length. Write in. for inch.
  12 in. = 1 ft

  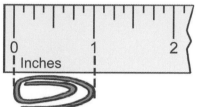

  The paper clip is 1 inch long.

  See **foot**.

- **is parallel to**

  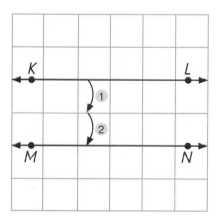

  Line *KL* is parallel to line *MN*.

- **is perpendicular to**

  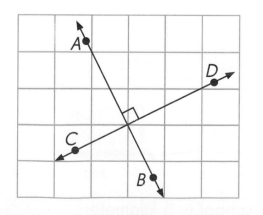

  Line *AB* is perpendicular to line *CD*.

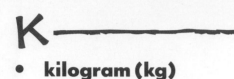

K

- ## kilogram (kg)

  Kilogram is a metric unit of mass.
  It is used to measure the mass of heavier objects.
  One kilogram is 1,000 times as heavy as 1 gram.
  Write kg for kilogram.
  1 kg = 1,000 g

  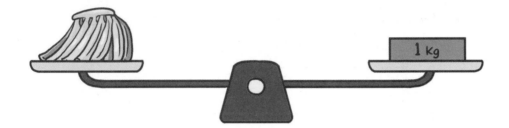

  The mass of the bananas is 1 kilogram.

  See **gram**.

- ## kilometer (km)

  Kilometer is a metric unit of length. It is used to measure length
  and distance. Write km for kilometer.
  1 km = 1,000 m

  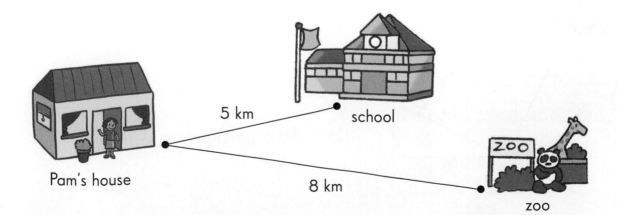

  The distance between Pam's house and the school is 5 kilometers.

L

- ## least

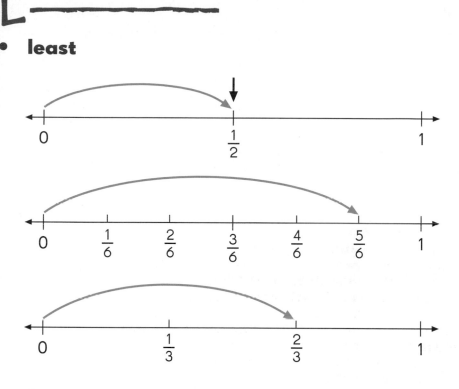

$\frac{1}{2}$ is the least fraction.

- ## less than (<)

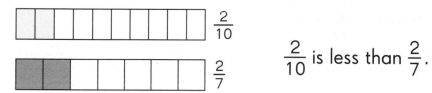

$\frac{2}{10}$

$\frac{2}{7}$

$\frac{2}{10}$ is less than $\frac{2}{7}$.

- ## like fractions

$\frac{1}{4}$ and $\frac{3}{4}$ are like fractions.

Fractions with the same denominators are like fractions.

See **unlike fractions**.

- **line**

  A line is a straight path. It goes on without end in both directions as shown by the arrowheads.

  This line passes through points *A* and *B*. This is line *AB* or *BA*.

- **line of symmetry**

  A line that divides a figure into congruent halves. The halves fit exactly over each other when folded along this line.

  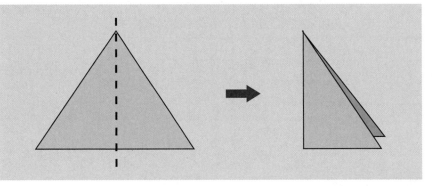

- **line plot**

  This is a line plot. It is a diagram that uses a number line to show how often an event happens.

  Number of Birthday Cards Received

  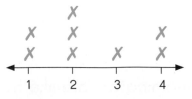

  Number of Birthday Cards

- **line segment**

  A line segment is part of a line. It has two endpoints.

  This is line segment *CD*.

- **liter (L)**

  Liter is a metric unit of volume and capacity. Write L for liter.
  1 L = 1,000 mL

  The measuring cup holds 1 liter of water.

M

- **meter (m)**

  Meter is a metric unit of length. Write m for meter.
  1 m = 100 cm

  See **centimeter**.
  See **kilometer**.

- **mile (mi)**

  Mile is a customary unit of length.
  Write mi for mile.

  A 1-mile brisk walk will usually take about
  20 minutes.

- **milliliter (mL)**

  Milliliter is a metric unit of volume and capacity. Write mL for milliliter.
  1,000 mL = 1 L

  The measuring cup holds 250 milliliters of water.

- **minute (min)**

  It is a unit of measurement of time.
  Write min for minute.
  60 min = 1 h

  Each small marking stands for 1 minute.
  The minute hand shows 5 minutes.

N

- **number line**

  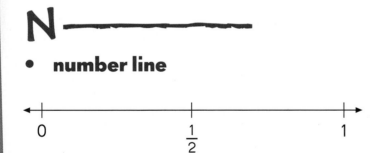

  This is a number line. Use a number line to help you find equivalent fractions and compare fractions.

numerator

It is the number above the line in a fraction. It shows the number of shaded parts in a whole.

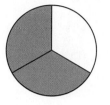

$\frac{2}{3}$ of the circle is shaded.

In the fraction $\frac{2}{3}$, 2 is the numerator.

O ――――――――――

octagon

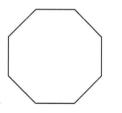

A polygon that has eight sides.
This is an example of an octagon.

See **polygon**.

open plane figure

A plane figure that does not start and end at the same point.

These are examples of open plane figures.

- **ounce (oz)**

  Ounce is a customary unit of weight.
  Write oz for ounce.
  16 oz = 1 lb

  The weight of one slice of bread is about
  1 ounce.

P

- **parallel lines**

  Two lines that will not meet no matter how long they are drawn.

  See **is parallel to**.

- **parallelogram**

  A quadrilateral with two opposite sides that are parallel.
  Only the opposite sides of a parallelogram need to be equal.

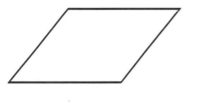

  These are examples of
  parallelograms.

  See **quadrilateral** and **parallel lines**.

- **past**

9:20 A.M. is 20 minutes past 9 A.M.

- **pentagon**

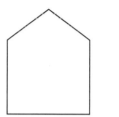

A polygon that has five sides.
This is an example of a pentagon.

See **polygon**.

- **perimeter**

Perimeter is the distance around a figure. Perimeter can be measured in linear units such as centimeters, inches, meters, and feet.

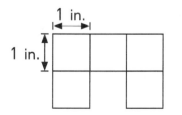

The perimeter of this figure is 12 inches.

- **perpendicular lines**

  Two lines that meet at right angles.

  See **is perpendicular to**.

- **pint (pt)**

  Pint is a customary unit of capacity.
  Write pt for pint.
  1 pt = 2 c

- **plane figure**

  A flat figure. It can be open or closed.

 These are examples of plane figures.

- **point**

  An exact location in space.

  •
  A   This is point *A* or *A*.

- ## polygon

  A closed plane figure formed by three or more line segments.

  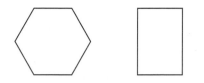

  These are examples of polygons.

  See **closed plane figures.**

- ## pound (lb)

  Pound is a customary unit of weight.
  Write lb for pound.
  1 lb = 16 oz

  The weight of the loaf of bread is about 1 pound.

Q

- **quadrilateral**

  Polygons with 4 sides and 4 angles.

  These are examples of quadrilaterals.

  See **polygon**.

- **quart (qt)**

  Quart is a customary unit of capacity.
  Write qt for quart.
  1 qt = 2 pt

R

- **rhombus**

  A parallelogram with sides that are equal in length.

  See **parallelogram**.

- **right angle**

  Angle *P* is a right angle. Use the corner of a folded paper to check for a right angle.

- **rotate**

  To change the position of a shape by turning about a point.

  See **turn**.

S

- ## scale

  The numbers that run along the vertical or horizontal axis of a graph.

  See **horizontal axis** and **vertical axis**.

- ## simplest form

  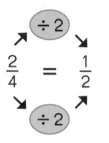

  $\frac{2}{4} = \frac{1}{2}$
  $\frac{1}{2}$ is a fraction in its simplest form.

- ## slide

  Move a figure in any direction to a new position.

  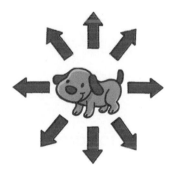

- ## square centimeter (cm²)

  Square centimeter is a metric unit of measure for area.
  Write cm^2 for square centimeter.

  This is a 1-centimeter square.
  Its area is 1 square centimeter (cm^2).

- **square foot (ft²)**

  Square foot is a customary unit of measure for area. Write ft² for square foot.

  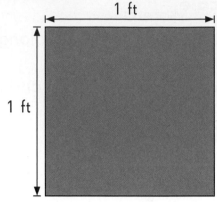

  A 1-foot square has an area of 1 square foot (ft²).

- **square inch (in.²)**

  Square inch is a customary unit of measure for area. Write in.² for square inch.

  This is a 1-inch square.
  Its area is 1 square inch (in.²).

  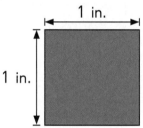

- **square meter (m²)**

  Square meter is a metric unit of measure for area. Write m² for square meter.

  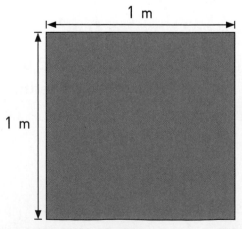

  A 1-meter square has an area of 1 square meter (m²).

- **square units**

  Units such as square centimeter, square inch, square foot, or square meter that are used to measure area.

- **survey**

  A method of collecting information or data.

- **symmetry**

  Occurs when two halves of a figure fit each other exactly when folded along a line.

T

- **tangram**

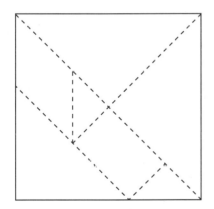

  A tangram is made up of seven polygons that can be put together to make a square.

- **temperature**

  A measure of how hot or cold something is.

- **thermometer**

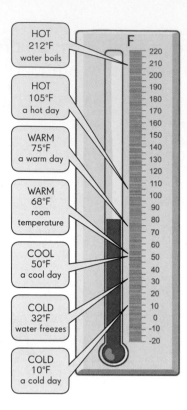

Thermometers are used to measure temperature.

- **time line**

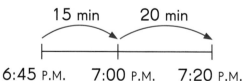

15 min   20 min

6:45 P.M.   7:00 P.M.   7:20 P.M.

Use a time line to help you find elapsed time.

See **elapsed time**.

- **to**

9:20 A.M. is 40 minutes to 10 A.M.

- **ton (T)**

  Ton is a customary unit of weight
  Write T for ton.

  The weight of a car is 1 ton.

- **turn**

  Rotate a figure about a point.

  See **rotate**.

U

- **unlike fractions**

  $\frac{2}{10}$ and $\frac{2}{7}$ are unlike fractions.

  Fractions with different denominators are unlike fractions.

  See **like fractions**.

V

- **vertex**

  A point where two sides of a polygon meet.

  vertex

- **vertical axis**

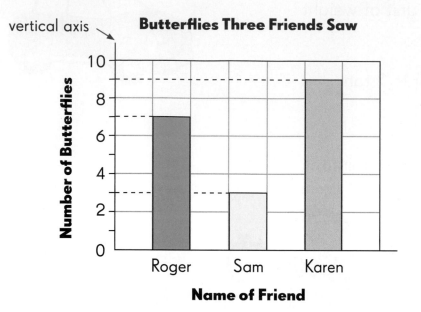

vertical axis

Butterflies Three Friends Saw

The value of the bars can be read from the vertical axis, which is marked 0, 2, 4, 6, 8, and 10.

See **axis**.

- **volume**

Volume is the amount of liquid in a container.

W

- **warm**

When the temperature outside is 75°F, it is warm.

See **cold**.

- **whole**

  A fraction is part of a whole.
  Divide a rectangular cake into 5 equal parts.

  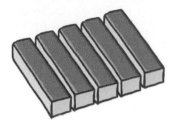
  $\frac{5}{5}$ is a whole.

Y

- **yard (yd)**

  Yard is a customary unit of length. Write yd for yard.

  This is a yardstick. →

  The height of the plant is 1 yard.

Index

Pages listed in black type refer to Pupil Book A.
Pages in blue type refer to Pupil Book B.
Pages in *black italic* type refer to Workbook (WB) A pages.
Pages in *blue italic* type refer to Workbook (WB) B pages.
Pages in **boldface** type show where a term is introduced.

Pages listed in black type refer to Pupil Book A.
Pages in blue type refer to Pupil Book B.
Pages in *black italic* type refer to Workbook (WB) A pages.
Pages in *blue italic* type refer to Workbook (WB) B pages.
Pages in **boldface** type show where a term is introduced.

139, 141, 143–148, 152, 155, 159, 161, 164–165, 169, 171–173, 177, 179, 191–193, 196, 201, 203, 205–206, 216–217, 221, 223, 225, 226, 228–229, 232–233, 243, 245, 247–248, 251–252, 255–256, 4–12, 15–20, 22, 25, 64–67, 70, 72–73, 87, 92–93, 98–99, 101, 118–120, 123–124, 127–128, 131, 134–136, 138, 140–141, 143, 149–154, 170, 174–175, 177–178, 180–181, 183, 187, 189, 192, 195, 199, 203–208, 224–225, 228–230, 233–234, 237–238, 242–245, 249, 252–253, 255, 267–270, 276–277, 281–282, 288–289, 304–305, 307, 310, 313, 316, 322, 324–325, 333, 348–349, 354–355, 357–358, 364, 366, 372, 375–377

H

Half-hour, 220, 247, 263

Half-inch, 171–175, 184, 212, 215; *WB 120–124, 135*

Hour, 220–222, **228**, 239–245, 247, 251–253, 255–256, 258–260, 262–263; *WB 151–162, 168–171, 173–174*

Hands-On Activities, 26, 57, 96, 179, 197, 13, 89, 102, 122–123, 132, 140, 178, 181, 190, 197, 208, 246, 271, 276, 277, 283, 290, 307–308, 312, 315–316, 325, 332, 349–350, 359, 367, 373, 377

I

Identity Property
for multiplication, *See* Multiplication – properties

Inequalities, *See* Algebraic Thinking

Integers
on a thermometer, 248–250, 254, 257, 263; *WB 163–166*

Interpreting remainders, *See* Division – remainder

Inverse operations,
relate addition and subtraction, *See* Addition and Subtraction
relate multiplication and division, *See* Multiplication and Division

J

Journal Writing, *See* Math Journal

K

Key, for a pictograph, 80, 82, 84, 108; *WB 61, 66, 87*

Kilogram, 42–47, 64, 67, 68, 71, 74, 76, 78; *WB 31–34, 42–45, 48*

L

Length, *See* Measurement

Let's Explore, 30, 82, 125, 140, 94, 145–146, 272, 305, 352, 369–370, 374

Let's Practice, 10–11, 19, 29, 44, 48, 52, 63, 68, 78, 83, 87, 96, 101, 106, 113, 126, 149–150, 157, 162, 167, 175, 177, 193, 198, 208–209, 218, 223, 226, 230, 234, 245, 249, 253, 258, 14, 23, 26, 68, 74, 90, 95–96, 103–104, 120, 125, 129, 144–145, 150, 154–155, 184–185, 199–210, 209–210, 227, 232, 236, 240, 247, 250, 255–257, 273–274, 278, 284, 291, 317–318, 327–328, 334–335, 351–352, 359–360, 368–369, 373–374, 379–380

Less than symbol (<), 20–24, 29, 34, 114, 116, 130–131, 133, 139, 144, 159, 192, 201; *WB 12*; *WB 103–105, 117, 139, 142*

Like fractions, *See* Fractions – like
adding, 116, 148–150, 159, 162; *WB 107–108, 140*
comparing, 133–135, 158; *WB 102, 106*
ordering, 135, 158; *WB 106*
subtracting, 149–150, 159, 162; *WB 109–112, 140*

Line
parallel, **285**–291; *WB 189–192, 255*
perpendicular, **279**–286; *WB 185–188*

Line of symmetry, **331**, 332–336, 339, 342; *WB 212, 247*

Pages listed in black type refer to Pupil Book A.
Pages in blue type refer to Pupil Book B.
Pages in *black italic* type refer to Workbook (WB) A pages.
Pages in *blue italic* type refer to Workbook (WB) B pages.
Pages in **boldface** type show where a term is introduced.

Line plot, *See* Graphs – line plots

Line segment, 170, 174–175, 184, 215, **266**–267; *WB 140, 177–178*
    as sides of angles, 267
    parallel, 285, 289, 290, 291
    perpendicular, 284

Liter, 48–58, 66–68, 73–76, 78; *WB 35–39, 42, 46*

M

Manipulatives,
    balance scale, 33, 166, 186, 188–189, 191–192, 194, 199, 216; *WB 127–128*
    base–ten blocks, 5–12, 14, 16–17, 20–23, 77, 79, 84–86, 94, 98–100, 102–105, 108–110, 194–195, 199–202, 204–205, 215, 227–228, 231–233; *WB 1, 9*
    clocks, *See* Clock
    fraction pieces, 140
    game cards, 207
    geoboard, 270, 272, 274, 278, 297, 312, 315, 325, 371–374
        grid paper, 81, 83, 85–96, 105, 107, 109, 123–124, 131–132, 146, 166, 281, 289, 297, 300, 302, 312, 337, 344, 346, 355, 360, 368–370; *WB 61, 63, 65, 67–74, 88, 217, 219–224, 227–229, 239*
    inch ruler, 165, 168–179, 184, 214, 217; *WB 119–122, 124–125*
    measuring cups, 48–58; *WB 254*
    measuring scale, 33–34, 42–47, 64, 166, 186–197, 199–200, 215; *WB 127, 142*
    meterstick, 32
    money set, 13
    number cards, 43, 47, 51, 81, 106, 156, 210, 222,
    number cubes, 16, 51, 156, 166, 222,
    question cards, 174, 197,
    spinner, 207, 222
    tangram, 293, 315; *WB 203, 213*
    yardstick, 179–181, 217

Math Journal, 31, 69, 88, 114, 257, 88–89, 147, 150, 211, *258, 329, 236, 361, 378*; *WB 35–36, 85–86, 118, 146, 156, 177–178*; *WB 19–20, 39, 83–86, 173–174, 193–194, 238*

Math Reasoning
    algebraic thinking
        adding in different ways, *See* Different Ways
        front–end estimation, *See* Front–end Estimation

missing number, 4, 6–11, 14–15, 18–19, 23–25, 28–32, 39–42, 44, 45–46, 48–50, 52, 55–56, 59, 61–62, 63,–64, 66–69, 72–73, 76, 78, 80, 82–83, 86–89, 91, 93–97, 101, 106, 111, 113–114, 116, 125, 127, 130–131, 136–137, 139–141, 143–150, 152, 155, 157, 159, 161–162, 164–165, 167, 169, 171–173, 175, 177, 179–180, 183–186, 190–193, 196, 198, 200–203, 205–210, 212–213, 215–221, 223, 226, 228–230, 232– 235, 238–239, 241–245, 247–248, 251–253, 255–258, 262–263; *WB 1–17, 19–33, 35, 37, 45–52, 55–58, 59–71, 73–79, 81, 87, 119–123, 127–135, 137–140, 93–98, 101–102, 104–106, 109–110, 112–115, 117–118, 147–153, 155, 159–162,167, 169–171, 173–180*
    multiplying in different ways, See Different Ways
    odd and even numbers, *See* Odd Numbers *and* Even Numbers

Mass. *See* Measurement

Measurement. *See also* Measurement Sense
    area, *See also* Area
        finding, 347–374, 384–387; *WB 215–230, 239, 242, 248–249*
        meaning of, **347**; *WB 230*
        square units, 347–352, 384, 387; *WB 215–218, 248–249*
    capacity, *See also* Capacity
        customary units, *See* Capacity
        metric units, 52–55; *WB 42*
    comparing measures, *See* Comparing – among measures
    converting
        customary units – *See* Converting – among customary units
        metric units, 35–37, 39–41, 46–47, 54–55, 63–66, 68, 69, 71, 74; *WB 23–28, 30, 32–33, 37–38, 41, 43–46, 49, 253*
    customary units, 165, 167–210, 212–218; *WB 119–136, 142–143*
    elapsed time, *See* Elapsed time
    estimate, *See* Estimate
    length
        benchmarks, 165, 167–185, 212–213, 215, 217; *WB 119–126*
        customary units, 165, 167–185, 212, 214–215, 217–218; *WB 119–126, 135, 140, 248–249, 251*
        metric units, 31–32, 34–41, 63–70, 74, 76–78; *WB 23–40, 41, 46–47, 49, 51*
        to the nearest half–inch, 171–175, 184, 212, 215; *WB 120–124, 135, 140*

Pages listed in black type refer to Pupil Book A.
Pages in blue type refer to Pupil Book B.
Pages in *black italic* type refer to Workbook (WB) A pages.
Pages in *blue italic* type refer to Workbook (WB) B pages.
Pages in **boldface** type show where a term is introduced.

P

Parallel lines, **285**–291, 310–313, 318, 341; *WB 189–193, 205–206, 245, 255*

Part-part-whole model
in addition, *See* Bar models
in subtraction, *See* Bar models

Patterns
addition, 5–11, 27–29; *WB 4, 14 39*
finding, to solve problems, *See* Problem-Solving
strategies – look for patterns
multiplication, *See* Multiplication
odd and even numbers, 224–226; *WB 151–152*
skip-counting, *See* Multiplication
subtraction, 133–143, 145–149, 163–164, 189; *WB 93–96, 150*

Pentagon, 306–308, 310, 317–318, 323, 329, 338, 340–341; *WB 199–202, 204, 206, 208–210*

Perimeter
meaning of, **383**

Perpendicular lines, **279**–284; *WB 185–188, 193–194, 245*

Pint, **203**, 204–210, 213–214, 216–218; *WB 131, 133–134*

Place value
expanded form, *See* Expanded form of whole numbers
hundreds, 12–14, 16–17, 19; *WB 5, 7, 9*
identifying, 12–19; *WB 5–10*
ones, 12–14, 16–17, 19; *WB 5, 7, 9*
standard form, *See* Standard form
tens, 12–14, 16–17, 19; *WB 5, 7, 9*
thousands, 12–14, 16–17, 19; *WB 5, 7, 9*
to compare and order, *See* Comparing *and* Ordering
word form, *See* Word form
zeros in, *WB 5–6, 9–10*

Plane figures. *See also* Angles; Line; Polygons; Quadrilaterals
classifying, 303–304
meaning of, **303**

Plot. *See* line plot

P.M., **220**

Polygons, **304**, **338**, 305–319, 340–342; *WB 199–206, 245*

Pound, 191–197, 199–201, 212, 214–216; *WB 127–129, 142, 256*

Practice
Guided Practice, *See* Guided Practice
Let's Practice, *See* Let's Practice

Prerequisite skills
Recall Prior Knowledge, *See* Recall Prior Knowledge
Quick Check, *See* Quick Check

Problem-Solving
Put on Your Thinking Cap!
strategies
act it out, 56, 75, 211, 292–293; *WB 135, 239–240*
before-after, *WB 38, 88; WB 175*
draw a diagram/model, 127, 27, 156, 259, 337; *WB 179–180; WB 22, 51–52, 195–198*
guess and check, 32, 69, 114, 181, 210, 259, 259; *WB 17–18, 37, 57–58, 69–72, 87, 117, 139–140, 157, 71–72; WB 117–118, 176*
look for patterns, 89, 210, 213–214, 242, 381
make a systematic list, 105, 156; *WB 118, 140, 158; WB 22, 136, 176, 239–242*
make suppositions, 259; *WB 89–90*
simplify the problem, 89,
solve part of the problem, 337; *WB 21, 87–88, 136, 175–176*
work backward, 32, 69, 114; *WB 17–18 37, 58, 69–71; WB 40*
write a number sentence, 89; *WB 38, 55, 58, 69–71, 185–186*
thinking skills
analyzing parts and whole, 89, 114, 259; *WB 18, 38, 72, 87–88, 118, 139–140, 157–158, 179–180; WB 22, 40, 175–176, 241*
classifying, 127, 56; *WB 55; WB 89–90, 214*
comparing, 69, 27, 56, 105, 156, 259, 381; *WB 17, 69–70, 117; WB 21, 87–88, 117–118, 136, 175–176, 213–214, 239, 242*
deduction, 32, 56, 105, 211, 259; *WB 37, 57; WB 22, 87–88, 136, 241*

Pages listed in black type refer to Pupil Book A.
Pages in blue type refer to Pupil Book B.
Pages in *black italic* type refer to Workbook (WB) A pages.
Pages in *blue italic* type refer to Workbook (WB) B pages.
Pages in **boldface** type show where a term is introduced.

Scale
graph, **85**, 86–88, 90, **107**, 108; *WB 63, 65, 67*

Set(s)
compare, 20–34; *WB 11–16*
fractions of, 151–155, 159, 162; *WB 113–116,*
140–141

Sides
of polygons, 299, **306**–308, 317, 338, 340–341;
WB 199–202, 204, 250
of quadrilaterals, 310–313, 317–319, 340–341;
WB 205–206
of triangles, 270, 299, 301, 306, 308, 317; *WB 201*

Skip counting, *See* Multiplication

Slides, **320**, 322, 327–328, 338, 342; *WB 207, 209*

Standard form, throughout, See, for example, 5–35; *WB 1–18*

Statistics, See Data; Graphs; Line Plots.

Strategies, See Problem-Solving – Strategies.
Subtraction,
across zeros, 108–113, 115–116; *WB 67–68*
checking, 95, 97, 100–101, 105–106, 111, 115
difference, 94–**95**, 100–101, 106, 113, 116;
WB 69, 71
estimating differences, 58, 60, 62–63, 65–68,
71–73; *WB 29–30, 32–36, 38*
four–digit numbers, 94–116; *WB 59–72*
fractions, 115–116, 149–150, 159, 162;
WB 109–110, 112, 140
inequalities, 20–24; *WB 11–12, 40*
inverse operations, 95, 100, 105
money, 15–23; *WB 7–12*
number bonds, 45–46, 2–10, 14–23; *WB 21–23,*
13–22
patterns, 27–29; *WB 14–16*
place value, 94–95, 98–100–110, 115–116;
WB 59–61, 63–65, 67–70
real–world problems, 111, 113, 116, 122–131,
24–27, 60, 65–66, 68, 70, 72, 73–74, 76–78;
WB 68, 71–72; WB 13–22, 43, 45–46, 48–49,
51–52, 262

regrouping in, 98–116; *WB 61–70*
relation to addition, 95, 100, 105
repeated to divide, *See* Division
three–digit numbers, 101, 106, 108–110, 112–113,
115–116, 65, 67, 70, 72–73; *WB 59–62,*
65–69, 71–72
time, 237–240, 263; *WB 157–158, 173, 250–251*
two-digit numbers, *WB 59, 65–66, 69, 72*
units of measure, 65–66, 70, 72–73, 76–77; *WB 43,*
45–46, 48–49, 51–52
with zero, 95, 97, 108–116; *WB 59–63, 65–70*

Sum
estimating, *See* Addition
meaning of, **77**

Symbol
cents (¢), 1–30; *WB 1–22*
dollars ($), 1–30; *WB 1–22*
equal to (=), *See* Equal sign (=)
is greater than (>), *See* Greater than symbol
is less than (<), *See* Less than symbol

Symmetry, line, *See* Line of Symmetry

Table, *See also* Tally chart
using data; from, 88, 97–98, 100–101, 104, 106–109;
WB 80, 83–86, 89–90, 144

Tally chart
making, 83, 89, 99, 102–103; *WB 62, 65, 78*
using, 81, 83, 87, 89, 97–99, 102–103; *WB 62–63,*
65, 78, 137

Tally mark, 81, 83, 87, 89, 97–99, 102–103; *WB 62–63,*
65, 78, 137

Temperature. *See* Measurement.

Tens, *See* Place value

Thermometer, 248–250, 261, 263; *WB 163–166*

Pages listed in black type refer to Pupil Book A.
Pages in blue type refer to Pupil Book B.
Pages in *black italic* type refer to Workbook (WB) A pages.
Pages in *blue italic* type refer to Workbook (WB) B pages.
Pages in **boldface** type show where a term is introduced.

Photo Credits